The Academic
Library in
the American
University

The Academic Library in the American University

Stephen E. Atkins

AMERICAN LIBRARY ASSOCIATION
Chicago and London 1991

Cover and text design by Stromberg Design

Composed by Digital Graphics, Inc. in Times, Gill Sans and Zapf Chancery using TEX. Reproduction copy set on a Varityper 4300P imagesetter.

Printed on 50-pound Glatfelter, a pH-neutral stock, and bound in 10-point C1S cover stock by Edwards Brothers, Inc.

The paper used in this publication meets the minimum requirements of American National Standard for Information Sciences—Permanence of Paper for Printed Library Materials, ANSI Z39.48-1984. ∞

Library of Congress Cataloging-in-Publication Data

Atkins, Stephen E.
    The academic library in the American university / by Stephen E. Atkins.
        p.   cm.
    Includes bibliographical references and index.
    ISBN 0-8389-0567-6 (alk. paper)
    1. Libraries, University and college—United States. I. Title.
Z675.U5A86   1991
027.7'0973–dc20   91-11296
                                                                        CIP

Printed in the United States of America.

95 94 93 92 91   5 4 3 2 1

CONTENTS

TABLES

FIGURES

Introduction

$\mathcal{T}$*HE IDEA OF THIS BOOK* originated at the University of Iowa in the late 1970s during some discussions in a higher education administration class that I was taking. At the time of these discussions, I was working as a copy cataloger in the Cataloging Department at the University of Iowa Library. Although I had held this job since 1974, my main preoccupations in those days had been finishing my doctorate in French history and finding a teaching position. My dissertation was completed in 1976, but because of a weak job market, my career as an academic was "on hold." Besides working in the library full-time, I was also teaching part-time in the Saturday and Evening Class Division at the University of Iowa.

Teaching positions were so scarce that most new degree holders were looking toward alternative careers. Most of my work experience had been in teaching, first at the University of Missouri–Columbia and then at the University of Iowa. While my coursework in higher education administration was stimulating, and I did consider it briefly as a new career possibility, my attraction to library work made me reconsider. My contacts with librarians at the University of Iowa Library had made me curious about the interaction between the library and the university, so I started asking questions of librarians, teaching faculty, and campus administrators. Although the librarians had extensive experience dealing with the teaching faculty and administrators, they seemed puzzled about the university environment and the library's role in it.

The professor in my university administration class had been on several occasions assistant to the president of the university, so I also asked him about the library, but he seemed more puzzled about the relationship than I did. My friends on the teaching faculty claimed a proprietary interest in the library, but they had no idea of how the library functioned nor even seemed to care. My contacts in the administration had an attitude that the library is a necessity, but just don't bother us with questions about things outside our expertise. The more that I studied the question of the library and the university, the more I felt that librarians had to make a stronger case for themselves and the library in the university, or else they would be ignored. Shortly afterward, my application for entry into the library science school at the University of Iowa was approved and I took this belief into my classes there.

Library science school offered a good technical education, but many of the broader issues of academic librarianship were left unclear. Because of state work rules, as a full-time employee of the state, I had to be a part-time student in the University of Iowa's Library and Information Science School, where I had the opportunity to take library science courses over a three and a half year period. In several of these courses I observed my fellow students' reaction to academic library concerns. The caliber of the students was high because of the selective admissions policy, but few of the students were interested in academic library issues. Most of them wanted jobs in a public or school library, but the few who were opting for academic libraries were job oriented rather than profession oriented. Several professors were concerned about the role of academic libraries in the university, but they merely expressed frustration without providing answers or solutions.

My first job after library and information science school was at the University of Illinois at Urbana-Champaign, where I arrived in 1983 in the midst of restructuring the library by the university librarian, Hugh Atkinson. Before his untimely death, I had several brief but stimulating conversations with him about his perceptions of the interaction between the library and the university. His attitude was that academic librarians had to function as equal partners with the teaching faculty, or else librarians would be second-rate partners in the educational process. By second-rate, he meant that librarians would have little or no status. He also expressed strong opinions that dual track systems don't work. Other colleagues at the University of Illinois Library shared similar or even more assertive ideas on this subject. Lengthy conversations were held on these types of issues, and I began to develop some ideas based upon my experiences as both a teacher and a librarian. The result was that I submitted a contribution to the Association of College and Research Libraries (ACRL) Conference at Baltimore in 1986, and this book is the result of interest in the subject displayed at the conference.

The ACRL Conference at Baltimore was the best conference that I have attended. Each author had to give two oral presentations, and the response was overwhelming. A representative of ALA Books contacted me at the conference and asked if I would consider broadening my remarks and paper into a book-length manuscript. Because I needed time to think about the ideas in my short paper, it has taken me several years to research and to write this work. Since I made the agreement to write this book, I received tenure at the University of Illinois, and this was soon followed by my position as head of the Resource Development Division at the Sterling C. Evans Library, Texas A&M University. My new job has allowed me to examine yet another university-library relationship.

Several people have been instrumental in motivating me to write this book. My former colleagues at the University of Illinois at Urbana-Champaign Library, especially Patricia Stenstrom, Dale Montanelli, Bart Clark, and Sue Griffiths, encouraged me at key stages. Bob Engel, Bob Felsing, and Tanja Lorkovic at the University of Iowa also helped me conceptualize some of the ideas of this book. Bettina MacAyeal, of ALA Books, encouraged me in this project from the first. Hugh Atkinson was an inspiration both as a librarian and as a friend; his death has been a great loss to the library profession. Finally, my family—Susan, Stephanie, Jordan; my two dogs, Budwyn and Beaver, and my cat, Natasha—have all contributed one way or another to the completion of this book.

CHAPTER ONE

History of the University and the Academic Library

1638 to 1945

THROUGHOUT THE HISTORY of American higher education, the academic library has supported the university in its educational mission. Colleges and universities evolved, over three hundred and fifty years, from institutions providing a restricted curriculum for a limited number of disciplines to serving a broad curriculum for a multitude of disciplines, and academic libraries followed the lead of their institutions by adapting to these changes. Beginning in the colonial period with small collections of books in the classics and religion for the instructional needs of teachers, the academic library has become a depository of materials that support faculty and graduate student research in an almost infinite variety of disciplines. This change in orientation, from acquiring collections to supplementing the teaching of a standard undergraduate and graduate curriculum, to the building of large collections for the research needs of faculty and students, began in the late nineteenth century and accelerated in the twentieth century. By the middle of the twentieth century, as most academic libraries were acquiring huge amounts of research materials to support advanced graduate programs, educational leaders began to recognize a direct correlation between the "educational effectiveness of a college and the growth of its library." [1]

Libraries became a source of pride for the administrators and faculty in the quality institutions—and a source of concern and disquiet for the faculty of institutions with small libraries. Academic libraries shared in the rapid expansion of colleges in the 1920s, and in most cases they matched the growth rates of their institutions. Only during the depression of the 1930s and World War II did the growth rate of academic libraries and their host institutions begin to slow, but these years proved to be an interlude before the postwar boom in higher education. The year 1945 constitutes the end of the first phase of the partnership between institutions of higher education and their academic libraries and the beginning of a new era.

Although the nine colonial colleges were founded in imitation of English models, each college had differences caused by the geographical and political environment of its region. Since nearly all of the early leaders of these institutions had been students at Cambridge and Oxford, these universities were the most obvious models.[2] An innovation was the adoption of the Scottish universities' practice of forming lay boards of trustees to oversee operations of the college. Exact duplicates of the English models were never attempted because financial resources in the colonies were inferior to those in England. Moreover, it is doubtful that English authorities would have granted the necessary royal charter for "duplicates" of Cambridge or Oxford in the New World.[3] British authorities assumed that the colonies had little need for such institutions, because Cambridge and Oxford universities were still available to provide a quality education for the colonists' sons. Consequently, the colonial colleges were founded more to fulfill the need for educated ministers than to provide a basic liberal arts education. Although a majority of the colonial colleges were started by religious denominations to train ministers, no religious test for college attendance was ever required.[4] The lack of such a requirement allowed the colonial colleges some flexibility when the educational environment changed in the eighteenth century.

The curriculum of the colonial colleges was again English in inspiration. English universities had long concentrated on producing clergymen and statesmen rather than scholars. Colonial colleges retained this emphasis on a general education, but with more intent to train ministers than statesmen. Students were products of private tutoring, or instruction by local ministers, and they were admitted to a college only after a lengthy oral examination. Throughout the colonial period the requirements for admittance to any of the colleges were a knowledge of Latin and Greek and evidence of good character. Two degrees were issued by the colleges—a bachelors and a masters. The bachelors was a four-year degree with few electives; in contrast, the masters was a three-year degree with no course and no residency requirements. The assumption of this system was that education was for gentlemen, and "a common core of central knowledge" was the best way to train such a person.[5]

The colonial college was an elite institution that attracted only a select few. A college education was always costly, and the colonial college's classical curriculum discouraged individuals interested in practical application of their education. The classics curriculum was never seriously challenged during the colonial period, but a growing interest in the natural sciences was apparent by 1750.[6] This interest in science corresponded to a drop in the number of ministers trained between the early and late eighteenth century, but the classical and theological composition of the curriculum remained unchallenged.[7] As more faculty and students became interested in the professions of law and business, the religious orientation of the colleges was weakened. All the colonial colleges remained small, with a peak pre–Revolutionary War enrollment at Harvard of 413 in 1770 and 338 at Yale.[8] Despite small enrollments, these institutions were able to serve as the training grounds for several generations of colonial leaders in education, religion, and government.

The libraries of the colonial colleges responded to the needs of their colleges by housing collections of the standard classics. Bibles and language textbooks were always the staples. None of the colonial institutions developed extensive book collections before the American Revolution because of the scarcity of printed materials in the colonies, the expense of acquiring books from Europe, and the problem of preservation. Dartmouth College, alone of the colonial colleges, had regular appropriations for the acquisition of library materials because it charged students a circulation fee.[9] Fire, the principal enemy of colonial libraries, destroyed several libraries during the eighteenth century. The most notable was the Harvard College fire in 1764, which destroyed a collection of 5,000 books.[10] Consequently, preservation of materials, rather than acquisition, seems to have been the practice among colonial college libraries.

While college library collections grew slowly during the eighteenth century, they experienced no undue strain because of the lack of demand for materials by faculty and students. Part of the reason for the lack of demand for larger libraries was that the predominant recitation mode of teaching placed few demands on the library.[11] This type of instruction depended upon close interaction between the teacher and the student, with the student reciting the assigned lesson from a common text. Each student had a personal textbook with which to prepare for the next day's recitation, and therefore students had little need to consult other books. A common practice in Latin and Greek classes was for the students to translate the difficult passages by writing in their books. Even the teachers had little need for large library collections since they had no research responsibilities and teaching was confined to the textbook. Consequently, the size of all collections in college libraries at the end of the American Revolution has been estimated at slightly more than 26,600 volumes.[12] Each colonial college library averaged fewer than 3,000 volumes, but with such weak demand, small collections imposed no hardship on either the teaching staffs or the students.

Lack of demand meant that few financial resources were devoted to the acquisition of library materials. Limited resources also meant that college libraries had to depend on outside sources for the acquisition of books and periodicals. Book printing in the colonies was producing a slow but steady supply of printed materials. The economics of printing, however, made book making secondary to newspaper and pamphlet work.[13] Consequently, books were scarce, and most had to be imported from abroad. Expensive European books and even the less expensive colonial books required more funds than colleges had available for book acquisition. Perhaps less than 10 percent of library books in colonial college libraries were acquired by direct purchase.[14] These factors resulted in libraries receiving the bulk of their books through donations. A significant portion of these donations was the product of solicitations by faculty members traveling in England, western Europe, and the colonies.

The libraries' books reflected the colleges' curriculum. Since the curriculum was heavily oriented toward Latin and Greek subjects, much of the library consisted of textbooks in those languages. Studies of the leading libraries in the eighteenth century show that nearly half of the books were on theological subjects, with history and literature a distant second and third.[15] This subject imbalance and the lack of books on scientific subjects was common in all colonial college libraries. Libraries reflected the curriculum of institutions that were intended to train ministers and to provide a liberal arts education for the rest of the student body.

Access to the library was severely restricted at every colonial college. While the faculty and a few trusted students were allowed access to materials in the library, they had only a brief time each week to use these resources. Limited access imposed little inconvenience on the faculty members because they had been recruited for theological soundness rather than scholarship; and scholarly activity was regarded "as an individual pursuit rather than an institutional one." [16] Since professors were rewarded for teaching rather than scholarship, few teachers spent much time on scholarly pursuits. Some college officials even considered research harmful to effective teaching.[17]

The custodian of the library was usually a part-time faculty member whose primary function was to preserve and keep track of the collection. By academic law and tradition, the librarian had the custodial responsibility to account for the books as property, and censure followed if that part of the job was neglected.[18] In the smaller institutions, it was not unknown for the college president to be the librarian.[19] Lack of access also had little impact on undergraduates because there were almost no books in the library of contemporary interest to students.[20] Instead, students formed literary societies to provide a place where they could build libraries filled with books of interest to them.

The American Revolution was an early watershed in the history of colleges and universities. Revolutionary activities had a severe impact on the operations of the nine colleges, because most of them were in areas that became war zones. Besides damaged buildings, lost endowments, and lowered enrollments, revolutionary fever caused changes in the educational curriculum.[21] The prewar curriculum was modified to emphasize the practical arts of science and public affairs; these reforms proved, however, to be of a limited nature, and they had little immediate impact on libraries. The creation of a federation of states meant that the former monopoly of the nine colonial colleges was broken, and it was no longer necessary to obtain a royal charter for new colleges. Consequently, nineteen new colleges were founded between 1782 and 1802, including a new type of institution, the state university.

Soon after these new postrevolutionary institutions started operation, they started libraries. Much as it had affected the colonial colleges, a lack of funds and the scarcity of materials hindered them from acquiring large library collections. The book trade was still in its infancy and few American books were produced in the period immediately following the American Revolution. Just how scarce books were can be seen in the estimate that only 39,162 publications had been published in the thirteen colonies and the new republic during the 1639 to 1800 period.[22] The first catalog of the American book trade (in 1804) listed only 1,338 books, many of which had been printed in previous years.[23] Efforts were still made to acquire books from abroad, but funds for book acquisition were almost nonexistent. College trustees often expressed opposition to spending scarce funds for books, and this opposition was hard to overcome.[24] These factors combined to restrict the size of the college library in the postrevolutionary era.

The educational mission of colonial colleges was transplanted westward in the first half of the nineteenth century by the founding of numerous new colleges. New institutions were founded as territories gained statehood, and citizens of these new states lobbied their legislatures for state colleges.[25] As a result of this lobbying, state legislatures endowed new state colleges and some private colleges with land provided by provisions of the Northwest Ordinance of 1787. A considerable number of these institutions were outgrowths of earlier "free schools or academies" that had provided the equivalent of a high school education.[26] It was less difficult to expand the curriculum and add faculty to these academies than to build a college from scratch. In addition, many of the larger communities sponsored a college in an effort to gain status and the educational benefits of such institutions. Colleges were considered such an asset that real estate speculators supported their foundation.[27]

Despite the benefits of a college for the community, the most significant reason for college expansion continued to be the rivalry among religious denominations.[28] Each denomination advocated college building as a way to compete with other sects.[29] Many of these new colleges resembled the established eastern colleges, not only because of their religious affiliations but because the founders modeled them after the most prominent eastern institutions.[30] The founding of colleges in the postrevolutionary era was followed by a brief interlude of consolidation before a further period of rapid expansion after 1820. Nineteen colleges were established between 1782 and 1802. Only eight colleges opened their doors in the next twenty years. The combination of population growth and local pride resulted in 217 full-time colleges by the late 1850s (see table 1.1).[31] Since forty colleges went bankrupt during hard times in the 1830s and 1840s, this figure represents 83 percent of the total number

Table 1.1: Enrollment in Liberal Arts Colleges, 1800–1860

Years	No. of Students	No. of Colleges	Avg. Student Size
1800–01	1,156	26	44.5
1809–10	1,939	31	62.5
1819–20	2,566	36	71.3
1829–30	4,647	53	87.7
1839–40	8,328	100	83.3
1849–50	9,931	129	71.3
1859–60	16,600	202	82.2

Source: Colin B. Burke, *American Collegiate Populations: A Test of the Traditional View* (New York: New York University, 1982), p. 13.

of colleges founded during this era.[32] These figures differ considerably from other estimates of the number of colleges during this period, but most of the confusion has been caused by the lag time between legislative action and the actual operation of the institution and by the confusion between the operations of high school academies and colleges.[33]

Most of the growth in higher education before the Civil War was among private colleges because the expansion of public institutions had been hindered by national and state politics. State universities languished after the U.S. Supreme Court decision in the Dartmouth College case in 1819.[34] This decision gave private colleges independence from any interference by a state legislature since it prevented state takeovers of private colleges, even if the state had previously provided financial assistance. By making state legislatures establish schools rather than taking over existing ones, states became reluctant to assume complete financial responsibility and support for these new institutions. Because of this court decision and the subsequent political fallout, resistance to supporting public education became widespread for almost two decades. Hostility of the denominational colleges toward state universities also contributed to the slow growth of public higher education. Intense lobbying by representatives of the denominational colleges against financial backing for state universities was always a factor during debates on public higher education. Only after some of this hostility died down, in the late 1830s, did a number of state legislatures authorize new universities, but, with a handful of notable exceptions, few of these new institutions prospered until after the Civil War.

Only a limited number of students took the opportunity to gain a college education in the nineteenth century. A small population base and the expense of a college education combined to keep the student population down. Tuition, fees, and room and board costs constantly increased in the period from 1800 to 1860, further reducing opportunities for all but those families able to afford the expense.[35] Nevertheless, many of the new states founded public institutions in the 1840s and 1850s in an effort to expand educational opportunity. The result of such a rapid explosion of new colleges and the dearth of students was that soon the number of colleges exceeded the demand for them. While several of the older eastern colleges prospered both academically and financially in this period, few of the newer private colleges and new state universities had the resources to operate at much more than a subsistence level.[36]

Most of the antebellum colleges were small operations. A number of these new schools had only one building and a small staff of instructors. While some of the established colleges had faculties larger than ten members, most institutions in the West and South had only four to six.[37] Few of the instructors were scholars, and most, in fact, were clergymen or had some theological training.[38] This religious orientation was reinforced by an overwhelming majority of the college presidents being ministers by training or practice.[39] "Moral character," rather than scholarship, was prized by these college presidents.[40] Salaries were kept low for the teaching faculty, and in such conditions there was little desire to excel in either scholarship or teaching.[41] Scholarship was not considered a requirement for teaching, and exposure to "wrong ideas" through scholarship could hurt an academic career.[42] Professors were so poorly paid that most needed independent means to supplement their salary.[43] Unpopular views were kept out of the classroom, and teachers could be fired for advocating any but "mainstream" ideas. Since venturing far from safe opinions was dangerous in such a teaching environment, intellectual innovations were stymied.[44] The earlier emphasis on recitation was gradually replaced by the lecture method, because the instructors felt that the lecture stimulated the student to "active" learning.[45]

Before the Civil War the financial situation in all but the most established institutions was precarious. Many of the colleges failed because of financial woes during the economic upheavals in 1837 and 1857, but others failed because of internal dissension and even natural disasters.[46] Evidence indicates that most of the institutional failures were in the 1840s and 1850s: twenty-eight of the forty-one bankruptcies, or 68.3 percent.[47] Some colleges were saved by benefactors providing endowments, but these sums were always insufficient to provide prosperity for the school. Another expedient was a public lottery to raise large sums for buildings.[48] Among other expedients was the selling of perpetual scholarships, but rather than use of these funds as an endowment, too often the money was spent for current expenses.[49] Regardless of these financial expedients, the success of a college most often depended upon the quality of its leadership. Capable presidents and a contented teaching faculty ensured the success of an institution, and an incompetent president or a series of weak leaders could cause the ruin of any college.

The lack of resources of these colleges meant that there was little money to buy materials for libraries. Most libraries were only the size of a modern reading room, access was limited, and almost no provisions were made for using books and journals in the library.[50] This lack of large libraries and limited access was in line with "the attitude that the college library was for reference rather than reading and for supplementing professors' libraries rather than operating as an active force in the education of students." [51] But almost as important to the libraries was the fact that the American book publishing industry was producing only a small number of expensive books. Theology was still the staple of the college curriculum, with the study of the sciences and the practical arts becoming more important. These factors combined to make the college library only of fringe interest to the faculty or students. Books of a more popular nature were collected by the literary societies.

The libraries of the literary societies filled the void left by the weak book collections of the college libraries. These undergraduate societies were literary in nature, and a college might have two to four such groups in competition with each other. One expression of these rivalries was in building competing library collections. Each literary society collected books on contemporary subjects, or for reference in preparing for debates and for leisure reading.[52] Only the natural sciences were weakly represented in the collections of the literary societies.[53] Often faculty members contributed support in the form of financial aid or in selecting materials to help build these collections.[54] These literary-society libraries served much the same function as the modern undergraduate library by providing easy access to popular books and journals. Many of these libraries became so large that most of the societies appointed a student librarian to enforce the rules for borrowing and the collection of fines.[55] Often these collections were equal to or larger than the college library (see table 1.2).[56] An examination of the sixteen colleges with large literary societies in the 1830s and 1840s shows the size and the importance of these libraries. Only at Harvard was the college library larger than the literary societies' libraries.[57] Many of the literary-society libraries at other colleges, however, were nearly equal in size to, or in several cases larger than, the main college library collection.

By the middle of the nineteenth century a natural sorting out of universities had taken place. Universities with solid financial backing were successful, and those without such support either had closed or were in danger of closing. The success of a college was often reflected in the size of its library, and a survey of academic libraries in 1849 gives a sample of institutions and the size of their libraries; however, information was gathered from only thirty-three of the 126 libraries surveyed.[58] While this low response is partly indicative of the communication problems of the day, it also shows that many universities may have been reluctant to give information on the size of their libraries. Consequently, the data reflect only the most successful libraries and those with ambitions to become larger. The data show that academic libraries were growing at

Table 1.2: Volumes in College versus College Society Libraries in 1830s and 1849

Colleges	Years	College Libraries	Society Libraries	Totals	Society Percentage
Harvard (founded 1636)	1833	45,000	4,500	49,500	9.9
	1849	56,000	12,000	68,000	17.6
Yale (1701)	1839	10,500	15,000	25,500	58.8
	1849	20,500	27,200	47,700	57.0
Princeton (1746)	1833	7,000	4,000	11,000	36.3
	1849	9,000	7,000	16,000	43.7
Brown (1764)	1833	6,000	5,600	11,600	48.3
	1849	23,000	7,200	30,200	23.8
Dickinson (1783)	1839	3,000	7,300	10,300	70.9
	1849	5,100	9,500	14,500	65.5
Franklin (1785)	1839	500	1,000	1,500	66.7
	1849	7,300	3,000	10,300	29.1
U. of North Carolina (1789)	1839	3,000	7,000	10,000	70.0
	1849	3,500	8,800	12,300	71.5
Williams (1793)	1839	3,000	3,200	6,200	51.6
	1849	6,000	4,600	10,600	43.6
Union (1795)	1839	8,150	8,450	16,600	50.9
	1849	7,800	6,800	14,600	46.6
Middlebury (1800)	1839	2,230	3,110	5,340	58.2
	1849	5,000	3,400	8,400	40.2
Ohio U. (1802)	1838	1,300	1,200	2,500	48.0
	1849	1,300	1,500	2,800	53.6
Miami U. (Ohio) (1809)	1839	1,681	2,671	4,352	61.4
	1849	3,500	3,300	6,800	48.5
Hamilton (1812)	1839	2,500	3,700	6,200	59.7
	1849	3,500	6,800	10,300	66.0
Amherst (1821)	1839	4,300	6,250	10,550	59.2
	1849	5,700	8,000	13,700	66.4
Hobart (1825)	1839	1,200	1,500	2,700	55.6
	1849	2,000	3,700	5,700	64.9
Pennsylvania (1832)	1839	2,000	3,000	5,000	60.0
	1849	1,800	4,600	6,400	71.8

Source: Catharine Penniman Sortie, *What Contributions Did the American College Society Make to the College Library: A Supplementary Chapter in the History of the American College Library* (Master's thesis, Columbia University, 1938), pp. 19–25.

a slow rate during the early nineteenth century (see table 1.3).[59] While this slow growth reflected the lack of demand on the libraries by faculties and students, a division between the larger prestige libraries and the smaller college libraries was beginning to appear. Several of the larger and more prestigious institutions were starting to build larger collections because they had the financial resources to build such collections and the alumni to donate materials. The libraries at Harvard, Yale, and Brown are obvious examples. In contrast, the less successful colleges lacked both the financial resources and the ability to attract donations. All the libraries that reported in 1849 counted the collections of the literary societies as part of the general library collection, despite the lack of institutional control over them.

An educational reform emerged late in the antebellum era that achieved most of its successes after the Civil War. The reformers were not united on a single program, but they coalesced around several common themes: colleges must reform their curricula to include new kinds of knowledge, especially the natural sciences; provide opportunity for career education; and establish some type of advanced study on Euro-

Table 1.3: Collections in Libraries in 1849 by Size

College	Size of Collection	College	Size of Collection
Harvard	68,000	Hamilton	10,300
Yale	47,700	Waterville	8,500
Brown	30,200	Middlebury	8,400
Georgetown	26,100	Emory and Henry	8,000
Bowdoin	21,500	Western Reserve	7,700
South Carolina	18,400	Georgetown (Ky.)	7,300
Virginia	18,400	Alabama	7,100
Princeton	16,000	Miami (Ohio)	6,800
Union	14,600	Marietta	6,400
Dickinson	14,500	Pennsylvania	6,400
Amherst	13,700	Geneva (N.Y.)	5,700
Columbia	12,700	Hobart	5,700
Vermont	12,300	Maryville	3,700
North Carolina	12,300	Ohio	2,800
Wesleyan	11,100	Emory	2,700
Williams	10,600	Bethany (Va.)	2,300
Franklin	10,300	Norwich (Vt.)	1,000

Source: Kenneth J. Brough, *Scholar's Workshop: Evolving Conceptions of Library Service* (Urbana: University of Illinois Press, 1953), pp. 14–15.

pean models.[60] Some progress was made in introducing natural sciences into the curricula of some of the prominent colleges before the Civil War, but the other reforms had to wait until after the war. Several leaders of the reform movement used the Civil War era to lobby for and to plan reforms, and these leaders were to become influential in the postwar reform of higher education.[61]

The Morrill Act of 1862, the first of the major reforms enacted, provided income from public lands for the establishment of land-grant institutions. While the intent of this legislation was to promote the study of science and technology for practical benefits to farmers and businessmen, this support gave a boost to all public higher education. The prewar reform movement's intent to change the classics curriculum to a scientific orientation coincided with a desire by many for institutions to promote improvements in the agricultural and mechanical arts. Southern opposition to land-grant legislation was removed by the Civil War, and the Morrill Act was passed in December 1861 and signed in 1862.[62] Despite government support, land-grant institutions grew slowly because only the interest from the grants could be used to finance the new schools. It took further legislation before these institutions could flourish. A series of federal legislation in the 1880s and 1890s (the Hatch Act of 1887 and the Morrill Act of 1890) helped consolidate the role of these institutions, but it was not until the turn of the century that the land-grant universities could be accounted a success. In the midst of the development of the land-grant schools, the movement for curriculum reform picked up momentum.

The reform of the college curriculum by the introduction of the "elective" system was so controversial that it was not settled until the early years of the twentieth century. Feelings were so intense over this issue that the debate has been characterized as "the central educational battle of nineteenth-century America." [63] Beginning with the introduction of the elective principle at William and Mary in the eighteenth century and its espousal by Thomas Jefferson at the University of Virginia, the debate over the elective system reappeared at regular intervals, but most institutions adhered to the rigid requirements of the older system until late into the nineteenth century. The official position against the elective system was the Yale Report of 1828, which defended the traditional classics curriculum for undergraduates.[64] A declining rate of college enrollment, in comparison to the growth in population in mid-century, was cited by educational reformers as a danger signal for higher education.[65] The need for a more flexible curriculum was proposed by reformers as a necessity if higher education was to become a significant force in American society. Many of these reformers were not so much opposed to a classical education as they were advocates of the need to introduce more scientific and technical subjects into the curriculum. Once these subjects entered the curriculum, however, the classical curriculum never recovered from the competition.

The spokesperson for this curriculum reform was Charles William Eliot, the president of Harvard College, who spent forty years, beginning in 1869, fighting for the elective system at Harvard and elsewhere. Subject requirements were removed at Harvard's colleges in graduated steps from 1872 until 1885. This policy of expanding the curriculum met with opposition both at Harvard and at other institutions, but by the turn of the century the elective system was in place at most of the major institutions. Exceptions were some of the state universities of the South and many of the small colleges. This curriculum change resulted in an expensive expansion in the size of the faculty, in the building of new laboratory facilities, and in a dramatic increase in the size of the libraries,[66] but the most notable effect was that it allowed the faculty and students to pursue research interests rather than merely teaching or learning designated subjects. This meant that the old recitation instructional method was now completely replaced by scholarly lectures and seminars, with their increased demand on both the faculty and students. A study of the curricula of ninety-seven institutions in 1900 found that the elective principle had become accepted in almost all types of institutions of higher education.[67] Later, several of the prestigious eastern universities rebelled against the free elective system in the interest of "liberal culture," but most of the curriculum reforms withstood the defection of these institutions.[68]

Even more significant than curriculum reform for the development of higher education in the nineteenth century was the adoption of the German style of graduate education by Johns Hopkins University, which was founded in 1876 as a graduate school for advanced study. For nearly forty years before 1876, American students had been attracted to the type of graduate education available in Germany, and it was at these German universities that American students, most of them college graduates, learned advanced research techniques in science and the humanities from world-famous German scholars. During the period in which these American students were visiting Germany, the German higher education system was at its peak in scholarship and in developing new research fields. An estimate is that more than ten thousand American students made "academic pilgrimages" to German universities in the nineteenth century, with the bulk of them after 1850.[69] Most of the leaders in American higher education in the late nineteenth century had spent at least one year at one of the most influential German universities—Göttingen, Berlin, Leipzig, or Halle.[70] These students returned to the United States to spread the advantages of this kind of study, but the first American prototype was Johns Hopkins University. It took the leadership and inspiration of Daniel Coit Gilman's presidency at Johns Hopkins to start an institution in the mold of the famous German universities, selecting teachers regardless of nationality and combining them with the best American graduate students. Among the new faculty at Johns Hopkins were several with German doctorates.[71] By 1884, nearly all of the fifty-three professors and lecturers at Johns Hopkins University had studied at German universities, and thirteen had been granted German doctorates.[72] The spirit of the new institution was to search for scientific truth through sophisticated research techniques. Monographs and articles in scholarly journals became the mediums through which the findings of research were communicated in the United States and abroad.[73]

The impact of the new emphasis on research was almost immediate. Before the 1870s, research played almost no role in American higher education, but by the early 1880s the popularity of research was apparent.[74] The consequences of the Johns Hopkins graduate program can be best seen in that 1,000 of its 1,400 graduates were on American college and university faculties in 1925.[75] This movement showed its popularity in the foundation of several new research-oriented universities in the late 1880s and early 1890s: Clark University, the University of Chicago, and Stanford University. Several presidents of the larger universities made it plain to their faculties that promotion was tied to scholarly research rather than teaching expertise. By 1910 it had become apparent that the prestige associated with research was indicative of the quality of the university. While the teaching role was still considered to be the primary mission of higher education at most institutions, research had become an end in itself, and it began a steady challenge to the former primacy of teaching.

Despite the fact that the first research institution, Johns Hopkins University, was private, it was in the state universities that the new research philosophy flourished. The University of Michigan, under Henry P. Tappan, had flirted with German educational principles in the 1850s and the early 1860s, but opposition from other educational leaders on campus and from the Michigan legislature hindered full implementation of his reforms. Although his efforts had gone unrewarded and unappreciated, the Johns Hopkins University experiment changed all this. Many leaders of the state universities, interested in developing research programs, had little difficulty in combining pure research on the German model with applied research for practical ends.[76]

The biggest obstacle for state universities in adopting the new emphasis on research was in attracting qualified faculty. One solution was to train researchers from the brightest students, but this necessitated recruiting quality students. Private colleges had a series of academies and feeder schools to prepare their students for college, but this avenue was too limited for the state universities. Instead, university leaders decided to tap the resources of the public school movement, and this they did by designing and sponsoring a certification program for public high schools.[77] While this system took a number of years to be implemented, the result was that by the first decade of the twentieth century the state universities had a large body of qualified students to recruit potential scholars from.[78] These students provided the raw material to allow the universities to expand their dual goal of research and teaching in the twentieth century.

The increase in the number of doctorate programs and the number of doctorates awarded marked the progress of the new orientation in colleges and universities. Yale College offered the Ph.D. in 1860, and it granted three doctoral degrees the following year. A list of the pre-1876 doctorate degrees awarded by American universities shows the slow growth in the granting of these degrees (see table 1.4).[79] Examination of the next twenty-five years reveals the influence of Johns Hopkins University, which continued to recruit promising graduate students by the economic lure of the academic fellowships.[80] Until the mid-1890s,

Table 1.4: Earned Doctorates Conferred by Colleges and Universities, 1861–1876

Year	Ph.D.s	Year	Ph.D.s
1861	3	1869	4
1862	1	1870	1
1863	0	1871	13
1864	0	1872	14
1865	0	1873	26
1866	4	1874	13
1867	1	1875	23
1868	0	1876	31

Totals: 134 Ph.D.s awarded, or 8.4 average for 16-year period

Source: American Council on Education, *Higher Education in the United States* (Washington, D.C.: American Council on Education, 1965), p. 154.

most colleges and universities had few professors with the doctorate on their faculties, but this began to change in the late 1890s as the supply of American doctorates began to catch up with the demand (see table 1.5).[81] An influx of new doctorates allowed universities to start recruiting them for their institutions. By the early twentieth century, most of the major universities expected candidates to have the doctorate in hand. The supply of new Ph.D.s had almost exceeded the demand for them by the second decade of the twentieth century.[82] With such an increase in research expertise, the new emphasis was on publication of research results. Publication became the avenue to promotion and success for the faculty.[83] Subsequently, a scholarly subculture developed, with faculty participating in learned societies and writing for scholarly journals.

The impact of these changes on the academic library was dramatic. A new emphasis on faculty scholarship meant that more materials had to be acquired and on a variety of subjects. At the same time, the shift from recitation to lectures and seminars meant that students needed to consult books other than basic textbooks.[84] Finally, accessibility to the collection had to be improved as new demands were made on the academic libraries. As late as 1869, the library of Columbia University was open only two hours each day.[85] Even in 1877, one in seven college libraries was not open for faculty or student use daily.[86] Increased de-

Table 1.5: Earned Doctorates Conferred by Colleges and Universities, 1877–1900

Year	Ph.D.s	Year	Ph.D.s
1877	31	1889	124
1878	32	1890	149
1879	36	1891	187
1880	54	1892	190
1881	37	1893	218
1882	46	1894	279
1883	50	1895	272
1884	66	1896	271
1885	77	1897	319
1886	84	1898	324
1887	77	1899	345
1888	140	1900	382

Totals: 3,801 Ph.D.s, or 159.3 average over 24 years

Source: American Council on Education, *Higher Education in the United States* (Washington, D.C.: American Council on Education, 1965), pp. 154–55.

mand for library materials resulted in a gradual expansion of library services. By the 1880s, both faculty and students were allowed greater access to libraries' collections by the relaxation of restrictive closing hours. Libraries were now open during daylight hours, but almost all libraries had rules against night use for the prevention of fires. The introduction of electricity into the library allowed libraries to extend their operations into nighttime hours.

Research demands were such that more financial resources were allocated toward building the library's collection. Academic libraries had been growing even before the new emphasis on research, but the growth was slow and directionless. Inadequate financial support was the main culprit since many libraries could only depend on a low student fee or sporadic state support.[87] As the main library collections grew, literary-society collections began to comprise a smaller portion of the total library resources of the institutions (see table 1.6).[88] It was also at this time that the large library collections housed by the literary societies were incorporated into the university library collections.[89] These transfers were made because the literary societies had become less popular and less financially viable.[90] Student interests had moved toward social fraternities and other extracurricular activities.

Because collections had become too large to remain in a single reading room of the old college, two solutions were devised to handle the overflow of books and journals: separate buildings and departmental libraries. Most library leaders opted for a large centralized structure to house the library, but materials so outstripped space that often institutions had both a large library building and department libraries. This administrative structure was so unwieldy that the president of Harvard, Charles William Eliot, proposed that "it would be better to throw away many of the books in the Harvard Library than spend money on a larger building to house them."[91] Fortunately for the future of the academic library, this view was never adopted, and the pressure for larger library collections became irresistible.

The growth in libraries corresponded to the professionalization of librarianship. Only 209 librarians of all kinds were reported in the 1870 census.[92] Demand for librarians able to handle the responsibilities of the new system meant that the older part-time librarian, with teaching responsibilities, began to be replaced.[93] Even at the prestigious libraries at Harvard, Yale, and Columbia, which had full-time librarians, little attention had been given to making the libraries accessible to patrons.[94] Moreover, the demand for larger libraries meant that more librarians were necessary, but they still had little input in library planning for

Table 1.6: Volumes in College versus College Society Libraries, 1876

Colleges	College Libraries	Society Libraries	Totals	College-Society Percentage
Harvard	212,050	15,600	227,650	6.9
Yale	95,200	19,000	114,200	16.6
Dartmouth	25,550	27,000	52,550	48.6
Princeton	29,500	12,000	41,500	28.8
Amherst	30,406	8,127	38,527	21.1
Bowdoin	22,760	13,100	35,860	36.5
Columbia	31,390	2,200	33,590	6.6
Georgetown	28,000	4,268	32,468	13.1
Michigan	27,500	900	28,400	3.2
South Carolina	27,000	1,250	28,250	4.4
Georgia	21,600	6,000	27,600	21.7
Dickinson	7,765	19,738	27,503	71.7
Williams	17,500	10,000	27,500	36.4
Marietta	15,130	11,570	26,700	43.3
Union	19,800	6,000	25,800	23.3
Pennsylvania	23,250	2,323	25,573	9.8
St. Louis	17,000	8,000	25,000	32.0
Kenyon	10,659	10,046	20,705	48.5
City College, New York	20,000	600	20,600	2.9
Vermont	13,521	2,500	16,021	15.6
Washington & Lee	11,000	5,000	16,000	31.2
Middlebury	12,000	3,500	15,500	22.6
Colby	11,100	3,000	14,100	21.3
Missouri	11,000	2,400	13,400	17.9
Kentucky	10,845	2,089	12,934	16.1
Holy Cross	11,000	1,000	12,000	8.3
Rutgers	6,814	3,800	10,614	35.8
Beloit	8,300	1,000	9,300	17.5
Wisconsin	6,670	1,800	8,470	21.1
Bates	6,800	1,600	8,400	19.1
Mississippi	6,129	2,000	8,129	24.6

Source: Thomas S. Harding, *The College Literary Societies: Their Contribution to Higher Education in the United States, 1815–1876* (New York: Pageant Press, 1971), p. 3.

buildings or collections.[95] The need for trained librarians and professional standards had been the reason for the founding of the American Library Association (ALA) in 1876, because there were around 3,700 libraries in existence and in need of professional help.[96] While academic librarians were only a minority in the organization, many of them were to become leaders in ALA. Library education soon followed, with the establishment of a library science school at Columbia University by Melvil Dewey. Dewey attempted to root his library school within the ALA organizational structure, but opposition formed to ALA sponsorship.[97] By the first decades of the twentieth century a number of new library science schools were beginning to turn out professional librarians in a slow but steady stream. Yet it was not until the 1920s that library education had a reasonably consistent form.[98] One of the criticisms of library education was its alleged overemphasis on practical matters and its "low intellectual quality."[99] It has taken over half a century of hard work to overcome this low-intellectual-quality reputation, which still exists in certain quarters.

The new scholarship and the search for truth produced enough controversy that the ideas of academic freedom and tenure assumed importance. Academic freedom had often been an issue in the older colleges, but it was for denominational rather than political reasons. The debate over Darwinism was the pivotal issue that caused much of the controversy on college campuses in the late nineteenth century.[100] Supporters of Darwinian ideas had to fight with educational, political, and religious leaders both inside and outside academia, and several professors lost their teaching positions because of controversy over their beliefs.[101] Cases of teachers fired for their unpopular views or research findings threatened the academic community. Again the supporters of academic freedom fell back on a German tradition. The German idea of *Lehrfreiheit*, or the right of the professor to freedom of inquiry and teaching, was advanced as a faculty right. While the German principle applied only to affairs within the academic environment, American professors extended this right to affairs outside the university. The classic statement in support of academic freedom and research is contained in the 1915 Report of the Committee on Academic Freedom and Tenure by the American Association of University Professors (AAUP).[102] It took several decades and more than a few collegiate controversies, but once the principle of academic freedom was established the field was wide open for any type of research. Tenure was always tied closely to academic freedom, because of the protection it gives the professor for research.

The spurt of growth by universities between 1890 and 1915 transformed the face of American higher education. This growth was sparked by funds released by the prosperity of American industry. Industry created a demand for specialty disciplines and the products of research, and this demand was translated into financial support for higher education.[103] Money and resources became available to build buildings and faculties on the campuses of established institutions, and in several cases founded new universities. Even the older colleges experienced growth, but at a lower rate. This growth can be seen in the rapid increase in the number of colleges and universities, especially in the 1880s and 1890s (see table 1.7).[104] One manifestation of these changes was the replacement of ministers on the boards of trustees with businesspeople. Perhaps the most significant reason for the rapid expansion of higher education was the series of strong university presidents. These individuals were said to be so dominant that "every university to rise to major status did so under the dominating influence of such a president." [105] One scholar of higher education history has even characterized the period from 1880 to 1930 as an era of "strong presidents." [106] These presidents had major control over all aspects of library operations, and some of these presidents utilized this authority to support the activities of the library.[107] As the boom in higher education progressed, universities began to compete for prestige with a combination of publicity, peer esteem, and pride.[108]

Another manifestation of the changes in higher education was the increase in college attendance. Educators had long noted a mid-nineteenth-century slump in the number of students attending college. Beginning after 1885, the number of students increased steadily. Perhaps it was the curriculum reforms, change of emphasis toward a career orientation, or simply a demographic upturn, but a significant segment of the younger populace began to see an academic degree as an important life goal. Consequently, more members of the middle ranks of society found the means to send their children to a college or university.[109] This

Table 1.7: Institutions, Faculties, and Student Enrollment by Decades, 1869–1940

Year	Institutions	Students	Average Size	Faculties	Average Faculty
1869–70	563	52,266	92.8	5,553	11.6
1879–80	811	115,817	142.8	11,522	14.2
1889–90	996	156,756	157.4	15,809	15.9
1899–00	977	237,592	243.2	23,868	24.4
1909–10	951	355,213	373.5	36,480	38.4
1919–20	1,041	597,880	574.3	48,615	46.7
1929–30	1,409	1,100,737	781.2	82,386	58.4
1939–40	1,708	1,404,203	874.8	146,929	86.0

Source: W. Vance Grant and Thomas D. Snyder, *Digest of Education Statistics, 1985–86* (Washington, D.C.: U.S. Government Printing Office, 1986), p. 110.

expansion of students and the founding of several new universities—the University of Chicago (1892), Clark University (1889), and Stanford University (1891)—created a demand for more teaching positions.

At the same time that higher education was booming, the publishing trade was also in an expansionary cycle. The improvement in printing presses in the post-Civil War era and the increasing demand for books combined to produce a flood of new book titles (see table 1.8).[110] It was not until the middle of the 1880s, however, that the increase became dramatic. The supply of books and periodicals from book publishers and printing houses more than met the demand from academic libraries for more research materials. Larger printing runs of significant books made more copies available at lower cost. The emphasis on a mass market and publishers' demand for cheap paper, however, were to produce preservation problems for libraries, but neither publishers nor librarians expressed any concern at the time. Periodicals also increased in number, so that by 1905 6,000 were published annually.[111]

By the early 1920s the reforms and the resulting expansion in higher education in the previous half century produced the outline of the modern university. While the smaller colleges were still the sanctuary of the liberal arts, the large private and public universities pursued the twin goals of scholarly research and advanced professional education. A constant flow of new doctorates filled old and new teaching vacancies (see table 1.9).[112] This increase in the number of new doctorates was spurred by the growing belief, by both institutions and national educational groups, that the number of doctorates on a faculty was an indicator of high collegiate standards.[113] The major characteristic of higher education in the 1920s, however, was the broad-based financial

Table 1.8: New Titles and Editions in Selected Years, 1869–1945

Year	New Titles	Year	New Titles
1869	2,602	1915	9,734
1880	2,076	1920	8,422
1885	4,030	1925	9,574
1890	4,550	1931	10,307
1895	5,469	1936	10,436
1900	6,356	1940	11,328
1905	8,112	1945	6,548
1910	13,470		

Source: Helmut Lehmann-Haupt, *The Book in America: A History of the Making and Selling of Books in the United States* (New York: Bowker, 1951), p. 321; and Downing Palmer O'Harra, *Book Publishing in the United States, 1860–1901* (Master's thesis, University of Illinois, 1928), pp. 145–46.

Table 1.9: Earned Doctorates Conferred by Universities and Colleges,
1901–1945

Years	Ph.D.s	Years	Ph.D.s
1901	365	1924	1,098
1902	293	1925	1,213
1903	337	1926	1,415
1904	334	1927	1,448
1905	369	1928	1,481
1906	383	1929	1,890
1907	349	1930	2,299
1908	391	1931	2,476
1909	451	1932	2,654
1910	443	1933	2,742
1911	497	1934	2,830
1912	500	1935	2,800
1913	538	1936	2,770
1914	559	1937	2,852
1915	611	1938	2,933
1916	667	1939	3,112
1917	699	1940	3,290
1918	556	1941	3,394
1919	395	1942	3,497
1920	615	1943	2,901
1921	648	1944	2,305
1922	836	1945	2,136
1923	960		

Source: American Council on Education, *Higher Education in the United States* (Washington, D.C.: American Council on Education, 1965), pp. 154–55.

support given to colleges and universities.[114] State appropriations for public institutions far outstripped student enrollments, and donations for private schools were at an all-time high.

The problems of college and university growth resulted in the creation of a host of new departments and a proliferation of academic administrators. This bureaucracy was a response to enrollment increases and to demands for new services.[115] An indication of the rate of increase in the number of administrative officers is that the median of thirty-two institutions of higher education in 1860 was 4, as compared to 30.5 in 1933.[116] It is ironic that the number of university administrators in the early twentieth century so outnumbered the professors and instructors of the nineteenth-century college.

The growth of the universities placed a strain on the academic libraries to keep up with the changes. Curriculum reforms had modified faculty and student expectations about the libraries, and now the faculty wanted more research resources, and students demanded duplicate copies of instructional materials. Financing library operations had become an annual responsibility of the institutions, and money was now available to acquire library materials.[117] Funds were insufficient for all needs, but the real problem was in the dual demand for materials for research and undergraduate instruction. Slowly, over a forty-year span, policies were adopted by academic libraries to provide more access to their collections by liberalizing lending practices to the faculty and students.[118] As the universities grew larger, increased demand by undergraduates caused libraries to consider various ways to match this demand. Some libraries, such as that at the University of Chicago, had resorted to rental library service.[119] This expedient was rarely attempted elsewhere, because it violated most librarians' belief in free service. Other libraries tried to ignore the problem altogether, since they preferred to allocate their resources for scholarly books and journals. All of the major universities attempted to build their collections by acquiring scholarly materials. Libraries had become associated with the quality of the university, and rivalries over the size of collections sparked further library growth (see table 1.10).[120] A Yale professor, Chauncy Brewster Tinker, publicized this view by stressing that the size and quality of a great library was instrumental in attracting and retaining outstanding professors and students.[121] For the smaller institutions, regional standardizing associations (such as the North Central Association of College and Secondary Schools and the Association of Colleges and Secondary Schools of the Southern States) and various state agencies stimulated them to increase the number of volumes in their libraries by establishing minimum collection standards.[122]

Library growth from 1912 to 1945 reflected both a drive by universities to expand and a necessity to react to political and economic events. Book expenditures closely reflected the economic conditions of the country, but expenditures responded somewhat slowly both to prosperity and depression.[123] A look at a graph on the average number of volumes added by the twenty-three largest libraries shows dramatic increases during prosperous times and retrenchment in hard times (see figure 1.1).[124] Events associated with World War I slowed the growth of libraries in the 1916–1918 period, and it took several years for appropriations to increase after 1918 for the next surge of acquisitions to start. This pattern lasted from 1919 to 1928. After a brief downturn in

Table 1.10: Growth of Leading Libraries by Size and Expenditures, 1912–1939

Library	1912–13	1917–18	1923–24	1928–29	1933–34	1938–39
Harvard	1,083,750	1,854,900	2,322,400	2,866,200	3,603,040	4,079,541
	($106,695)	(N/A)	($156,598)	($636,666)	($215,757)	($248,458)
Yale	1,000,000	1,130,000	1,644,516	1,922,157	2,325,540	2,850,349
	($27,674)	($35,955)	($85,731)	($135,369)	($171,917)	($167,733)
Columbia	516,774	711,416	893,147	1,166,621	1,443,307	1,662,843
	($37,548)	($32,709)	($82,202)	($147,151)	($142,882)	($173,783)
Cornell	423,570	557,931	710,575	804,239	917,942	1,036,404
	($28,000)	($18,224)	($40,360)	($53,299)	($52,774)	($66,036)
Chicago	402,503	545,890	694,000	871,276	1,077,633	1,271,296
	($42,374)	($34,462)	($67,470)	($139,651)	($102,306)	($120,861)
Pennsylvania	375,109	466,769	578,293	692,421	811,303	901,164
	($25,730)	($29,217)	($40,131)	($70,416)	($52,324)	($52,251)
Princeton	355,897	409,159	545,413	630,885	709,450	939,017
	($17,243)	($13,472)	($61,492)	($67,322)	($61,361)	($69,092)
Michigan	322,040	400,830	570,806	718,425	900,671	1,060,784
	($34,533)	($32,000)	($91,550)	($142,940)	($122,528)	($140,860)
California	259,737	374,269	544,449	735,718	869,475	1,039,447
	($36,538)	($15,000)	($72,618)	($102,074)	($102,300)	($156,000)
Illinois	233,586	403,257	567,787	800,330	978,212	1,175,692
	($45,000)	($59,143)	($106,210)	($117,599)	($94,648)	($138,859)
Brown	232,000	245,000	305,427	384,427	462,922	558,291
	($23,766)	($10,553)	($24,310)	($55,688)	($46,798)	($51,112)
Stanford	221,720	298,856	375,903	511,034	610,737	739,879
	($42,658)	($21,475)	($35,590)	($59,896)	($55,460)	($63,519)
Wisconsin	204,000	253,000	327,980	(N/A)	462,560	472,061
	($31,306)	($21,000)	($50,630)	(N/A)	($57,358)	($47,583)
Minnesota	177,500	266,000	425,000	573,489	757,807	1,061,965
	($38,796)	($28,993)	($60,084)	($148,514)	($52,358)	($139,097)
Johns Hopkins	174,777	208,237	266,637	354,774	463,260	552,850
	($16,064)	($13,280)	($29,121)	($50,034)	($54,618)	($40,413)
Texas	(N/A)	148,160	282,048	430,082	473,837	618,856
	(N/A)	($29,834)	($37,659)	($46,500)	($69,992)	($105,274)
Ohio State	126,034	191,100	253,295	335,950	422,970	528,000
	($20,000)	($20,761)	(N/A)	($51,496)	($51,653)	($42,861)
Missouri	118,617	161,470	209,043	268,795	309,917	380,649
	($15,000)	($10,500)	($23,187)	($42,883)	($18,397)	($106,337)
Nebraska	105,451	136,670	187,993	233,845	285,820	341,870
	($16,000)	($15,000)	($35,000)	($36,000)	($30,079)	($49,200)
Northwestern	93,402	175,431	236,946	327,092	719,041	612,425
	($8,083)	($9,941)	($27,963)	($69,748)	($71,991)	($79,125)
Indiana	91,591	126,013	166,000	197,787	269,438	329,451
	($9,975)	($5,649)	($18,500)	($24,347)	($25,962)	($51,605)
Kansas	86,235	123,817	167,500	212,000	257,874	309,777
	($10,000)	($17,800)	($28,000)	($26,603)	($33,937)	($37,418)
Washington	52,614	84,809	132,007	198,757	275,820	398,819
	($9,800)	($7,000)	($43,935)	($40,170)	($27,044)	($73,138)

Source: J. T. Gerould, *Statistics of University Libraries* (Princeton, N.J.: Princeton University, 1913–1940), pp. 7–13.
(N/A) = not available

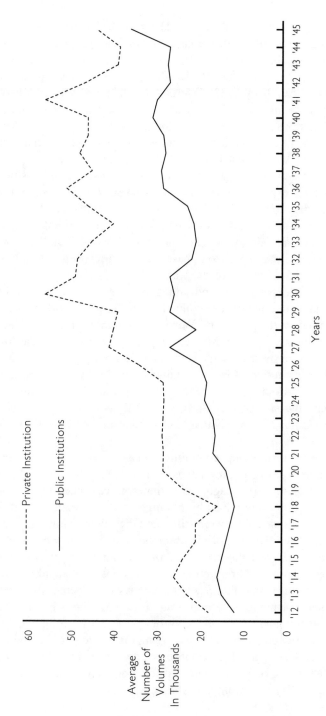

Figure 1.1: Average Number of Volumes Added to Public and Private Universities, 1912–1945

1928–29, private schools resumed their growth, but public universities were slower to break out of the early stages of the depression. Because of lag time in appropriations, 1931 was the peak year in the twenty-year growth of expenditures cycle.[125] While the depression caught up with private schools by 1933, differences in financial resources between private institutions made the impact differ according to their ability to withstand the loss of large private donations. Major donations became more infrequent after the start of the depression.[126] It was only on the eve of World War II that it seemed that library growth was going to continue at a slow but expanding rate. It was noted that universities did not raise their expenditures for materials so rapidly or so high as they raised the rate for all educational purposes.[127] After all, there was a backlog for salary increases, new equipment, and new buildings, all of which needed attention first. The outbreak of World War II ended this rebuilding from the depression phase, and libraries went into a holding pattern until after the end of the war.

Data on expenditures and added volumes indicate that differing institutional commitments determined library growth patterns in the interwar period. In the pre–World War I era, certain institutions—Harvard, Illinois, Stanford, Chicago, Minnesota, Yale, Columbia, and California–Berkeley—were spending large sums to build library collections. In contrast, other institutions—Brown, Indiana, Kansas, Washington, Northwestern, Johns Hopkins, and Iowa—were allocating barely enough funds to maintain the size of their library collections. Several institutions—Princeton, Cornell, Pennsylvania, and Wisconsin—took the middle path of moderate effort.

Different institutional commitments also characterized the next period of rapid expansion in the 1920s. Harvard, Yale, Illinois, California–Berkeley, Columbia, Chicago, and Minnesota continued to be leaders, but this time they were joined by Michigan and Princeton. Brown, Indiana, Missouri, and Kansas were still receiving minimal financial support for their libraries. The rest of the libraries were expanding but at a moderate rate. In view of the prosperity of the mid-1920s, it is surprising that the expansion of library collections was not more rapid.

At the same time that academic libraries prospered, the need for librarians to assume more administrative responsibilities became apparent. The requirement for daily control of the activities of the library resulted in more emphasis upon managing the collections. As more academic disciplines gained acceptance in the university curriculum, the library had to respond to the demand for more subject specialties. This type of specialization meant that library administrative functions needed autonomy roughly parallel to that of other academic departments.[128] Because of this close identity with the academic mission of the university, special emphasis was placed on hiring librarians with scholarly reputations.[129] This was in marked contrast with the large number of technically trained librarians graduating from library science schools. Tension developed between the teaching faculty members' emphasis on acquiring materials and the librarians' concentration on cataloging and reference services.[130] This incompatibility of outlook and the influx of women into librarianship hindered attempts of librarians to gain political control over library functions.[131] Women were recruited in great numbers into librarianship because well-educated women were available and because they would accept subordinate positions and low pay.[132] The consequences of these practices and policies are still with us in the library profession.

The depression caused a sharp break in the growth of colleges and universities, and retrenchment soon followed the reduction in enrollments. Faculty salaries were cut, sometimes in a series of reductions. While the depression hit public institutions much more quickly and harder than private ones, private schools had fewer financial resources to survive such an economic downturn. Many small colleges were unable to survive the financial stress, and a number of them closed their doors. Students reacted to the bad times by protesting over social and educational issues. Only toward the end of the 1930s did collegiate life regain some of its earlier confidence. A further impact was that students had become more career oriented than before the depression. One positive accomplishment of the thirties, however, was that most of the major universities had been able to build large central libraries to house their collections.[133]

About the time that the colleges and universities were beginning to recover from the economic effects of the depression, World War II broke out. Research efforts and scientific facilities were reoriented toward military subjects.[134] Other efforts were made to provide military education for male students. As these students graduated, enrollment dropped as all able-bodied males either joined or were drafted into military service before they entered college. Joining the students, faculty and staff were mobilized for military service. By the middle of the war, even the large universities were hurt by the lack of military-age students.

The academic library also shifted functions. Responding to calls for assistance by the government, libraries began to function as information centers rather than as depositories of scholarly materials. The demand for technical literature to support the war effort became so heavy that libraries had difficulty in matching demand.[135] Much of this reference service was confidential in direct support of military authorities.[136]

The era from 1638 to 1945 was one of uneven growth for institutions of higher education, but the relationship between the library and its host institution was always close. Colleges and their libraries grew slowly in the first two hundred and fifty years, but this changed in a dramatic fashion beginning in the 1870s. Academic libraries grew in size and holdings at the same rate as the rest of the college or university. The key ingredient was strong presidential leadership, which made a small number of elite private colleges and an equally small number of public universities expand their libraries to become the trendsetters. By the early twentieth century the differences in size and mission between the large university research libraries and the liberal arts college libraries were such that there was a growing separation in functions. The role and size differences only increased during the rest of the first half of the twentieth century. Other major changes that caused the academic library to adjust were the reforms in instruction and curriculum, the introduction of graduate degrees, and the shift toward research. The full impact of these changes, however, was to fall on higher education and academic libraries in the postwar era. After a slow start, library education began to produce a steady flow of competent librarians, but the problems of low pay and lack of status were already apparent.

𝒩OTES

1. Fremont Rider, *The Scholar and the Future of the Research Library: A Problem and Its Solution* (New York: Hadham Press, 1944), p. 8.
2. Emmanuel College at Cambridge University was the model for Harvard College, and Queen's College at Oxford University for the College of William and Mary (Frederick Rudolph, *The American College and University: A History* [New York: Knopf, 1965], p. 24).
3. John S. Brubacher and Willis Rudy, *Higher Education in Transition: A History of American Colleges and Universities, 1636–1976* (3d ed.; New York: Harper and Row, 1976), p. 4.
4. Brubacher and Rudy claim that the desire for "a literate, college-trained clergy" was the most important factor in the founding of colonial colleges. See their *Higher Education in Transition*, p. 6.
5. Richard Hofstadter and C. DeWitt Hardy, *The Development and Scope of Higher Education in the United States* (New York: Columbia University Press, 1952), pp. 11–12.
6. Brubacher and Rudy, *Higher Education in Transition*, p. 16.

7. Hofstadter and Hardy, *Development and Scope of Higher Education*, pp. 6–7.
8. Charles F. Thwing, *A History of Higher Education in America* (New York: Appleton, 1906), p. 105.
9. Arthur T. Hamlin, *The University Library in the United States: Its Origins and Development* (Philadelphia: University of Pennsylvania Press, 1981), p. 18.
10. Louis Shores, *Origins of the American College Library* (Nashville, Tenn.: George Peabody College Press, 1934), p. 51.
11. Brubacher and Rudy, *Higher Education in Transition*, p. 98. Recitation was an oral quiz of nearly in hour, held daily throughout the academic year. Its intent was to see whether the student had memorized the assigned text. See Laurence R. Veyser, *The Emergence of the American University* (Chicago: University of Chicago Press, 1965), p. 37.
12. David Kaser, "Collection Building in American Universities," in *University Library History: An International Review* (New York: Saur, 1980), p. 35.
13. Helmut Lehmann-Haupt, *The Book in America: A History of the Making and Selling of Books in the United States* (New York: Bowker, 1951), pp. 29–30.
14. Shores, *Origins of the American College Library*, p. 109.
15. Joe W. Kraus, "The Book Collections of Early American College Libraries," *Library Quarterly* 43 (1973): 156–57.
16. James A. Perkins, "Organization and Functions of the University," in *The University as an Organization*, edited by James A. Perkins (New York: McGraw-Hill, 1973), p. 6.
17. Walter P. Metzger, *Academic Freedom in the Age of the University* (New York: Columbia University Press, 1955), p. 12.
18. Kenneth J. Brough, *Scholar's Workshop: Evolving Conceptions of Library Service* (Urbana: University of Illinois Press, 1953), p. 19.
19. Brubacher and Rudy, *Higher Education in Transition*, p. 27.
20. Thomas S. Harding, *The College Literary Societies: Their Contribution to Higher Education in the United States, 1815–1876* (New York: Pageant Press, 1971), p. 3.
21. Rudolph, *American College and University*, pp. 34–35.
22. Clifford K. Shipton, *American Bibliography of Charles Evans: A Chronological Dictionary of All Books, Pamphlets and Periodical Publications Printed in the United States of America from the Genesis of Printing in 1639 Down to and Including the Year 1800 with Bibliographical and Biographical Notes* (Worcester, Mass.: American Antiquarian Society, 1955), vol. 13, p. 281.
23. E. Byrne Hackett, *Trade Bibliography in the United States in the Nineteenth Century* (New York: Brick Row Book Shop, 1939), p. xv.
24. Howard Clayton, "The American College Library, 1800–1860," *Journal of Library History* 3 (April 1968) 2:121–22.
25. Rudolph, *American College and University*, p. 51.

26. Thwing, *History of Higher Education in America*, p. 203.
27. Brubacher and Rudy, *Higher Education in Transition*, p. 60.
28. Rudolph, *American College and University*, p. 54. Burke presents figures to show that 86 percent of the colleges in 1850 had a denominational affiliation. Colin B. Burke, *American Collegiate Populations: A Test of the Traditional View* (New York: New York University Press, 1982), p. 21.
29. Metzger, *Academic Freedom in the Age of the University*, pp. 20–21.
30. Hofstadter and Hardy, *Development and Scope of Higher Education*, p. 13.
31. Burke, *American Collegiate Populations*, p. 14.
32. Ibid., p. 50.
33. Tewksbury estimated 600 to 800 colleges were founded during the pre–Civil War era. Donald G. Tewksbury, *The Founding of American Colleges and Universities before the Civil War* (Hamden, Conn.: Archon Books, 1965), p. 17. He also surveyed the number of colleges surviving the war and found an 81 percent failure rate (p. 28).
34. This case arose out of a dispute between the president of Dartmouth College, John Wheelock, and the board of trustees over the control of Dartmouth College. Thwing, *History of Higher Education in America*, pp. 273–78.
35. Burke, *American Collegiate Populations*, p. 50.
36. Clayton, "American College Library," p. 121.
37. Burke, *American Collegiate Populations*, p. 48.
38. Tewksbury, *Founding of American Colleges*, p. 24.
39. George Schmidt, *The Old Time College President* (New York: Columbia University Press, 1930), pp. 184–86.
40. Veyser, *Emergence of the American University*, p. 45.
41. Clayton, "American College Library," p. 121.
42. Orvin Lee Shiflett, *Origins of American Academic Librarianship* (Norwood, N.J.: Ablex, 1981), p. 19.
43. Veyser, *Emergence of the American University*, pp. 6.
44. Metzger, *Academic Freedom in the Age of the University*, pp. 8–9.
45. Shiflett, *Origins of American Academic Librarianship*, pp. 23–24.
46. Rudolph, *American College and University*, pp. 158–60.
47. Burke, *American Collegiate Populations*, p. 25.
48. The most famous lottery was for Union College in 1814. Two hundred thousand dollars was raised for Union—$100,000 for building, $50,000 for scholarships, $30,000 for debt, and $20,000 for the library for books and equipment. Thwing, *History of Higher Education in America*, p. 329.
49. Shiflett, *Origins of American Academic Librarianship*, p. 6.
50. At the University of Indiana in the 1830s and 1840s the library was open only on Saturdays, and was not equipped with tables and chairs. Thomas D. Clark, "Building Libraries in the Early Ohio Valley," *Journal of Library History* 6 (April 1971) 2:109.
51. Shiflett, *Origins of American Academic Librarianship*, p. 29.
52. Harding, *College Literary Societies*, p. 26.
53. Hamlin, *University Library in the United States*, p. 39.

54. Mary D. Herricks and N. Arvin Rush, "Early Literary Societies and Their Libraries in Colby College, 1824–78," *College and Research Libraries* 6 (December 1944) 1:61.

55. Harding reports that a student was paid $55 and furnished with room, wood, and lights. Harding, *College Literary Societies*, p. 61.

56. Catharine Penniman Sortie, *What Contributions Did the American College Society Make to the College Library: A Supplementary Chapter in the History of the American College Library* (Master's thesis, Columbia University, 1938), pp. 19–25.

57. Clayton, "American College Library," pp. 129–30.

58. Brough, *Scholar's Workshop*, pp. 11–12.

59. Ibid., pp. 14–15.

60. Roger L. Geiger, *To Advance Knowledge: The Growth of American Research Universities, 1900–1940* (New York: Oxford University Press, 1986), p. 4.

61. Ibid., pp. 4–5.

62. Richard G. Axt, *The Federal Government and Financing Higher Education* (New York: Columbia University Press, 1952), pp. 38–39.

63. Brubacher, *Higher Education in Transition*, p. 100.

64. Ibid., pp. 104–5.

65. Hofstadter and Hardy, *Development and Scope of Higher Education*, p. 29.

66. Rudolph, *American College and University*, p. 300.

67. E. D. Phillips, "The Elective System in American Education," *Pedagogical Seminary* 8 (June 1901): 206–30.

68. Princeton and Yale were the leaders in this reaction, but Harvard soon followed with the inauguration of of A. Lawrence Lowell as president in 1909. Veyser, *Emergence of the American University*, pp. 249–51.

69. Everett Walters, "The Rise of Graduate Education," *Graduate Education Today* (Washington, D.C.: American Council on Education, 1965), p. 6. Part of the reason for this influx of American scholars was that it was cheaper to study at German than at American universities. Veyser, *Emergence of the American University*, p. 130.

70. Thwing gives a list of the prominent American educators who studied for at least a year in Germany. Thwing, *History of Higher Education in America*, p. 320.

71. Rudolph, *American College and University*, pp. 270–71.

72. Charles F. Thwing, *The American and the German University* (New York: Appleton, 1928), p. 43.

73. Geiger, *To Advance Knowledge*, p. 8.

74. Veyser, *Emergence of the American University*, pp. 174–75.

75. Rudolph, *American College and University*, p. 336.

76. Metzger, *Academic Freedom in the Age of the University*, pp. 8-9.

77. Rudolph, *American College and University*, pp. 284–85.

78. Ibid., p. 160.

79. American Council on Education, *Higher Education in the United States* (Washington, D.C.: American Council on Education, 1965), p. 154.

80. Rudolph, *American College and University*, p. 337.
81. American Council on Education, *Higher Education in the United States*, pp. 154–55.
82. Shiflett, *Origins of American Academic Librarianship*, p. 105.
83. Brubacher and Rudy, *Higher Education in Transition*, p. 98.
84. Brough describes the stigma associated with the older recitation method, for which instructors substituted the "library method" (i.e., making library assignments). Brough, *Scholar's Workshop*, p. 61.
85. Thwing, *History of Higher Education in America*, p. 413.
86. Ibid.
87. Edward G. Holley, "Academic Libraries in 1876," *College and Research Libraries* 37 (January 1976) 1:22–23.
88. Harding, *College Literary Societies*, pp. 272, 279, 291.
89. Ibid., pp. 296–97.
90. Herricks and Rush, "Early Literary Societies," p. 63.
91. This quote is taken from Veyser, *Emergence of the American University*, p. 96.
92. Holley, "Academic Libraries in 1876," p. 35.
93. Veyser reports that as late as the 1890s Eliot at Harvard would give controversial radicals posts in the library rather than regular faculty positions. Veyser, *Emergence of the American University*, p. 97.
94. Brough's treatment of John Langdon Sibley at Harvard, Addison Van Name at Yale, and Beverley Robinson Betts at Columbia shows that they were good at collection development and conservation of materials, but deficient in library service. Brough, *Scholar's Workshop*, p. 21.
95. Shiflett, *Origins of American Academic Librarianship*, pp. 44–45.
96. Dennis Thomison, *A History of the American Library Association* (Chicago: American Library Association, 1978), p. 12.
97. W. Boyd Rayward, "Melvil Dewey and Education for Librarianship," *Journal of Library History* 3 (October 1968) 4:306.
98. Shiflett, *Origins of American Academic Librarianship*, p. 176.
99. Ibid., pp. 193–94.
100. Metzger, *Academic Freedom in the Age of the University*, pp. 46–90.
101. Ibid., pp. 67-68.
102. Ibid., pp. 133–38.
103. Hofstadter and Hardy, *Development and Scope of Higher Education*, p. 31.
104. W. Vance Grant and Thomas D. Snyder, *Digest of Education Statistics, 1985–86* (Washington, D.C.: U.S. Government Printing Office, 1986), p. 110.
105. E. E. Duryea, "Evolution of University Organization," in *The University as an Organization*, edited by James A. Perkins (New York: McGraw-Hill, 1983), p. 23.
106. Burton A. Clark, *The Academic Life: Small Worlds, Different Worlds* (Princeton, N.J.: Carnegie Foundation for the Advancement of Learning, 1987), p. 15.
107. Hamlin, *University Library in the United States*, pp. 112–14.

108. Geiger, *To Advance Knowledge*, p. 10.
109. Ibid., p. 13.
110. This table is a combination of data from Lehmann-Haupt's *The Book in America*, p. 321, and Downing Palmer O'Harra's *Book Publishing in the United States, 1860–1901* (Master's thesis, University of Illinois, 1928), pp.145–46.
111. Frank Luther Mott, *A History of American Magazines, 1885–1905* (Cambridge, Mass.: Belknap Press, 1957), p. 11.
112. American Council on Education, *Higher Education in the United States*, pp. 154-55.
113. Walters, "Rise of Graduate Education," p. 19.
114. Geiger, *To Advance Knowledge*, p. 123.
115. Rudolph, *American College and University*, p. 434.
116. Earl James McGrath, *The Evolution of Administrative Offices in Institutions of Higher Education in the United States from 1860 to 1933* (Chicago: University of Chicago Libraries, 1938), p. 190.
117. Hamlin, *University Library in the United States*, p. 49.
118. Shiflett, *Origins of American Academic Librarianship*, pp. 131–33.
119. Brough, *Scholar's Workshop*, pp. 66–67.
120. J. T. Gerould, *Statistics of University Libraries* (Princeton, N.J.: Princeton University Press, 1913–40), pp. 7–13.
121. C. B. Tinker, "The University Library," *Yale Alumni Weekly* 33 (February 1924): 650.
122. Floyd W. Reeves and John Dale Russell, "The Relation of the College Library to Recent Movements in Higher Education," *Library Quarterly* 1 (January 1931) 1:57–58.
123. Ralph E. Ellsworth, "Trends in University Expenditures for Library Resources and for Total Educational Purpose, 1921–41," *Library Quarterly* 14 (January 1944) 1:7.
124. Robert E. Moyneux, *The Gerould Statistics, 1907/08–1961/62* (Washington, D.C.: Association of Research Libraries, 1986), pp. 103–6.
125. Ellsworth, "Trends in University Expenditures," p. 3.
126. Ibid., p. 7.
127. Geiger, *To Advance Knowledge*, p. 53.
128. Shiflett, *Origins of American Academic Librarianship*, pp. 151–52.
129. Ibid., p. 152.
130. Ibid., p. 261.
131. Ibid., pp. 261–62.
132. Barbara Elizabeth Brand, "Sex-Typing in Education for Librarianship, 1870–1920," in *The Status of Women in Librarianship: Historical, Sociological and Economic Issues*, edited by Kathleen M. Heim (New York: Neal-Schuman, 1983), pp. 46–47.
133. Hamlin, *University Library in the United States*, pp. 63–64.
134. Evelyn Steel Little, "War Activities of College and Research Libraries," *College and Research Libraries* 4 (June 1943) 3:179.

135. Herbert A. Kellar, "American Reference Libraries in the Postwar Era," *College and Research Libraries* 3 (September 1942) 4:285.
136. Little, "War Activities of College and Research Libraries," p. 184.

CHAPTER TWO

The University and the Academic Library in the Postwar World

1945 to Present

THE POSTWAR ERA has been one of unprecedented growth in both higher education and academic libraries, and this growth has been most apparent in student enrollment levels. Both the financial health and the social functions of American higher education have been influenced by the fluctuations of student enrollments.[1] Before 1945, a college education was restricted to a small portion of the U.S. population, and it was a combination of the return of World War II veterans in the late 1940s and the subsequent baby boom of the 1960s and 1970s that has forced higher education to come to grips with the country's needs for an educated work force. Each decade since 1945 has witnessed a greater percentage of high school graduates going to college. It is this increasing demand for higher education that has made dire predictions about the demographic downturns, such as the "bottoming out" of students in the mid-1980s, prove to be less drastic than anticipated. While higher education has never been immune from the vagaries of economic booms and busts, the steady flow of undergraduate and graduate students has meant that the demand for educational services has remained high. Even the financial downturns of the mid-1970s and (to a lesser extent) the mid-1980s, which caused contractions of educational services, have only been aberrations in an era otherwise known for expansion of colleges and universities. The result of these financial downturns, however, has been the "stretching" of financial resources of most institutions of higher education. A weaker financial base and the movement for more financial accountability by state and local governments have combined to place many institutions in an unenviable position of declining resources at a time when the burdens of expanding enrollments and the need for new programs are increasing.

Although the overall pattern has been one of growth, higher education has gone through three distinct phases in the postwar world. The first phase was unrestrained growth, as society dictated that new programs and different types of institutions be developed. Federal support for scientific and technological research also stimulated expansion at the larger institutions. This era lasted from the end of World War II until the mid-1960s. Colleges and universities adapted themselves admirably to the requirement to grow and prosper.[2] New schools and programs proliferated at an ever increasing rate, until the political environment changed suddenly because of political unrest.

The second phase was one of critical self-examination that unrestrained growth did not solve all of society's problems. This period was shorter, lasting only from the mid-1960s to the mid-1970s. Student turmoil and pressures for "humanizing" education combined to make it a troubled decade for higher education.[3] The political scene became so troubling that it was not uncommon to witness university presidents resigning and teaching faculties splitting along ideological lines. One side effect was that the overwhelming public acceptance of higher education was replaced by a more skeptical attitude. Public disfavor of political turmoil on campus manifested itself in the era of critical examination.

The third phase has been one of critical examination of all aspects of higher education by outsiders. This phase started in the mid-1970s and is still operating in the 1990s. Public agencies, both federal and state, have devoted increasing attention to the issues of higher education. Fiscal accountability and control have become fashionable themes in governmental circles. While public colleges and universities have been most affected by the accountability trend, the increased dependence of private institutions on federal funds has also involved them.[4] The experience of the postwar world suggests that a certain tension always exists between the demands of society and the goals of higher education.

Academic libraries experienced expansion at almost the same rate as their host institutions, and the postwar expansion in higher education placed severe strains on the resources of even the largest academic libraries. Most of the great prewar libraries had been built around the humanities and social sciences.[5] Wartime expansion and the Cold War rivalry created a demand for more science and engineering materials, and libraries acquired these materials at an accelerated pace. Most prewar library buildings were too small to hold the new materials, so almost every institution had to build new buildings or expand its library space with new branch libraries.

Besides acquisition of traditional research materials, libraries had to find funding to acquire materials on a variety of new types of technology. Information on new technologies was expensive, and an almost endless demand on finite resources made libraries explore ways for resource sharing. Recently, libraries have also had to adapt to new library technologies, and this has also had a hefty price tag. Finally, the monopoly of the library on the university's information needs ended with the emergence of a serious rival for financial support, the university computer center. Together, these factors have made the last forty-five years an era of rapid change for academic libraries—and it is still in progress. Despite the fluctuations of library support from colleges and universities, the feeling remains among leaders in higher education and the teaching faculty that "no university can be great unless it has a great library." [6]

Academic libraries also shared the various phases of support experienced by higher education, but the libraries have differed in their degree of change and intensity. Both moral and financial support for libraries was strong from the mid-1950s to the mid-1960s. Library collections were able to expand at a rate beyond the capability of most institutions to house them, and the growth of student enrollments meant the need for more librarians and especially support staff. On the eve of the baby boom in 1957, a survey of academic libraries stated that they were understaffed by about 10 percent, with 500 to 800 unfilled positions.[7] A special campaign to recruit librarians was launched by libraries and library science schools, but it soon turned into a recruitment of men for upper-level administrative positions.[8] While this campaign to recruit librarians was successful, as a higher percentage of men than women entered the profession in the years from 1950 to 1960, the long-term impact was to cause a division within the profession between male administrators and female librarians. The problem of finding more librarians for all the openings remained. Only gradually, as new library and information science schools opened and new graduates entered the work force, did the shortage of librarians begin to end.

By the late 1960s, the academic library began to experience some of the dislocation brought on by the political troubles of student and staff unrest. The turmoil of the late 1960s and early 1970s caused librarians anxiety over the physical safety of the collections. Despite political upheaval, institutional support in terms of building collections and housing materials remained constant. It was in the accountability phase of the mid-1970s and 1980s that library leadership had to cope with reduced expectations and resources. Again, the academic library has been sheltered by college and university administrators from the full impact of cuts, but the rate of growth for library materials and personnel has lessened. An ongoing problem has been that demand for library materials and services has continued to grow, beyond resources, causing considerable stress to library administrators and staff. Demands for new technology also surfaced when resources had been reduced by inflation and lagging financial support.

Initial growth in higher education was stimulated by a number of changes in the postwar environment. American colleges and universities were unprepared to handle the influx of students after World War II. Reputable economists predicted in 1945 that only a small percentage of the eligible war veterans would take advantage of the new G.I. Bill.[9] Instead of the expectation of higher education administrators of an increase in student enrollment from 150,000 to 700,000, 2,232,000 veterans attended college under the World War II G.I. Bill.[10] War veterans mixed with high school graduates to form a student body that almost overwhelmed institutions of higher education. While this was especially true with public colleges and universities, and less so with private institutions, all schools experienced the education boom of the late 1940s and early 1950s. More students meant the need for more professors and more space for teaching. Much of the lack of postwar planning by higher education officials was because the planners had heeded the pessimistic predictions of the leading economists of the day, that another period of economic downturn was approaching.[11] An interlude in the mid-1950s gave colleges and universities a brief respite from high student enrollments, but many harassed higher education officials misinterpreted this lull as a return to the prewar environment of smaller enrollments. Few institutions were ready for the great influx of the baby-boom generation, starting in the early 1960s. Demographic projections foretold a large number of young adults reaching college age, but it took almost a decade for higher education to prepare room for the overwhelming number of students.

At the same time that higher education was attempting to cope with the growth of the student body, the federal government expanded its role in supplying funds for scholarly research in science and technology. The wartime experience of the government made officials receptive to spending federal funds in sponsoring research and development at the university level. While some federal money had been spent on science projects before the war, "crash" programs during the war allocated huge outlays for applied scientific research. This experience made it easy for the federal government to continue to fund scientific research in the postwar years; but support developed within the university community for basic rather than applied research.[12] Thus the difference or tension between basic and applied research has continued to haunt relations between the federal government and the university community.

   Commitment to research had become an integral part of American higher education earlier in the century, but now research had support from both inside and outside the university. Universities continue to benefit from the close working relationship between the federal government and the academic scientific community. The ebb and flow of federal funds to support research has depended on the changes in national priorities during the last forty-five years. While academic research still consumes a significant portion of the total higher education expenditures, it has had, in the past, even a higher percentage of the expenditures (see table 2.1).[13] The effort has stabilized in the last decade at about 8.5 percent. This level, however, contrasts unfavorably with the research effort in the middle 1960s, which was in the high teens.

Table 2.1: Organized Academic Research as a Share of Higher Education Expenditures, 1946–1985 (In Milllions of Dollars)

Years	Total Expenditures	Organized Research	Percentage
1946	$ 1,088	$ 87	7.9
1950	2,246	225	10.0
1956	3,499	501	14.3
1960	5,601	1,022	18.2
1966	12,509	2,448	19.5
1970	21,043	2,144	10.1
1974	35,058	3,132	8.9
1977	45,971	3,920	8.5
1980	64,053	5,773	9.1
1983	81,993	6,724	8.2
1985	97,536	8,437	8.6

Source: U.S. Bureau of Statistics, *Historical Statistics of the United States, Colonial Times to 1970* (Washington, D.C.: Bureau of the Census, 1975), p. 145; and Thomas D. Snyder, *Digest of Education Statistics, 1987* (Washington, D.C.: Center for Education Statistics, 1987), p. 236.

Federal support for applied scientific research became another chapter in the ongoing conflict between adherents of liberal arts education and applied science. Proponents of both sides reside on university campuses, and they jockey for influence within the university administrative power structure. The creation of so many new professional schools caused tension between supporters of the traditional academic disciplines and those of the new professional schools.[14] This tension has been slow to diminish, especially after these professional schools have prospered and grown.

This division between the applied and the theoretical has had its impact on the academic library. Scientific research is an extension of technology, and its research materials are costly. Currency of information becomes the key principle in the acquisition of materials for science and technology. In contrast, supporters of the liberal arts want the largest and most accessible collection of books and journals possible. Quality of scholarship, rather than currency of information, is the guiding principle. These supporters of the library subscribe to the "storehouse of knowledge" role of the academic library.[15] The issue of large collections of materials to support scholarship for the humanities and the social sciences, or the need for access to information for the sciences, has become a source of contention among teaching faculties and academic libraries alike. Rare is the academic library that can afford to build large collections of specialized research materials and also buy all the databases and CD-ROM products to support access to existing collections.

The debate over the direction of higher education is part of the failure of American higher education to decide upon its true mission. Ideals about educating an intellectual elite conflict with training students to make a living, and it is in this latter function that American higher education has been most successful.[16] After all, most parents send their children to college to better their position in the world. This fact alone is responsible for the dramatic surge in the size of postwar college enrollments, and it also accounts for the errors of forecasting drops in enrollment during demographic downturns. Each decade, a higher percentage of high school graduates goes to college than in the previous decade. This drive for betterment has also played a role in the dramatic growth of graduate and professional education.

The academic library was not unchanged by developments in higher education in the postwar world. An "information explosion" after World War II meant that librarians had to cope with new and different kinds of materials. Librarians adjusted to these new conditions by adopting the philosophy of utilization of library materials, rather than their conservation on the shelves for scholarly use only.[17] New demands on curriculum meant that library leadership had to make serious choices on the dividing of finite resources. At the same time that these hard financial decisions had to be made on the direction of the academic library, a new generation of library leaders appeared. A comparative study of university librarians in 1933 and 1948 showed that the latter were younger, more educated, and had more exposure to library positions than their 1933 counterparts.[18] This new leadership had to respond to a series of new challenges. These challenges were to provide more library services for a faculty with expanding scientific and technological interests, a growing student body, and a changing university curriculum as more and more new disciplines were being added. The growth of layers of administrative offices between the university president and the library director ended the former close relationship between them. It became a constant battle for the library director to keep in touch even with lower-rank academic officers on decisions affecting the library.[19]

Besides dealing with the growth in demand for library services, new research specialties had to be integrated into the library. Two areas of special concern were science and area studies (East Europe, Middle East, Far East, etc.).[20] Resources were difficult to obtain, because libraries were failing to hold their own in an inflationary cycle. A comparison of library expenditures between 1939 and 1949 indicated that while university budgets as a whole tripled, the library budgets of these research institutions only doubled.[21] This story continued in the 1950s, until a renewed interest in education appeared after 1959. Projected enrollments made leaders in the library world nervous, because they recognized that more students meant more students in the library.[22]

At the same time as all the new developments in higher education, new types of institutions were forming with distinct clienteles. Historically, the development of American higher education has produced a variety of institutions, such as the four basic types of institutions that emerged earlier in the century: (1) the liberal arts college, (2) the research university, (3) teachers' colleges, and (4) the junior college. Each type of institution had a secure educational place, with a curriculum attracting a different kind of student clientele. The liberal arts college has had a long history, and despite bad economic times during the 1930s depression, most colleges were still providing students a solid liberal arts education. It was the growth of the large research universities, both private and public, that had made the major impact on the prewar higher educational scene. These institutions had large student bodies, famous faculties, commitment to research, and the reputation of providing the educational leadership for the nation. In contrast, teachers' colleges had the task of training teachers for elementary and secondary schools, and while many of these colleges were large, the curriculum was devoted almost exclusively to teachers' training. The junior colleges had an educational mission to conduct remedial education and to train students in technical subjects, but they attempted to carry out these functions in only two years. Most of these schools were new and had started playing an important educational role only in the decade before World War II.

The postwar world has seen an expansion in the number and types of institutions of higher education. While the four types of prewar institutions retained their place in the postwar era, they now had rivals. The liberal arts college began as the most numerous type of higher educational institution in the United States, but by the late 1950s the junior college (now renamed "community college") had overtaken it. Liberal arts institutions, however, continued to provide a liberal arts education following the nineteenth-century model of classical humanism, tempered by an emphasis on Christian ethics. These schools have been able to retain their prominent place in higher education, but during periods of economic downturn many of them have suffered a loss of endowments and some have had to close their doors.

The community college has become an important factor in higher education in the postwar world. Few of these two-year colleges were in existence in 1945, but by the early 1960s they were numerous enough to constitute an impressive educational force. These colleges assumed even greater importance, because they were "a direct result of numerous scientific, industrial, and technological changes which demand more trained technicians at the sub-professional level."[23] These colleges also expanded beyond remedial and technical curricula to develop a liberal arts curriculum. Their emphasis on undergraduate education at the introductory level meant that generalist instructors were more in demand than disciplinary specialists.[24] Consequently, the number of instructors holding doctorates had only increased from around 10 percent in the 1950s to about 20 percent in the mid-1980s.[25] These schools have also allowed access for new types of students—women, middle-aged people, senior citizens, and minorities—"left out" of the traditional institutions.[26]

The research university has become the most prestigious institution in higher education. Although outnumbered by the liberal arts colleges, these universities dominate both practical and theoretical learning. By offering a liberal arts education, profession training, and direct service to the public, universities have assumed a paramount place in American higher education. A relatively small number of great universities, perhaps as few as fifty institutions, are the most influential and prestigious.[27]

Their success is reflected in their spectacular growth. But these institutions also have suffered stress in reconciling the traditional objectives of higher education with the diversity in interests and qualifications of many disciplines and programs.[28]

By the end of the 1960s the four earlier types of institutions had been further subdivided, according to educational functions. The Carnegie Foundation for the Advancement of Teaching and its subordinate unit, the Carnegie Commission on Higher Education, had determined by the early 1970s that ten types of institutions of higher education were in existence (see appendix). These ten were listed in the following order: research universities I, research universities II, doctoral-granting universities I, doctoral-granting universities II, comprehensive universities and colleges I, comprehensive universities and colleges II, liberal arts colleges I, liberal arts colleges II, two-year colleges, and specialized institutions (see table 2.2).[29] The criterion for each category has changed slightly over the last decade and a half and

Table 2.2: Carnegie Classification of Institutions in Years 1973, 1976, 1987

| | | | | | Years | | | | |
| Type of | | 1973 | | | 1976 | | | 1987 | |
Institution	Pub.	Priv.	Total	Pub.	Priv.	Total	Pub.	Priv.	Total
Research universities I	30	22	52	29	22	51	45	25	70
Research universities II	27	13	40	33	14	47	26	8	34
Doctoral-granting universities I	34	19	53	38	18	56	30	21	51
Doctoral-granting universities II	17	11	28	19	11	30	33	25	58
Comprehensive univ. and coll. I	223	98	321	250	131	381	284	140	424
Comprehensive univ. and coll. II	85	47	132	104	109	213	47	124	171
Liberal arts colleges I	2	144	146	0	123	123	2	140	142
Liberal arts colleges II	26	547	573	11	449	460	30	400	430
2-year colleges	805	256	1,061	909	238	1,147	985	382	1,367
Specialized schools	64	357	421	70	490	560	66	576	642
Totals	1,313	1,514	2,827	1,463	1,605	3,068	1,548	1,841	3,389

Source: Carnegie Foundation for the Advancement of Teaching, *A Classification of Institutions of Higher Education* (Berkeley, Calif.: Carnegie Commission on Higher Education, 1987), pp. 1–5.

institutions have been able to move upward or downward according to fixed standards. Each type of institution has been successful by responding to a specific need in higher education. At the same time, a hierarchy of quality was established, with each college and university seen as high, medium, or low.[30] This hierarchy, besides determining rank, gives these institutions the hope that by improving faculty, facilities, and funding they could move up in the quality ranking.[31] Among lower-ranking institutions, this drive for improvement in ranking has become a priority.

In the shift between the private and public sectors in higher education, the latter sector has grown at a faster rate during the last thirty years than the former (see table 2.3).[32] Private institutions outnumbered public ones by almost two to one in the 1950s, but this was changed by the large number of public institutions that opened in the 1960s and early 1970s. While growth in the public sector leveled off in the 1970s and a slight reduction took place in the early 1980s, the gain in the public institutions rose from about 35 percent to 40+ percent in the mid-1980s (see table 2.4).[33] The number of private institutions is still larger than the number of public ones, and unless economic conditions deteriorate, little further change is expected.

The growth in number of institutions is reflected in the huge increases in the number of students attending institutions of higher education. Leaders in higher education recognized the problem of the postwar baby-boom crowd reaching college age, but still they were unprepared

Table 2.3: Institutions of Higher Education by Type of Control and 5-Year Intervals, 1950–1986

| | | | Type of Control | | | |
| | Public | | Private | | Totals | |
Year	No.	Pct.	No.	Pct.	No.	Pct.
1950–51	636	34	1,216	66	1,852	100
1955–56	650	35	1,200	65	1,850	100
1960–61	700	35	1,321	65	2,021	100
1965–66	821	37	1,409	63	2,230	100
1970–71	1,089	43	1,467	57	2,556	100
1975–76	1,219	44	1,546	56	2,765	100
1980–81	1,334	44	1,722	56	3,056	100
1985–86	1,326	42	1,829	58	3,155	100

Source: Thomas D. Snyder, *Digest of Education Statistics, 1987* (Washington, D.C.: Center for Education Statistics, 1987), p. 165.

Table 2.4: Enrollment in Private and Public Institutions of Higher Education by 5-Year Intervals, 1965–1985 (In Millions)

Types of Institutions	Years									
	1965		1970		1975		1980		1985	
	Enroll.	Pct.	Enroll.	Pct.	Enroll.	Pct.	Enroll.	Pct.	Enroll.	Pct.
Universities	2,332	39	3,077	36	2,838	25	2,902	24	2,871	23
Public	1,658	28	2,350	27	2,124	19	2,154	18	2,141	18
Private	675	11	727	8	714	6	748	6	730	6
Other 4-year institutions	2,458	41	3,345	39	4,377	39	4,669	39	4,845	40
Public	1,299	22	2,024	23	2,874	26	2,974	25	3,068	25
Private	1,159	19	1,321	15	1,503	14	1,694	14	1,777	15
2-year institutions	1,173	20	2,227	26	3,970	35	4,526	37	4,531	37
Public	1,041	17	2,102	24	3,836	34	4,329	36	4,270	35
Private	132	2	125	1	134	1	198	1	261	2
All types of institutions	5,920	100	8,649	100	11,185	100	12,097	100	12,247	100
Public	3,970	67	6,476	75	8,835	80	9,457	78	9,479	77
Private	1,950	33	2,173	25	2,350	20	2,639	22	2,768	23

Source: Thomas D. Snyder, *Digest of Education Statistics, 1987* (Washington, D.C.: Center for Education Statistics, 1987), p. 165.

for the great number of students ready for college in the middle 1960s. Combining with the demographic boom was the belief among Americans that a college degree was important and useful. The general public, however, was insistent that "higher education must be democratized, broadened, and made a national as well as state priority."[34] Suddenly, not only were more students of college age, but also a higher percentage of high school graduates wanted to go to a college or university. In the decade between 1960 and 1970, five million new students attended colleges and universities, 500 new campuses were constructed, and 250,000 added faculty were employed.[35] Public institutions were the most affected by the surge of new students (see table 2.5),[36] but private schools were not immune from the pressure (see table 2.6).[37] Most of the growth in privately controlled institutions of higher education has been in the four-year schools.

Academic libraries were not immune from the demand for more services caused by the increase in the number of students. Library leaders were aware, before the fact, that library buildings were too small to house the collections or provide the necessary study space for the projected enrollment increases.[38] Building programs were launched on

Table 2.5: Publicly Controlled Institutions of Higher Education by 5-Year Intervals, 1950–1986

	4-Year		2-Year		Totals	
Year	No.	Pct.	No.	Pct.	No.	Pct.
1950–51	341	54	295	46	636	100
1955–56	360	55	290	45	650	100
1960–61	368	53	332	47	700	100
1965–66	401	49	420	51	821	100
1970–71	435	40	654	60	1,089	100
1975–76	447	37	772	63	1,219	100
1980–81	465	36	869	64	1,334	100
1985–86	461	35	865	65	1,326	100

Source: Thomas D. Snyder, *Digest of Education Statistics, 1987* (Washington, D.C.: Center for Education Statistics, 1987), p. 165.

Table 2.6: Privately Controlled Institutions of Higher Education by 5-Year Intervals, 1950–1986

	4-Year		2-Year		Totals	
Year	No.	Pct.	No.	Pct.	No.	Pct.
1950–51	971	80	245	20	1,216	100
1955–56	987	82	213	18	1,200	100
1960–61	1,063	80	258	20	1,321	100
1965–66	1,150	82	259	18	1,409	100
1970–71	1,230	84	237	16	1,467	100
1975–76	1,320	86	226	14	1,546	100
1980–81	1,396	81	326	19	1,722	100
1985–86	1,454	80	375	20	1,829	100

Source: Thomas D. Snyder, *Digest of Education Statistics, 1987* (Washington, D.C.: Center for Education Statistics, 1987), p. 165.

many campuses, but the rate of construction always seemed to lag behind the need for more space. Impetus for library building came from grants from the Higher Education Facilities Act of 1963. While these grants were discontinued in 1969, their result was 605 separate library buildings at colleges and universities receiving funding.[39] Similar dire forecasts concerned the need to build larger library collections, but the funds were not always forthcoming. Funding had to come from state sources, and these funds were not as large as the federal grants for library buildings. An earlier projection, that student increases would mean the ratio of professional librarians to clerical staff would decline, proved to be true.[40] The small number of library schools was unable to graduate enough librarians to match the demand.

The turmoil surrounding the political unrest in the late 1960s and the early 1970s caused higher education to go through a period of painful self-examination. Colleges and universities had concluded a tacit alliance with the federal government to produce research for products useful for defense and military purposes. In exchange for plentiful federal grants, scientific and technical researchers devoted their attention to research and development projects. At first, it was only antiwar protestors who challenged this arrangement; then, racial unrest hit the campus. Although radical students affiliated with the new left orchestrated many of the original protests, the issues became a concern for enough other students that campus unrest became general. Many humanities and social science professors began to question the interdependence of the university and the war effort. Together, the civil rights and antiwar causes and questions about the lack of a response from higher education to these issues made college and university administrators uneasy. For nearly five years, from 1967 to 1972, higher education felt itself under attack. A siege mentality developed, and federal troops on college campuses were not an unfamiliar sight. The unrest ceased, but only because the students and their faculty allies achieved so many of their demands, and because a new generation of less politically active students arrived on college campuses.

The final result of the political agitation of the late 1960s and early 1970s was the demise of the ivory tower image of academia. No longer was the campus a refuge away from life's problems. Academia was now challenged by the philosophy of making education relevant. Practical rather than liberal arts education became more popular, and professional programs flourished on college and university campuses. Curriculum reforms meant that the undergraduate curriculum became a supermarket, and some academic departments prospered and others declined.[41] The division between the applied professions and the liberal arts widened, with considerable fear and resentment from the liberal arts side. Finally, student activism and the quasi-protected status of draft deferments for college students changed the public's attitude toward higher education.[42] Disenchantment with higher education became widespread among the general populace, and the decline of the national economy exacerbated the feeling of malaise on college campuses.

The expansion of higher education in the 1960s was followed by contraction in the early 1970s. Although the number of students going to college was still growing, the combination of student unrest and the economic downturn began to take a toll on the expansion of colleges and universities. A list of institutions of higher education that went bankrupt between 1960 and 1983 shows the bulk of the closures were between 1967 and 1975 (see table 2.7).[43] A total of 151 out of 254 schools, or 59.4 percent, failed in this eight-year period. In comparison, only 103 closed their doors in the other fifteen years. By far the majority of these failures were in private institutions. This low failure rate in public institutions is not surprising, because it takes a political decision for a public institution to go bankrupt.[44] Instead of bankruptcy, public institutions tend to struggle along with increasingly inadequate financial resources. The litany of reasons for the lack of financial health in colleges and universities includes higher instructional costs, with little or no increase in productivity; higher building costs; higher maintenance and security expenditures; more student services; and inflation.[45] Tuition and fee increases had been implemented, but the higher education market could handle only so many such hikes. At the same time that the financial picture worsened, education demographers noted that the number of college-age students would start decreasing in 1979 and remain low until the middle 1990s.[46] Since student enrollments and the financial health of most colleges and universities were so closely intertwined, educational planners began to downscale plans for expansion and, instead, contemplated retrenchment.

Academic libraries continued to expand in the mid-1960s to mid-1970s, but the rate of growth slowed. Booming student enrollments had

Table 2.7: Number of Defunct Public and Private Institutions of Higher Education in 5-Year Intervals, 1960–1983

	Public		Private		
Years	4-Year	2-Year	4-Year	2-Year	Totals
1960–64	0	6	4	15	25
1965–69	0	11	29	30	70
1970–74	0	17	48	33	98
1975–79	1	1	28	13	43
1980–84	0	0	21	5	26
Totals	1	35	130	96	262

Source: Thomas D. Snyder, *Digest of Education Statistics, 1987* (Washington, D.C.: Center for Education Statistics, 1987), p. 166.

caused the same kind of dislocation in the academic library as elsewhere in the university. Frantic efforts were made by library administrators to spread the resources to cover a greater variety of patron demands. Library work was still labor intensive, with professional librarians still heavily involved in nonprofessional tasks. Academic libraries had not been able to meet the requirement of the Downs formula: a professional-clerical ratio of one to three.[47] Earlier heavy demand for librarians began to slacken, and for several years in the mid-1970s library jobs became scarce. Also, library resources were beginning to be mobilized for library technology, but only at a few trend-setting libraries. Some of the violence of the late 1960s and early 1970s reached even into academic libraries. Arson, bombings, and destruction of books and card catalogs were experienced at a number of academic libraries.[48] Extraordinary measures were taken to safeguard collections and card catalogs, including making backup copies.

Toward the end of the campus disturbances, librarians began to consider major changes in the cataloging rules. These changes also had an impact on the functioning of the academic library. The second edition of the *Anglo-American Cataloguing Rules* (AACR2) was intended to consolidate earlier cataloging rules, but, in modifying the rules, academic libraries had to solve the problem of combining the new rules with the old.[49] Dissatisfaction with a mixed card catalog and an increasing patron demand resulted in library administrators becoming more receptive to the possibility of online computer systems. These systems were still in a developmental phase, but the need for something to replace the old system was recognized by leaders in the academic library community.

Higher education has come under increasing scrutiny since the mid-1970s. Both federal and state governments have been reluctant to give higher education a blank check. Higher education had been the recipient in the postwar era of what has been called the "liberal consensus" on the benefits of education as a public good.[50] This consensus depended, however, on a "near-boundless confidence" in the ability of the national government to deploy its resources to achieve educational and societal goals.[51] In a sense, it was the success of this coalition of national political leaders, education leaders from public and private institutions, theorists from think tanks, and labor union leaders that mobilized a conservative opposition. Although higher education has been successful in educating large numbers of students, insatiable demands for more money and the collapse of the liberal consensus has caused the public to lose confidence in higher education.[52] A conservative estimate placed the reduction at 15 percent in total enrollment head count.[53] The lack of public confidence and the eminent demographic downturn combined to produce a readiness in government agencies to make higher education more accountable. For higher education, accountability was interpreted to mean making colleges and universities responsible for their graduates, much as a business is responsible for its products.[54] One president, William Gerberding at the University of Washington–Seattle, called "the combination of hard times, the tax revolt, and the de-mystification of higher education" lethal to the cause of higher education.[55]

At the same time that this accountability debate was in progress, financial pressures on colleges and universities intensified. Inflationary pressures in the mid-1970s and the change of philosophy during the Reagan administration also played a role in reducing the interest in funding higher education at higher levels. Higher education administrators have resented detailed budget and accounting procedures and comprehensive regulations. They have argued, instead, for more flexibility in dealing with management problems.[56] Several states have allowed for some financial flexibility, but most have retained tight control over their institutions.

These funding problems have also had an impact on the academic orientation of colleges and universities. A two-track institutional system has emerged: narrowly academic and broadly educational.[57] The narrowly academic are those institutions in the Carnegie categories of research universities and doctoral-granting universities. These institutions have a traditional orientation toward research, and they strive for quality. The remainder of the colleges and universities are nontraditional and more interested in a broad educational mission. A scholar in the field has even distinguished a difference in common terms between the traditionalists and nontraditionalists:

Traditionalists	Nontraditionalists
standards	diversity
regular students	new students
quality	opportunity
authority	adaptiveness
sequences	units
content	competencies
community	individualism [58]

A further fact has been a shift in student attitudes from traditional to applied fields. This shift is best documented in a 1984 survey of intended areas of study in college comparing student responses in the years

1975 and 1984 (see table 2.8).[59] Almost all of the traditional areas of study—history, biological sciences, philosophy and religion, mathematics, education, foreign languages, physical sciences, and English and literature—have lost in popularity. In contrast, computer science, engineering, business, communications, and health and medical subjects have become more popular. While fluctuations may occur between these fields, the general shift from the traditional liberal arts to the applied fields has had a major impact on the curricula of colleges and universities.

The academic library has suffered in this accountability trend. Reduction in financial resources at the university level has been felt at the library level. State governments have funded libraries at the national rate of inflation, or slightly below that level, but the rate of inflation in publishing has been double or even triple the national rate. Moreover, the strength (or lack of strength) of the American dollar in international

Table 2.8: National Changes in Intended Areas of Study in College, Comparison between 1976 and 1984

Field	1975 No.	% of Total	1984 No.	% of Total	% of Change
WINNERS					
Computer sciences	13,006	1.6	85,254	9.7	+555.5
Engineering	54,463	6.7	105,468	12.0	+93.7
Business	93,482	11.5	167,871	19.1	+79.6
Communications	21,948	2.7	32,519	3.7	+48.2
Health/medical	121,120	14.9	132,715	15.1	+9.6
Psychology	29,264	3.6	30,716	3.5	+5.1
Social sciences	62,592	5.1	64,160	7.3	+2.5
LOSERS					
Art	30,890	3.8	29,883	3.4	-3.3
Undecided	52,837	6.5	38,672	4.4	-26.8
English/literature	16,258	2.4	11,426	1.3	-29.7
Physical sciences	22,761	2.8	14,941	1.7	-34.4
Foreign languages	11,380	1.4	7,031	0.8	-38.2
Education	73,972	9.1	40,430	4.6	-45.3
Mathematics	19,509	2.4	9,668	1.1	-50.4
Phillosphy/religion	5,690	0.7	2,637	0.3	-53.7
Biological sciences	65,031	8.0	27,246	3.1	-58.1
History	11,380	1.4	4,395	0.5	-61.2

Source: Jan Krukowski, "What Do Students Want? Status," Change 17 (May–June 1985) 3:24.

exchange has also had an impact on library budgets. The result has been periods of financial uncertainty followed by short periods of stable funding. Part of the problem has been that the lessening of support for academic libraries has taken place during an era of rapid technological change in libraries.

Despite some of these financial problems, academic libraries have continued to grow, both in size of collections and in the number of faculty and students served. While collections have been expanding at a slower rate during the last few years, the major research libraries are still adding books and journal volumes at a steady rate. The two major problems in the last decade have been the rapidly increasing price of serials and the closing of several of the most prominent library science schools. Most academic libraries have had at least one spate of cancellations during the 1980s because of serial price increases. These increases are in part a result of the federal government's monetary policies, and some of the increases have to do with the nature of scientific publishing. Either way, serial price increases have devastated the materials budgets of most research libraries. Serial cancellations have also caused concern among scholars, learned societies, book and journal publishers, foundations, and the government.[60] Despite study of the problem, no solutions have been forthcoming, except the recommendation to spend more money; but even this open-the-pocketbook approach has been subject to criticism.[61] An irony is that academic librarians have been more bothered by the financial state of the scholarly communication system than the scholars themselves.[62]

The closing of several of the most prominent library science schools has more long-term effects. Some of the closings in the early 1980s were the product of lost political battles on campus.[63] Inept political leadership and declining financial resources combined to doom these schools. However, the recent loss of two of the most prestigious library science schools, Columbia University and the University of Chicago, is more serious. These closings or transfers reflect on the future of librarianship because, in both cases, the universities cast off prestigious programs rather than spend funds to keep them. Even a change of emphasis within the library profession (to information science) has not been enough to save them. The long-range impact is hard to gauge, but it is possible that there will be severe shortages of librarians within the next decade. This shortage could come at a time when the technological revolution will have created a demand for more (rather than fewer) librarians with information science backgrounds.

The technological revolution has been slower in developing in higher education than in other professional areas. Part of the problem has been the withdrawal of the federal government from its leadership role in higher education and the slowness of the states to see the advantages of a major state-financed effort in higher education.[64] Information technology is still in the process of development, and higher education is participating at an expanding rate. According to one analyst, participation in technological advancement goes through three distinct phases:

1. We continue to do familiar and traditional things we have always done, but we do them better and faster. In other words, we mechanize.
2. During the second stage, the tasks themselves change because technology has revised what we do, and things are done that were never done before.
3. Finally, in the last stage, technology causes our society itself to change, and fundamental changes in life-styles and institutions occur.[65]

This has caused some commentators to predict that further advancement in information technology will transform the face of the university by reducing the learning time of college-age students.[66] In such a scenario, the overall size of higher education institutions will become smaller, and fewer students will cause a redistribution of teaching.[67] Another scenario is that technology has so shortened the time between basic research and applied research that universities have lost their monopoly on basic research.[68] Most of this type of analysis remains conjecture, but the microcomputer explosion is having an undeniable impact on the university both in research and teaching.

The academic library has been in the midst of a technological revolution during the last two decades. Libraries had long been organized along functional lines—acquisitions, cataloging, reference, etc.—but this task-oriented organization has been challenged by the imposition of the new technology.[69] The appeal of the new technology to leaders in the library world was such that development and experimentation with computer systems began in academic libraries in the mid-1960s.[70] Academic library leaders adopted computer technology with enthusiasm, and the library was usually the first academic unit on campus to adopt computer systems.[71] These systems, however, were concentrated in technical services and out of the sight of most patrons, and high cost and nonawareness of computer systems were limitations that slowed progress in the 1970s.[72] Another limiting factor was the complexity of programming for the type of information necessary for an academic library: transaction-oriented data and complex library data structures.[73] Nevertheless, it was the escalating cost of creating and maintaining always larger manual files that provided the impetus for the adoption of computer technology.[74]

Academic libraries had to decide to change from manual to automated systems, but this transition had to take place without closing the library to install the new system. Incremental rather than revolutionary progress was therefore adopted by most academic libraries. Too often the new technologies were merely grafted onto the traditional, functional ways, and no effort was made to modify old ways of doing things. Library operations had long been labor intensive, especially in technical services, so university and library administrators were intrigued with the possible use of computers to perform routine library functions.[75] The promise of library automation was that the new technology would solve several long-standing library problems: storage, personnel shortages, declining budgets, rising overheads, and repetitious procedures.[76]

Much of this early promise proved illusory, because the only clear advantage of automation has been a significant increase in library productivity.[77] Routine tasks have been delegated to nonprofessional staff, releasing librarians to perform more administrative and service-oriented tasks. This lack of cost cutting has confused university administrators, who expected redistribution of the library budget (away from personnel costs) to result from automation.[78] Part of their confusion is that many library directors mistakenly promised lower operating expenses in the future to justify the heavy capital expenditures necessary for library automation.[79] Some political difficulties for academic libraries have resulted from this fact. Moreover, some library staff have suffered from the fear of job loss and staff displacement.[80]

A key factor in the growth of library automation was the founding of computer-based bibliographic-data cooperative networks. Before these utilities could exist, however, some type of standardized bibliographic format had to be devised; so the Library of Congress (LC) started in 1969 the MARC (Machine-Readable Cataloging) project. The MARC format has proven to be the library profession's primary communication format.[81] Soon afterward, a new company, the Ohio College Library Center (OCLC), started a nationwide cooperative based on using the new cataloging format. Another network, the Research Libraries Information Network (RLIN), started in the late 1970s with a more selective membership but also sharing cataloging data. About the same time, the Washington Library Network (WLN) came into existence, but its membership was restricted to the libraries of the Northwest United States. Together, these networks have provided an impetus for shared cataloging in a computerized environment.

Academic libraries have had to make a large capital investment in the new technology, and this has meant gaining the support of the university administration. At the beginning of the 1970s, libraries had either to invest in a vendor-sponsored turnkey system for routine circulation and technical services or to develop a unique specialized system. By 1979 nine commercial vendors were marketing their turnkey systems, but more than one academic library found these systems unsatisfactory in performance. The other approach of developing an individualized system was costly and only as good as the designers of the new system. Most of the designers understood computer applications, but they were less knowledgeable about library operations. Some libraries were never successful in designing an individualized system, and lost their capital investment without having a workable system in place. Many head librarians waited to see the fallout from the pioneering systems before venturing to consider any system.

Only in the 1980s has a second generation of more reliable systems been developed and attracted more academic libraries to consider "buying into" a system. These Online Public Access Catalogs (OPACs) have become more sophisticated and popular. One of the more successful systems in the mid-1980s has been NOTIS (Northwestern Online Total Integrated System), which was developed and marketed at Northwestern University; but other systems have also been adopted by academic libraries.

Before adopting any system, the library administration must persuade the campus administration of the benefits of an automated system for the library and the institution. Since an investment in any system has a hefty price tag and comes with recurring expenses, the new technology has been a delicate "selling job" for library administrators. Moreover, the long-term financial decisions for library automation are taking place in an era when public colleges and universities are experiencing uncertain financial support from state legislatures. Private colleges and universities have had fewer financial fluctuations to consider in purchasing automated systems for the library, but changing federal tax laws on donations to education have made financial planning more uncertain. Nevertheless, both private and public institutions have been receptive to the adoption of new technology for libraries as long as the library administration makes an effective case for it.

An ongoing problem has been that library automation needs constant updating. Library automation was accepted by the college and university administrators as a onetime expenditure, but library automation needs updating as systems improve.[82] A 1989 survey by Cahners Publishing revealed that 40 percent of college and university libraries had upgraded their automated systems, mostly in the preceding two or three years, and the demand is growing to either upgrade or change systems.[83] An industry standard is that computer systems last about seven years, but the computer systems in academic libraries have an effectiveness span of *less* than seven years.[84] A better benchmark is five years. Since the library will have to compete with other university constituents for scarce funding, updating library automation becomes a serious political problem. As one commentator states, "The library is everyone's second priority."[85] The future of further library automation resides in the ability of library administrators to compete in the political arena on a campus-to-campus basis. A key figure in the future of library automation remains the chief information officer (CIO). This person oversees campus computer functions, and the library's priority in acquiring new technology will be determined by how important the operations of the library are to this individual. Every effort needs to be made by librarians to educate the CIO about the computer requirements of the library and on the extent to which library work has been altered by computers.

Adoption of the computer into library operations has changed the academic library from emphasizing the custodial function to dealing with information. Besides making routine tasks easier, computers have also made a vast body of information accessible for manipulation.[86] The duality of automating and information technology has been a source of confusion in the business world, and this confusion has extended into the library environment. Library automation has been implemented without an understanding of the differences between automating and informating. Automating is the adoption of computer technology for routine tasks to be handled at the lowest level of production, and libraries have adjusted to this aspect of automation efficiently. Informating is the next step of computer technology, to transform operations and the product so as to improve library service and, ultimately, decision making. The academic library community has been less successful in implementing informating.

The future of the academic library has been a "hot" discussion topic among librarians and other interested parties. Terms such as the *paperless society* have been debated, and predictions of all types have been made for the next century.[87] In one scenario the academic library will wither away, as patrons will have little need for the library except as a museum.[88] A 1985 survey of opinion from library science professors, scientists, library networkers, publishers, Association of Research Libraries (ARL) directors, law school deans, and directors of law libraries on the impact of technology on academic research libraries and law school libraries was conducted by the Legal Information Center of the University of Florida and asked fifty-one questions on the nature of these libraries in the next decade and beyond. Despite a disappointing return of only 30.3 percent, the results of the survey show differences in perception of the future of library technology.[89] Most significant was the conservative attitude toward technology by ARL directors and library science faculty in comparison with the more positive outlook of the others. The consensus among the respondents, however, was that books will continue to be published, but more and more information will be available in electronic and multimedia formats.[90] Book collections will not be reduced in size as more electronic information becomes available, but the collections will not grow as fast and fewer duplicates will be purchased.[91] The library of the future will provide more information services without relinquishing its traditional role of providing access to books and periodicals.[92] In the immediate future, the most informed opinion forecasts tighter integration of the central "information server" with the large databases and the individual's microcomputer workstation to exploit more technically advanced information systems.[93] And perhaps the most exciting development for librarians is the possibility that the storage of full text (in digitized form) will become widespread.[94] Some critics are of course still uncertain about the inevitability of the "information age," and they question both the rate and the nature of the transformation.[95]

Other problems also confront the advent of the information age. Electronic systems will run afoul of current copyright legislation. Unless the current law is modified or some type of compensation is worked out, the copyright law will retard further progress on these systems.[96] And besides copyright law, publishers are fearful about an adulteration of texts, which they feel will hurt their reputation.[97]

The scholarly world is just beginning to realize the potential (and some of the limitations) of electronic publishing. A single record can provide the same access function of many printed book and journal copies, because a copy can be secured electronically wherever the user resides.[98] This convenience, however, has the potential to upset the traditional functions of publisher, reviewer, and editor, without replacing them with something new.[99] Until this scholarly relationship is somehow resurrected, scholars will approach electronic publishing with a certain hesitation. Various ideas on how the new scholarly relations will evolve have been advanced, and one of the more interesting is a proposal for an electronic network (the Scholarly Communication System) that would replace scholarly journals with an interactive system including both the author and reviewers.[100] The experience of Brown University and its

Scholar's Workstation in the mid-1980s shows some of the pitfalls, especially the cost and changes in expectations.[101] A British experiment with a prototype, the BLEND experiment in the mid-1980s, revealed some problems with electronic publishing; but the timetable seems to call for electronic publishing to be integrated into on-demand printing and retrieval systems in the next twenty years or so.[102]

Electronic publishing will present academic libraries with several new problems. One of the more serious will be pricing, since direct and obvious costs tend to be higher than in paper publication.[103] With library budgets already overstretched, it will be difficult to absorb these higher costs into the budget. Several publishers have indicated that they will price these new systems as high as the market will allow. Recent restructuring of publishing companies has resulted in many of them becoming subsidiaries of larger companies with no previous tie to publishing. Some publishers are even discussing the feasibility of charging a fee for browsing.[104] Maintenance of integrity and physical preservation of electronic databases are other issues that need to be addressed.[105] Two other perplexing problems will be whether collection development will be driven solely by demand, rather than based on a rational collecting plan, and the dependence on library relationships to trade materials.[106]

Finally, the question remains: Will the scholar in the electronic environment turn to libraries only for archival materials and depend on access to current materials directly from electronic vendors?[107] The future of such scholars may depend more on a to-be-determined price structure by vendors than on academic library policies. CD-ROM products, however, will for the immediate future continue to be the medium of choice for the publishing industry because of "its capability to provide quick access to large quantities of information while minimizing any tampering or modification of that data." [108] The danger to academic libraries from CD-ROM is that publishers will market it to the general information user rather than academic libraries.[109] It is this bypassing of the library that has caused so much concern for the future by academic librarians.[110]

The postwar era in higher education has been one of growth and ferment. Educators and librarians alike look back to the expansion of the 1960s with nostalgia, but with the realization that those days are gone forever. Higher education and academic libraries are in the middle of a different kind of expansion. The costs to higher education of the new technology are high, and many academic and library leaders have become frustrated at the slow pace of acquisition and implementation of new systems. While the pace remains slow, it gives everyone an opportunity to study how these new systems fit into the educational framework. It also allows the doubters some breathing room before the next round of technological advance.

The history of technology recounts various periods of rapid technological change, followed by longer interludes of refinement of the new technology to practical uses. Such interludes appear to have accelerated in the twentieth century, and the library world appears to be at the end of a computer interlude. The academic library has been an active participant in the new technology, but not everyone has been happy with this fact. Librarians have to realize that, to many teaching faculty, library automation is confusing and troublesome. The merging of the library's need for automation and the education of its clientele to the benefits of these new systems will be the major selling job in the next decade.

NOTES

1. Martin Trow, "American Higher Education: Past, Present, and Future," *Educational Researcher* 17 (April 1983) 3:13.
2. William R. Brown, *Academic Politics* (University: University of Alabama Press, 1982), p. 2.
3. Ibid., p. 3.
4. Ibid., p. 4.
5. Dorothy M. Crosland, "The Growing Giant: The Science-Technology Library," in *The Library in the University*, edited by John David Marshall (Hamden, Conn.: Shoe String Press, 1979), p. 225.
6. James D. Hart, "Search and Research: The Librarian and the Scholar," *College and Research Libraries* 19 (September 1958) 5:366.
7. Wayne S. Yenawine, "Education for Academic Librarianship," *College and Research Libraries* 19 (November 1958) 6:479.
8. Nancy Patricia O'Brien, "The Recruitment of Men into Librarianship following World War II," in *The Status of Women in Librarianship: Historical, Sociological, and Economic Issues*, edited by Kathleen M. Heim (New York: Neal-Schuman, 1983), p. 65.
9. Thomas N. Bonner, "The Unintended Revolution in America's Colleges since 1940," *Change* 18 (September–October 1985) 5:46.
10. Ibid.
11. M. A. Stewart, "The Duality of Demand on University Libraries," *College and Research Libraries* 8 (October 1947) 4:396.
12. Charles B. Osburn, *Academic Research and Library Resources: Changing Patterns in America* (Westport, Conn.: Greenwood Press, 1979), pp. 9–10.
13. U.S. Bureau of Statistics, *Historical Statistics of the United States, Colonial Times to 1970* (Washington, D.C.: Bureau of the Census, 1975),

p. 145; Thomas D. Snyder, *Digest of Education Statistics, 1987* (Washington, D.C.: Center for Education Statistics, 1987), p. 236.

14. *Universities, Information Technology, and Academic Libraries*, edited by Robert Mayo Hayes (Norwood, N.J.: Ablex, 1986), p. 13.

15. Kenneth J. Brough, *Scholar's Workshop: Evolving Conceptions of Library Service* (Urbana: University of Illinois Press, 1953), p. 26.

16. Richard Hofstadter and C. DeWitt Hardy, *The Development and Scope of Higher Education in the United States* (New York: Columbia University Press, 1952), p. 165.

17. Arthur M. McAnally, "Status of the University Librarian," in *Research Librarianship: Essays in Honor of Robert B. Downs*, edited by Jerrold Orne (New York: Bowker, 1971), pp. 24–25.

18. Joe W. Kraus, "The Qualifications of University Librarians, 1948 and 1933," *College and Research Libraries* 11 (January 1950) 1:17–21.

19. Arthur T. Hamlin, *The University Library in the United States: Its Origins and Development* (Philadelphia: University of Pennsylvania Press, 1981), p. 70.

20. Luther H. Evan, "The Librarians' Agenda of Unfinished Business," *College and Research Libraries* 12 (October 1951) 4:310.

21. Ralph H. Parker, "Libraries in an Inflationary Cycle," *College and Research Libraries* 12 (October 1951) 4:338.

22. Clifton Brock, "The Rising Tide: Some Implications for College and University Libraries," *College and Research Libraries* 19 (January 1958) 1:14.

23. Edward Mapp, "The Library in a Community College," *College and Research Libraries* 19 (May 1958) 3:194.

24. Burton R. Clark, *The Academic Life: Small Worlds, Different Worlds* (Princeton, N.J.: Carnegie Foundation for the Advancement of Teaching, 1987), p. 87.

25. Ibid.

26. Arthur M. Cohen and John Lombardi, "Can the Community Colleges Survive Success?" *Change* 11 (November–December 1979) 8:24.

27. Osburn, *Academic Research and Library Resources*, p. 24.

28. *Universities, Information Technology, and Academic Libraries*, p. 13.

29. Carnegie Foundation for the Advancement of Teaching, *A Classification of Institutions of Higher Education* (Berkeley, Calif.: Carnegie Commission on Higher Education, 1987), pp. 1–5.

30. Clark, *Academic Life*, p. 59.

31. Ibid., p. 61.

32. Snyder, *Digest of Education Statistics, 1987*, p. 165.

33. Ibid.

34. Bonner, "Unintended Revolution," p. 48.

35. Ibid., p. 49.

36. Snyder, *Digest of Education Statistics, 1987*, p. 165.

37. Ibid.

38. Bonner, "Unintended Revolution," p. 49.

39. Hamlin, *University Library in the United States*, p. 74.

40. Brock, "Rising Tide," p. 14.
41. Irving J. Spitzberg, "It's Academic: The Politics of the Curriculum in American Higher Education," in *Libraries and the Search for Academic Excellence*, edited by Patricia Senn Breivik and Robert Wedgeworth (Metuchen, N.J.: Scarecrow Press, 1988), p. 146.
42. Bonner, "Unintended Revolution," p. 49.
43. Snyder, *Digest of Education Statistics, 1987*, p. 166.
44. Douglas J. Collier, "Making Financial Assessments More Meaningful," *New Directions in Higher Education* 38 (June 1982): 88.
45. William W. Jellema, "Financial Status," in *Efficient College Management*, edited by William W. Jellema (San Francisco: Jossey-Bass, 1972), p. 108.
46. Trow, "American Higher Education," p. 13.
47. Robert B. Downs, "Are College and University Librarians Academic?" *College and Research Libraries* 15 (January 1954) 1:13–14.
48. Hamlin, *University Library in the United States*, p. 78.
49. Helen H. Spalding, "Recent Developments in Technical Services and Their Implication for Access to Scholarly Information," in *Access to Scholarly Information: Issues and Strategies*, edited by Sul H. Lee (Ann Arbor, Mich.: Pierian Press, 1985), p. 47.
50. Chester E. Finn, "The Future of Education's Liberal Consensus," *Change* 12 (September 1980) 6:26.
51. Ibid., p. 26.
52. Paul L. Dressel, *Administrative Leadership: Effective and Responsible Decision Making in Higher Education* (San Francisco: Jossey-Bass, 1981), p. 23.
53. Fred E. Crossland, "Preparing for the 1980s: Learning to Cope with a Downward Slope," *Change* 12 (July–August 1980) 5:20–21.
54. Robert J. Grossman, "The Great Debate over Institutional Accountability," *College Board Review* 147 (Spring 1988): 6.
55. *Universities, Information Technology, and Academic Libraries*, p. 21.
56. James A. Hyatt, "Incentives and Disincentives for Effective Management," *NACUBO Business Officer* 18 (October 1984) 4:19.
57. Warren Bryan Martin, "The Limits to Diversity," *Change* 10 (December–January 1978) 11:41.
58. Ibid., p. 43.
59. Jan Krukowski, "What Do Students Want? Status," *Change* 17 (May–June 1985) 3:24.
60. *Scholarly Communication: The Report of the National Enquiry* (Baltimore: Johns Hopkins University Press, 1979), p. 2.
61. Ibid., p. 12.
62. Ibid., p. 5.
63. Marion Paris, *Library School Closings: Four Case Studies* (Metuchen, N.J.: Scarecrow Press, 1988). This study of four library closings gives a good picture of the academic politics involved.
64. Francis Dummer Fisher, "Higher Education circa 2005: More Higher Learning, but Less College," *Change* 19 (January–February 1987) 1:42.

65. Dilys E. Morris, "Electronic Information and Technology: Impact and Potential for Academic Libraries," *College and Research Libraries* 50 (January 1989) 1:58.
66. Fisher, "Higher Education circa 2005," p. 44.
67. Ibid., p. 45.
68. Louis Vagianos and Barry Lesser, "The Jewel in the Temple: University Library Networks as Paradigms for Universities," in *Libraries and the Search for Academic Excellence*, edited by Patricia Senn Breivik and Robert Wedgeworth (Metuchen, N.J.: Scarecrow Press, 1988), p. 108.
69. The philosophic problems of functional organization are described in Eugene E. Graziano, " 'Machine-Men' and Librarians, an Essay," *College and Research Libraries* 28 (November 1967) 6:404–5.
70. Hugh F. Cline and Loraine T. Sinnott, *The Electronic Library: The Impact of Automation on Academic Libraries* (Lexington, Mass.: Lexington Books, 1983), p. 14.
71. Barbara B. Moran, "The Unintended Revolution in Academic Libraries: 1939 to 1989 and Beyond," *College and Research Libraries* 50 (January 1989) 1:28.
72. Cline and Sinnott, *Electronic Library*, p. 14.
73. Ward Shaw, "Technology and Transformation in Academic Libraries," in *Libraries and the Search for Academic Excellence*, edited by Patricia Senn Breivik and Robert Wedgeworth (Metuchen, N.J.: Scarecrow Press, 1988), p. 137.
74. Spalding, "Recent Developments in Technical Services," p. 44.
75. Barbara B. Moran, *Academic Libraries: The Changing Knowledge Centers of Colleges and Universities* (Washington, D.C.: Association for the Study of Higher Education, 1984), p. 7.
76. Rodney K. Waldron, "Implications of Technological Press for Librarians," *College and Research Libraries* 19 (March 1958) 2:123.
77. James A. Hyatt and Aurora A. Santiago, *University Libraries in Transition* (Washington, D.C.: NACUBO, 1987), p. 15. This lack of cost cutting is despite efforts to claim monetary benefits from library automation (Malcolm Getz, "More Benefits of Automation," *College and Research Libraries* 49 [November 1988] 6:534-44).
78. David W. Adamany, "Research Libraries from a Presidential Perspective," in *Issues in Academic Librarianship: Views and Case Studies for the 1980s and 1990s*, edited by Peter Spyers-Duran and Thomas W. Mann (Westport, Conn.: Greenwood Press, 1985), p. 13.
79. Moran, "Unintended Revolution in Academic Libraries," p. 29.
80. Marcia J. Nauratil, *The Alienated Librarian* (New York: Greenwood Press, 1989), p. 70.
81. D. Kay Gapen, "Myths and Realities: University Libraries," *College and Research Libraries* 45 (September 1984) 5:351.

82. Betty W. Taylor, Elizabeth B. Mann, and Robert J. Munro, *The Twenty-first Century: Technology's Impact on Academic Research and Law Libraries* (Boston: Hall, 1988), p. 2.
83. Cahners Publishing Co., "Upgrading Systems, Software, and Microcomputers," *Library Journal* 114 (15 September 1989): 57–58.
84. Susan K. Martin, "Information Technology and Libraries: Toward the Year 2000," *College and Research Libraries* 51 (March 1990) 2:401. Cahners Publishing discovered in its survey that the need for upgrading has dropped from the seven- or eight-year cycle of a few years ago to a two- to four-year cycle now (Cahners, "Upgrading Systems, Software, and Microcomputers," p. 59).
85. Martin, "Information Technology and Libraries," p. 400.
86. Shoshana Zuboff, *In the Age of the Smart Machine* (New York: Basic Books, 1988), pp. 9–10.
87. J. Wilfrid Lancaster, *Toward Paperless Information Systems* (New York: Academic Press, 1978), pp. 153-59.
88. J. Wilfred Lancaster, "Whither Libraries? or, Wither Libraries," *College and Research Libraries* 39 (September 1978): 355.
89. Taylor, Mann, and Munro, *Twenty-first Century*, p. 43.
90. Ibid., p. 67.
91. Ibid., pp. 68–69.
92. Carolyn Bucknall, "Conjuring in the Academic Library: The Illusion of Access," in *Access to Scholarly Information: Issues and Strategies*, edited by Sul H. Lee (Ann Arbor, Mich.: Pierian Press, 1985), p. 67.
93. Howard Curtis, "Microcomputers: Venue of Computing in the '90s," in *Technology for the '90s: Microcomputers in Libraries*, edited by Nancy Melin Nelson (Westport, Conn.: Meckler, 1990), p. 25.
94. Ibid., p. 27.
95. Paul Olum, "Myths and Realities: The Academic Viewpoint I," *College and Research Libraries* 45 (September 1984) 5:365.
96. Richard M. Dougherty, "Libraries and Computing Centers: A Blueprint for Collaboration," *College and Research Libraries* 48 (July 1987) 4:294.
97. Daniel Eisenberg, "Problems of the Paperless Book," *Scholarly Publishing* 21 (October 1989) 1:14–15.
98. Eldred Smith, *The Librarian, the Scholar, and the Future of the Research Library* (New York: Greenwood Press, 1990), p. 34.
99. Ibid., p. 35.
100. Sharon J. Rogers and Charlene S. Hurt, "How Scholarly Communication Should Work in the 21st Century," *College and Research Libraries* 51 (January 1990) 1:5–8.
101. Barbara B. Moran, Thomas T. Suprenant, and Merrily E. Taylor, "The Electronic Campus: The Impact of the Scholar's Workstation Project on the Libraries at Brown," *College and Research Libraries* 48 (January 1987) 1:5–16.

102. Priscilla Oakeshott, "The 'BLEND' Experiment in Electronic Publishing," *Scholarly Publishing* 17 (October 1985): 28–29.

103. Donald B. Simpson, "Electronic Publishing: Important Issues for Co-operating Libraries," in *Issues in Academic Librarianship: Views and Case Studies for the 1980s and 1990s*, edited by Peter Spyers-Duran and Thomas W. Mann (Westport, Conn.: Greenwood Press, 1985), p. 90.

104. Martin, "Information Technology and Libraries," p. 403.

105. Peter Briscoe et al., "Ashurbanipal's Enduring Archetype: Thoughts on the Library's Role in the Future," *College and Research Libraries* 47 (March 1986) 2:124.

106. Simpson, "Electronic Publishing," p. 91.

107. Ibid.

108. Norman Desmarais, "Optical Information Systems: Pioneering with Potential," in *Technology for the '90s: Microcomputers in Libraries*, edited by Nancy Melin Nelson (Westport, Conn.: Meckler, 1990), pp. 63–64.

109. Eric Rumsey, "The Power of the New Microcomputers: Challenge and Opportunity," *College and Research Libraries* 51 (March 1990) 2:96.

110. Martin, "Information Technology and Libraries," pp. 399–400.

CHAPTER THREE

The Impact of the Academic Library on the University Budget

THE ACADEMIC LIBRARY'S financial demands on the university budget are only a small portion of the total university budget, but these demands are a source of concern to academic administrators. Each year the library administration proposes a budget for consideration by the institution's financial officers, then these officers evaluate this budget request with reference to other institutional needs. Often a demand for increased funding for the library comes from the same individuals, deans and department heads, who are lobbying for more funds for other programs.[1] Faculty salaries and departmental programs are favored by them over library allocations.[2] Budget officers find the library is relentless in its pursuit of resources, and many of them are uncomfortable in dealing with this seemingly bottomless pit of demand. Until the 1960s, no other agency or center on campus was a serious rival for large-scale financial allocations directed toward the library, but this has changed with the emergence of the university computer center. Now the library has a rival to its role as *the* dispenser of information and consumer of large sums of money. In good financial times this competition is restrained, with both the library and the computer center sharing in resources, but the rivalry can become fierce during periods of economic crisis. Because of this and the increasing size and diversity of the universities, decreasing financial support for academic libraries has resulted. Moreover, even for libraries that have escaped cuts over the years, administrators are insisting more and more upon objective evaluations of library services before committing higher levels of financial support.

Modern institutions of higher education have had to develop ways to manage their financial resources. Colleges in the nineteenth century dealt with comparatively small budgets, and most educational institutions lived precariously from one enrollment period to the next, with cash-flow problems considered natural.[3] Even as late as the early 1920s, few institutions operated on any kind of a budget system,[4] but the surge of growth in higher education from the 1920s onward made it imperative that ways be found to manage the financial affairs of colleges and universities. Growth meant problems of planning and allocation of resources. At first, financial parity existed between public and private universities since state contributions to public institutions were the equivalent of the endowment income for private ones.[5] Gradually, however, differences emerged between public and private institutions as state financial support became more generous than private schools' endowment income.[6] Although tuition income was important to both types of schools, this income was expected to be approximately half of the university budget for faculty salaries in private institutions.[7] Public institutions had to depend more and more on tuition income also, because state support slowly diminished as a percentage of the total budget during the 1930s.

Financial problems became even more dramatic in the post–World War II era. Relative affluence in the three decades after 1945 was replaced by tightened budgets from the middle 1970s onward. Taxpayer and legislative demands for accountability have resulted in fiscal regulations for public institutions in many states. The most common regulation is the postaudit of funds.[8] Private institutions have escaped these types of regulations, but they have experienced economic dislocation from many of the same factors as the public schools. Both types of institutions now depend more on grants and private gifts than in the past.

Goals developed by institutions of higher education play a critical role in determining collegiate costs. Every college and university has a unique history and behavior pattern, but certain guiding principles unite all of them. A scholar of higher education has determined the following "laws of higher education costs":

1. The dominant goals of institutions are educational excellence, prestige, and influence.

2. In quest of excellence, prestige, and influence, there is virtually no limit to the amount of money an institution could spend for seemingly fruitful educational ends.
3. Each institution raises all the money it can.
4. Each institution spends all it raises.
5. The cumulative effect of the preceding four laws is toward ever increasing expenditure.[9]

These goals are all part of the constant drive of major research universities for a national reputation for excellence.

Academic libraries have had little difficulty in adjusting to these so-called laws of higher education costs. Excellence, prestige, and influence are all goals that the major research libraries subscribe to without reservations. Even the second echelon of academic libraries aspires to such goals. Each spring the statistical ranking of the Association of Research Libraries (ARL) is eagerly awaited. Changes in rankings are noted not only by librarians but by university administrators. Library administrators make certain that university leaders are notified about both good and bad news. As far as expenditures go, no academic library has ever had as much funding as the librarians know that it needs; spending money on materials and equipment is something that every librarian can do readily. The problem for most librarians is dealing with a limited or no-growth budget.

Each institution has to formulate an annual budget as a method of planning, and this budget is a way of matching anticipated income with expected expenses. While the actual outcomes will be different from planning figures, mostly because of unanticipated factors, this exercise is both a mandated requirement and a way of planning for routine functions. Each budget is comprised of a request budget and an expenditure budget. In the request budget, each administrative level seeks the necessary funds to run its programs at an optimal rate. In contrast, the expenditure level only allocates the funds actually available for the operation of a program. This is in keeping with the experience that the request budget always exceeds the expenditure budget.[10] Besides allocation, the budgeting process also serves as an instrument for achieving internal and external accountability.[11] Regardless of types of budgetary planning, the primary need for any budget is income.

All colleges and universities have similar ways of attracting funding. The three fundamental methods are the enrollment cycle flow, the institutional reputation flow, and the research reputation flow.[12] Most of the resources for the enrollment cycle flow come from funds gathered from student enrollments.[13] Tuition and fees are the most common way for institutions to obtain financial support for administrative and teaching functions. Certain subsidies, mainly from the state and federal governments for public schools, and donations from families for private schools, are tied to the enrollment cycle.[14] All institutions depend upon enrollment-generated funds regardless of size and prestige. Yet, fees paid by students provide only a small portion of the total budget of a university.[15] Even combining state appropriations (based on enrollment) with student fees, state universities gain only about 50 percent of their necessary educational and operational funding.

The institutional reputation flow is a consequence of past successful efforts to gain resources from outside agencies. Foundations, legislatures, and private donors are all approached for funding.[16] Only institutions with a reputation for quality are able to utilize this approach. Most of the larger, quality, private universities and a few of the state universities are successful in using reputation to attract outside funding, but this process has left out the majority of the smaller private and public institutions. Moreover, many of these funds appear in the form of endowments, and these resources are often left to the discretion of the president of the institution.[17]

The research reputation flow is the final approach to gaining more resources for an institution. This time, however, it is the reputation of the individual researcher or group of researchers that attracts the funding.[18] Research "stars" are able to attract grants from the federal government for specific projects. Most of the funds go to support their project, but their institutions benefit by gaining overhead costs, and these overhead costs can provide a substantial bonus for the institution. Again, the larger research institutions benefit most from this process, but it is possible that a professor from a small institution can receive this type of grant. Individuals who participate in "research grantsmanship" are eagerly sought after, and sometimes they take their grants with them after their recruitment by another school. The sciences and engineering benefit most from this type of funding flow, but other disciplines also gain in this process because of the accumulated prestige of these grants.

Certain internal factors must be considered before an institution begins to allocate resources. These internal factors are common in every institution of higher education, but each institution will have a different type of input from each variable, as follows:

1. The *governance* of the institution, from the trustees to the students: the legal bases of the college, the policy-making process, the power structures, the administrative functions.

2. *Faculty* matters: policies and assumptions on faculty loads, ratios, tenure, ranks, salaries, fringe benefits, research time, sabbaticals, publishing required, and many other concerns affecting budgeting decisions.
3. The *student body*: its composition, life styles, economic levels, attrition rates, services provided, activities and organizations, and many other areas of assessment.
4. *Curriculum* matters: teaching studies, technological influences, policies on class size, grading practices, number of programs, degrees offered, and other class operation matters.
5. The *library* and its service; the *public service*; the *support service*; the computer capability, nonprofessional and support staff considerations; as well as *general services* such as communication, printing, and other functions.
6. *Physical plant usage*: data on maintenance costs, rehabilitation requirements, care of grounds, security.
7. The *financial situation*: investment policies, tuitions, financial aid programs, sources of support, purchasing policies, general distribution of funds, and other considerations.[19]

This list of internal factors is imposing, but every institution must take these factors into consideration before making financial decisions.

The above list also is indicative of where the academic library fits into the overall budgetary scheme of an institution. Library funding requirements are considered in relation to a multitude of other competing financial requirements. The positioning of the library with other public service components and computer services is no accident. While the library may have a broad constituency that it serves on campus, and sometimes this helps in the political arena, it has to compete with a variety of other constituencies in financial affairs. Some of these other constituencies have powerful supporters.

After the receipt of funding and a study of internal factors, the problem becomes the internal allocation of resources. Various types of allocation systems have been tried, but two types have been adapted for higher education: management models and computer simulation models. Almost all of the management systems have been borrowed from the business world, with varying degrees of success. The computer simulation models are more recent, and most of them have been designed exclusively for use in higher education.

The most common system still in use is the uniform percentage adjustment, or incremental budgeting. Increments are calculated as uniform percentage adjustments for every line item. Across-the-board increases or decreases, based on historical patterns of support, have always been popular in higher education, mostly because educational administrators feel that there is little need for fluctuations in support for academic programs. Although this approach is based on the presumed collective wisdom of precedent, it suffers from inflexibility, unless the administrative leaders decide to fight the necessary political battles on a case-by-case basis.[20] This system still retains its popularity, despite attempts to incorporate more sophisticated systems into college and university planning. Part of the attractiveness of incremental budgeting for administrators is that it requires the least amount of work and analysis of any of the systems.[21] Lack of analysis, however, is also its weakest feature: past inequities are passed along without serious study, and changes in educational priorities are slow to be funded.

Another method close to incremental budgeting is formula budgeting, which attempts to achieve equity in the allocation of resources by relating allocation to "standard, consistent measures of activity." [22] Similar resources are provided for similar programs, either within an institution or in a multi-institution system. A majority of state formulas are based on enrollment measurements,[23] and while this allocation system can routinely make difficult decisions, it fails to treat each funding request on its merits.[24] This allocation scheme is often used by state agencies to distribute funds to institutions in a multi-institution or multicampus system, but it has also been utilized by individual institutions. Approximately half of the state governing boards use some variation of a formula approach for the allocation of funds.[25] Formulas are criticized most frequently because they "perpetuate poor practices and funding levels of the past." [26] Formula budgeting is unpopular at some state universities because the state routinely refuses to fund the budget at the highest levels of the formula. It becomes too easy for legislatures to reduce funding by lowering formula limits.

A method that has had some popularity in the past is called Planning, Programming, and Budgeting Systems (PPBS). Although this system is most closely identified with Robert McNamara's tenure at the Department of Defense in the early 1960s, it was first formulated by the Rand Corporation. The fundamental idea behind PPBS is that budgeting should start with goals.[27] PPBS bases resource allocations on clearly defined objectives of the organization, with a cost-benefit dimension to aid in planning decisions.[28] In short, program budgeting compares the costs and benefits of every program with those of every other program on a continuing basis.[29] PPBS became so popular in the early 1970s that several state governments forced the system upon colleges and universities with short advance notice.[30] The problem for higher education has been that program objectives have proven difficult to identify and to isolate.[31] Much of the criticism of this system has been that it works well for single-function organizations such as the Department of Defense, but that it has not proven adaptable to organizations with multiple missions. Consequently, PPBS has not been successfully applied to budget planning for higher education.[32] A side benefit of this system has been that, because it required certain advanced tools of analysis, computer models, and matrices, higher education officials started thinking about cost effectiveness and benefit analysis models.[33]

An early rival in popularity to PPBS and a system with greater staying power was Management by Objective (MBO). MBO originated in the business world in the 1940s, and by the 1950s it had been successfully used in profit-making organizations. This system has been characterized as "managing by results," [34] and it requires that an organization establish goals and objectives in order to evaluate success and failure rates. Each objective should have an outcome, a time frame, and a measurement of accomplishment.[35] Higher education became interested in MBO in the late 1960s and early 1970s, but the success rate was uneven. Part of the problem was the lack of higher education administrators who could understand and use the system effectively.[36] Instead of assigning tasks and responsibilities to people within the organization and linking rewards to achievement, administrators used MBO only for planning exercises.[37] This revamping of MBO made it a method of evaluation rather than a management tool. Finally, MBO relies upon a formal structure of authority (i.e., supervisor and subordinate) that is lacking in the collegial management environment. These reasons explain why MBO has been more successfully utilized on the nonacademic or business side in most colleges and universities.[38]

Another system that had its adherents in the 1970s was Zero-based Budgeting (ZBB), which was developed by Peter Phyrr and used at the Texas Instruments Company. ZBB focuses on a complete justification of all expenditures each time this system is used.[39] It is a way to reallocate funds tied up by outmoded functions, but the key to its successful functioning is the identification of decision units. Once these units have been identified, the next step is creation of a decision package, which includes rationale, benefits, costs, and alternatives.[40] In the college or university environment, each academic department would have to justify its budget allocation each fiscal year, but since many educational expenses are fixed in an educational environment, this system becomes only partially operational. Moreover, the amount of paperwork, time, and difficulty in delineating priorities makes this system burdensome for an academic organization.[41] Also, since educational administrators dislike having to justify policies and programs on an annual basis, they have been lukewarm about this system. Finally, even a partial ordering of academic program priorities is opposed by most faculties, and departments will try various schemes to preserve budget levels.[42]

The first of the computer simulation models of planning for resource allocation is the Resource Requirement Prediction Model (RRPM). Higher education officials perceived the need for more sophisticated tools for planning, so the Western Interstate Commission for Higher Education (WICHE) requested and received a federal grant through the National Center for Higher Education Management Systems (NCHEMS) to design a new system. The result was RRPM, which is a computer-based cost-estimation model dedicated to study variables over time.[43] Two products of this model are the student flow model and the Induced Course-Load Matrix (ICLM). Both subsystems were developed as ways to compare instructional loads in the discipline fields.[44] By studying student enrollment by majors, the university can make allocation decisions to reflect changes in course-work patterns. These systems also allow administrators to make long-range predictions.[45] The problem of this approach, however, is that it has been identified as useful for less than 40 percent of the institution's budget. Consequently, RRPM has been found more useful for institutions that are more teaching than research based.[46]

A close rival to RRPM is the Comprehensive Analytical Methods for Planning in University Systems (CAMPUS), developed by System Dimensions Limited (SDL) of Canada. Although both systems are concerned with cost prediction, CAMPUS is better suited for large research universities than its rival.[47] Another significant difference is that CAMPUS is much more expensive than RRPM. Because of high cost and a limited market, this system has not been as successful in attracting clients in the higher education market as other systems.

Another product of the National Center for Higher Education Management Systems is the Costing and Data Management System (CADMS), a software system developed out of funding from federal grants. It is designed to provide colleges and universities a general management tool. This system is a way of studying historical costs and using the data to forecast future costs.[48] It has been used as the basis for interinstitutional information exchange regarding the costs of degree programs.[49] Because this system is based on historical data and makes predictions based on past and possible future trends, it has been one of the more successful of the computer simulation models in academia.

The most recent trend has been the adoption by a number of colleges and universities of interactive modeling systems. Most popular of these systems has been the EDUCOM Financial Planning Model (EFPM), which was developed by EDUCOM with grant funding from the Lilly Endowment. EFPM is a model which allows the user to display alternative forecasts of outcomes.[50] Much of EFPM's popularity is because it is available over telephone networks from a host computer at Cornell University,[51] and this telecommunication system makes EFPM available at a lower cost than other models. Low costs and ease of accessibility are reasons why more than one hundred colleges and universities in the United States, Australia, Belgium, and Canada have subscribed to this model since its introduction in 1978.[52] Refinements of this model will make it a candidate for adoption by even more institutions.

Another interactive modeling system that has attracted attention in higher education circles is the resource allocation application of the Decision Support Systems (DSS). DSS is an outgrowth of research on organizational decision making conducted at the Carnegie Institute of Technology and the Massachusetts Institute of Technology in the 1960s.[53] A modification of DSS to limit it to budgeting and resource allocation resulted in the Group Decision Support Systems (GDSS) model.[54] This model allows benefit-cost ratios to be calculated and compared with each other for budgeting purposes.[55] The advantage of this model is that it is especially useful in handling complex allocation problems involving scarce resources.[56] College and university administrators have found GDSS and its variant models invaluable in dealing with the complex budgeting problems of the 1980s, and the popularity of the GDSS models is still growing.

These various systems for internal allocation of resources have had only moderate success in higher education. Only among top administrators at select institutions has much enthusiasm been displayed about adopting management models. Much more interest has been expressed in the computer simulation model systems. The demand is constant for even more sophisticated models to be developed for budget planning. Two major problems of computer simulation models have been noted: all variables have to be reducible to quantitative format, and faculty have been reluctant to accept these systems. Since only certain aspects of college and university affairs are quantifiable, this deficiency has limited the acceptability of these models. More serious, however, is the reluctance of faculty in accepting the legitimacy of computer-based models. Faculties are notorious in not accepting planning models, especially in so sensitive an area as assessment of educational programs. An ominous development has been the seizure of these models by state regulatory agencies as a way to impose fiscal accountability on public institutions. Too often these regulatory agencies have been using these models in retrenchment scenarios to study which programs have the weakest case for retention.[57] Retrenchment planning, rather than management applications, has cooled many educational administrators' enthusiasm for these systems.[58] Consequently, many institutions have adopted financial management packages that have planning as only a side benefit of the package. This way, planners have financial data for planning, but these data are used internally so as to avoid the view of overseers.

The academic library has little recourse but to follow any internal allocation scheme adopted by the institution. Since the adoption of any institution-wide allocation system has to have the active support of high-level administrators, the president and the administration's fate will be tied to the success or failure of the adopted system. The library is included in any broad allocation system, but the semiautonomous position of the academic library within the institution still allows the library administration considerable freedom to consider alternatives after the original allocation decision is made.

Each budget allocation scheme is capable of having a different impact on library operations. Across-the-board increases rarely match the needs of library operations because costs always seem to exceed the available funds. The rate of inflation in the domestic and foreign book trade has exceeded the national inflation rate by several percentage points a year over the last decade. Moreover, the line-item budget has the disadvantage that it has no mechanism for reviewing the effectiveness of library operations.[59] Yet it is this combination of historical and incremental budgeting that most universities use in allocating funds to their academic libraries.[60] Formula budgeting also offers little for academic libraries in the present environment because it works best during periods of growth, not retrenchment.[61] Most academic libraries have experienced so little recent growth that this type of budgeting becomes frustrating both to library administrators and staff.

Two types of library formula methods are used in twelve states: rate per student and percentage of instruction.[62] In theory, the library could prosper in the PPBS system, if the library had a high enough priority in university planning. Otherwise, if the institution had higher priorities, the library might suffer or, at best, be ignored. Efforts to adapt

PPBS for internal library operations have been disappointing, and most libraries have dropped PPBS.[63] MBO is a system that works better in areas where verifiable figures are available. Library operations, such as technical services, fit this requirement, but if goals and timetables are not met, does this mean the department should be punished? Library administrators have been intrigued by MBO as a management tool for evaluating internal operations, but they have been slow in adopting it for general library use.[64] ZBB is a system that makes little sense for libraries unless mandated from above as part of a university-wide exercise. Academic libraries have fixed functions, and always having to justify these functions for budgetary reasons is time consuming or, at best, paper exercises with little meaning. Adaptations of ZBB by individual libraries have been more successful than PPBS and MBO, however, because the adaptations allow flexibility for integrating new programs.[65]

The computer simulation models are intriguing, both in theory and practice, to the academic library community because they have predictive features that the library could find useful in long-range planning. Unfortunately, almost all of the software deals with instructional rather than library-related issues. Since the DSS models have applications both to decision making and resource allocation, these models may have the most potential for future library use. Universities and academic libraries will continue to experiment with these systems because of the ongoing need to evaluate functions and programs.

Some university administrators have become critical of the ways libraries allocate their resources. They are especially cool toward the traditional 60-30-10 allocation rule: 60 percent of the library budget for personnel, 30 percent for acquisition of library materials, and 10 percent for all other costs.[66] Library automation is seen by some university administrators as changing this standard, and they expect funds saved from reductions in personnel costs to be transferred to other parts of the library budget.[67] Library administrators, however, have not seen reductions in personnel costs because of lower library budgets and increased patron demand. Library automation has increased productivity, but it has not lessened the work load.

Planning for academic libraries has long been recognized by library leaders as a necessity. During periods of financial growth, little effort was devoted to long-range planning, but this earlier reluctance has been changed by events. Budgetary squeeze, caused by less university support, has combined with the need for capital to fund new technology to promote planning for resource allocation. Academic libraries have been left out of university planning except in the most general terms.

Consequently, academic libraries have only cautiously engaged in planning activities. Penalties for the failure to plan are numerous:

> Services are interrupted, financial support is lost or poorly utilized, which is virtually the same thing, patrons are inconvenienced, future development and growth is handicapped, the influence and usefulness of the library is diminished, and the respect and support of the community for the library is usually lost, to cite a few examples.[68]

Although these penalties are recognized as real by most library leaders, it is still difficult for library administrators to engage in full-scale planning. With chronically understaffed libraries, it is difficult to find the time or the people to conduct planning. Nevertheless, library literature is always full of articles advocating specific management planning schemes to improve library operations, but no consensus has emerged. Academic libraries are still more concerned with conducting daily operations than with planning, and until this changes, "planning" will be more a reaction to events than anticipating the future.

The most important person in the early stages of the budget decision-making cycle is the college or university business officer, or chief financial officer (CFO). A survey of CFOs from 171 universities in 1983 indicates that this person is trained mainly in business administration and management, and the CFO is one of the three or four officers most involved in major institutional decision making.[69] The CFO's function is to gather intelligence on the general economic climate and to manage the institution's portfolio of investments. Another part of the business officer's responsibilities is to alert the president and other appropriate officers to any economic news that may impact on the institution.[70] An important aspect of the job is to educate his or her colleagues and the faculty about the economic realities of an educational institution. Besides preparing yearly budgets, the business officer has the responsibility for long-range planning.[71] Finally, the budget officer has to monitor the institution's budget. A budget is, after all, merely a forecast of income and expenditure for a particular year, and, as in all forecasts, changing situations make for constant tinkering. Most institutions have to resort to considerable shifting of funds to cover unexpected income and expenses.[72] A common expedient is the creation of a contingency fund to handle these types of fluctuations. While the business officer is involved in the formulation of contingency fund lines, the final decision on the shifts comes from higher administrative levels.

The library budget officer is the counterpart of the university's budget officer. They have a similar function, except the library budget officer oversees a more specialized budget. Also, this officer reports to the library director in much the same fashion as the university budget officer reports to the university president. The major difference is that most often the library budget officer is a librarian rather than a professional budget specialist. Library budgets have many of the complexities of those of a mid-size not-for-profit corporation. Efficiency of operations, rather than the "bottom line," marks the essential difference between the two types of operations. The library budget officer works closely with the library director because success or failure in handling the budget can have a direct causal relationship to the tenure in office of the library director. Loss of control of the budget places the library director in a precarious situation with the campus administration. Weakening financial support for libraries, combined with increasing costs for materials and supplies during the last decade, has made life difficult for both the budget officer and the library director. Although the library budget is outside the institution's budget cycle after the initial allocation, sometimes the library is involved in the internal transfer of funds at the instigation of the central administration. Near the end of the annual budget cycle the college or university may have unspent funds available for dispersal, and the library is always a ready consumer of such funds. Or, more ominously, when the state requires return of funds in a state budget crisis, the library often supplies a portion of the money. Either way, the library and the library budget officer become participants in the institution's budget plans.

Institutions of higher education spend their funds along prescribed lines. Universities spend nearly a third of their budgets on instruction (see table 3.1).[73] Auxiliary enterprises, hospitals, institutional support, research, physical plants, and academic support functions assume such importance that they often rival the educational mission, especially in the large universities. Significant differences appear, however, between public and private institutions. More attention is given by public institutions to providing funds for instruction, research, academic support, and public service (see table 3.2).[74] In contrast, private schools give more financial backing to institutional support, scholarships, and fellowships (see table 3.3).[75] Such differences only reflect the aspirations and needs of differing types of institutions.

Budget officers have learned that institutional costs never remain static, that three types of costs are always present: uncontrollable, controllable, and mixed. Uncontrollable costs consist of books and periodi-

Table 3.1: Average Expenditures in Higher Education by Purpose, 1985–1986

Types of Expenditures	Funds	Percentage
Instruction	$31,032,099	31.8
Research	8,437,367	8.7
Public service	3,119,533	3.2
Academic support	6,667,392	6.8
Libraries	2,551,331	2.6
Student services	4,562,938	4.7
Institutional support	9,350,786	9.6
Operation and maintenance of plant	7,605,226	7.8
Scholarships and fellowships	4,160,174	4.3
Mandatory transfers	1,192,449	1.2
Total Educational and General Expenditures	$76,127,965	78.1
Auxiliary enterprises	$10,528,303	10.8
Hospitals	8,692,113	8.9
Independent operations	2,187,361	2.2
Total Expenditures	$97,535,742	100.0

Source: Thomas D. Snyder, *Digest of Education Statistics, 1989* (Washington, D.C.: Center for Education Statistics, 1989), p. 301.

Table 3.2: Average Expenditures in Public Institutions of Higher Education by Purpose, 1985–1986

Types of Expenditures	Funds	Percentage
Instruction	$21,880,782	34.6
Research	5,705,144	9.0
Public service	2,515,734	4.0
Academic support	4,693,543	7.4
Libraries	1,685,052	2.7
Student services	2,927,758	4.6
Institutional support	5,667,144	9.0
Operation and maintenance of plant	5,177,254	8.2
Scholarships and fellowships	1,575,909	2.5
Mandatory transfers	735,695	1.2
Total Educational and General Expenditures	$50,872,962	80.5
Auxiliary enterprises	$ 6,830,235	10.8
Hospitals	5,358,699	8.5
Independent operations	131,956	0.2
Total Expenditures	$63,193,841	100.0

Source: Thomas D. Snyder, *Digest of Education Statistics, 1989* (Washington, D.C.: Center for Education Statistics, 1989), p. 302.

Table 3.3: Average Expenditures in Private Institutions of Higher Education by Purpose, 1985–1986

Types of Expenditure	Funds	Percentage
Instruction	$ 9,151,318	26.6
Research	2,732,222	8.0
Public service	603,799	1.8
Academic support	1,873,849	5.7
Libraries	866,279	2.5
Student services	1,641,180	4.8
Institutional support	3,683,642	10.7
Operation and maintenance of plant	2,427,972	7.1
Scholarships and fellowships	2,584,266	7.5
Mandatory transfers	456,754	1.3
Total Educational and General Expenditures	$25,255,003	73.5
Auxiliary enterprises	$ 3,698,067	10.8
Hospitals	3,333,414	9.7
Independent operations	2,055,405	6.0
Total Expenditures	$34,341,889	100.0

Source: Thomas D. Snyder, *Digest of Education Statistics, 1989* (Washington, D.C.: Center for Education Statistics, 1989), p. 303.

cals for the library, equipment, supplies and materials, and utilities—all of which have increased between 120 and 300 percent over the last decade.[76] Less dramatic and more manageable are the controllable costs of contracted services, faculty and professional staff salaries, and non-professional wages and salaries.[77] Cutbacks can be implemented in any of these areas, but the political fallout is always serious. The largest mixed costs concern employee benefits, which combine some flexibility of choice at the beginning with fixed cost afterwards.[78]

College and university libraries consume significant resources of their parent institutions. Academic libraries spend between 2.5 and 7.5 percent of the total university education budget.[79] This financial load varies considerably according to the size of the institution and the importance of the library to the school's educational mission. Another factor is that as the university adds functions (i.e., computer center, research institutions, etc.), the proportional size of the financial commitment to the library is reduced. The median for institutional support of academic libraries in 1986 was 3.4 percent of educational expenses, but this figure has fluctuated over time (see table 3.4).[80] These figures show that institutional support was slowly shrinking in the middle 1980s, after an era of strong support in the 1970s. Even in the 1970s, institutional budget shortfalls caused a drastic drop in support during the 1974–75 academic year. A recovery was attempted in subsequent years, but since then financial support has declined from 4 percent in 1975–76 to 3.4 percent in 1984–85. This reduction has been at a time when heavy demands have been placed on academic libraries by greater patron needs and by the necessity to acquire new technologies. Library managers continue to seek a proportional share of the university budget, but this share is still declining. Justification for library budget increases has been based on past performance in satisfying faculty and student needs, but arguments such as these are obviously not enough to persuade academic

Table 3.4: Library Expenditures and Share of Higher Education Expenditures, 1949–1986 (In Millions of Dollars)

Year	Educational Expenditures	Library Expenditures	Libraries' Percentage of Share
1949–50	1,706	56	3.3
1951–52	1,921	61	3.2
1953–54	2,271	73	3.2
1955–56	2,766	86	3.1
1957–58	3,604	110	3.1
1959–60	4,513	135	3.0
1961–62	5,768	177	3.1
1963–64	7,425	237	3.2
1965–66	9,951	346	3.5
1967–68	13,190	493	3.7
1969–70	15,789	653	4.1
1971–72	19,201	765	4.0
1973–74	23,257	939	4.0
1975–76	30,599	1,224	4.0
1977–78	36,257	1,349	3.7
1979–80	44,543	1,624	3.7
1980–81	50,073	1,760	3.5
1981–82	54,849	1,922	3.5
1982–83	58,929	2,040	3.5
1983–84	63,741	2,231	3.5
1984–85	70,061	2,362	3.4
1985–86	76,128	2,551	3.4

Sources: Martin M. Cummings, *The Economics of Research Libraries* (Washington, D.C.: Council on Library Resources, 1986), p. 13; and Thomas D. Snyder, *Digest of Education Statistics, 1987* (Washington, D.C.: Center for Education Statistics, 1987), p. 238.

administrators of the necessity for more funding. This weakening of the financial base of the library also means that more attention needs to be paid to financial planning. Universities are requiring academic libraries to participate in campus strategic planning, and many of these strategic plans envisage tighter financial control over libraries.

Private and public institutions have been injured partners in the decline of funding for academic libraries, but they have experienced this drop at different levels. Public institutions have funded libraries at a lower percentage than the university average (see table 3.5).[81] This lower rate has been consistent in the period since 1975. Private institutions have been funded slightly higher during the same time (see table 3.6).[82] This trend seems to be stable and a permanent feature of academic life.

Lower support for academic libraries has meant that library administrators have had to lower their expectations. Rather than planning for large-scale growth, these managers have had to administer with low- or no-growth funding. A survey of thirty-eight academic library administrators in the early 1980s had these officials rate eleven areas of the library's budget in terms of their importance over the next decade.[83] They identified these areas in the following order:

Table 3.5: Library Expenditures and Share of Higher Education Expenditures in Public Institutions, 1975–1986 (In Millions of Dollars)

Year	Educational Expenditures	Library Expenditures	Libraries' Percentage of Share
1975–76	21,283	825	3.9
1977–78	25,149	901	3.5
1979–80	30,627	1,115	3.6
1980–81	34,173	1,187	3.5
1981–82	37,171	1,288	3.5
1982–83	39,707	1,338	3.4
1983–84	42,594	1,464	3.4
1984–85	46,874	1,558	3.3
1985–86	50,873	1,685	3.3

Information unavailable for 1976–77 and 1978–79.

Source: Thomas D. Snyder, Digest of Education Statistics, 1987 (Washington, D.C.: Center for Education Statistics, 1987), pp. 238–39.

1. Cost of periodicals
2. Cost of books
3. Cost of equipment
4. Librarian salaries
5. Staff salaries
6. Cost of audio/visual materials

7. Cost of supplies
8. Cost of binding
9. Part-time salaries
10. Cost of maintenance and repair
11. Cost of custodial services [84]

These answers indicate that these administrators were most concerned about the cost of materials and the impact of the costs on their collections. They were also asked about the areas of the university budget of most concern to their institution's top administrators,[85] and these were the areas so identified:

1. Organized research
2. Automation
3. Faculty salaries
4. Periodical subscriptions
5. Books to be purchased
6. Equipment, including automation

7. Binding
8. Staff positions
9. Librarian positions
10. Supplies
11. Maintenance and repair [86]

Table 3.6: Library Expenditures and Share of Higher Education Expenditures in Private Institutions, 1975–1986 (In Million of Dollars)

Year	Educational Expenditures	Library Expenditures	Libraries' Percentage of Share
1975–76	9,316	399	4.3
1977–78	11,108	448	4.0
1979–80	13,915	509	3.7
1980–81	15,901	573	3.6
1981–82	17,678	635	3.6
1982–83	19,222	702	3.7
1983–84	21,148	768	3.6
1984–85	23,188	804	3.5
1985–86	25,255	866	3.4

Information unavailable for 1976–77 and 1978–79.

Source: Thomas D. Snyder, *Digest of Education Statistics, 1987* (Washington, D.C.: Center for Education Statistics, 1987), pp. 238–39.

The differences between these lists indicate a divergence in priorities between library administrators and their bosses. Library managers have to realize the implications and make adjustments accordingly. Probably the greatest "adjustment" of all has been acknowledgment of the university computer center and its impact on the academic library.

The major budgetary rival to the academic library on most campuses has been the university computer center. Universities became interested in computer systems nearly thirty years ago, initially for their advanced research potential and later for their administrative applications.[87] Computer information systems to support administrative functions—class registration, student billing, donor solicitations, etc.—had become widespread in most colleges and universities by the early 1980s.[88] Information-processing technologies have been popular in the college and university environment because the United States is fast becoming an information-based economy. The increased capacity of computer hardware and the decrease in cost have made collegiate administrators receptive to spending the large sums necessary to purchase the hardware. Moreover, academic computing to support instruction and research has accelerated in the last decade. Decreased emphasis on a single, large mainframe computer and the advent of the inexpensive microcomputer have stimulated computer instruction and research. At present, the number of computers sold to institutions of higher education is approaching 40 percent of the computer market.[89] Most of the large institutions are in the process of implementing large-scale, campus-wide networks. A system at the University of California–Berkeley will accommodate a network of 20,000 workstations with 40,000 ports, as well as electrical wires and cables for seventy-five buildings.[90]

The importance of academic computing has resulted in the creation of a new agency for computer administration, and two models of computer administration are presently in vogue: a director of academic computing and a coordinator of campus-wide computing.[91] The director of academic computing, who is usually a Ph.D. with a highly technical background, administers a computing facility and staff to support the instructional and research mission of the institution. In contrast, the coordinator of campus-wide computing is normally *not* an academic and is at least one step above the director's level—often a vice-president reporting directly to the president. These administrators have been given the title chief information officer (CIO), or they are characterized as "computer czars."[92] At last count in 1987, there were about one hundred of these so-called czars in higher education, and their numbers continue to grow.[93] Indeed, a centralized computer center has become the recipient of considerable institutional resources, and despite efforts by the academic library to participate in the computer planning process, these centers are challenging the funding of the library on most academic campuses. Such a rapid expansion of computer services means that computer and information technology may be twice as costly as the academic library.[94]

Academic libraries have been slow to respond to the challenge of the computer centers. The center and its related information technology organization, after all, is part of a dynamic international growth industry and has "its own distinctive high-tech professional culture."[95] In the early stages of the development of computer centers, only a few library leaders believed that computer technology had a natural home in the academic library, but they were unable to mobilize enough support from inside or outside the institutions to become involved in long-range planning. Even when such leaders attempted to intervene, they were bypassed by university planners because "libraries were passe; computers were 'sexy.' "[96] In any event, academic libraries have adopted the new computer technology piecemeal, and the major decisions on computer applications are now made at the campus level. A segment of academic leadership has asked why computer centers have developed outside of the library system, and they mistakenly attribute lack of aggressiveness on the part of the library as the reason.[97] Some library leaders believe that the greatest danger for academic libraries from the computer center will be in having the library report to a person in charge of information technology rather than to the chief academic officer.[98] Another layer of bureaucracy will only further isolate the library from campus decision making.

Efforts have been made to integrate computer and library functions at various universities, but the jury is still out on how effective this alliance will be. A variety of academic leaders think that it makes sense to link communications, or the computer center, with the library.[99] Part of this reasoning has been based upon the belief that if the academic library competed for resources with the computer center in the academic political arena, the library would probably lose.[100] Some speculation is that the recent trend toward decentralized computing will weaken the financial base of the computer center and make possible a blending of general computing and library operations.[101] Several difficulties in any such merger have been identified, such as differences in skills, attitudes, and motivation between individuals working in computer centers and libraries.[102] Librarians tend to be people oriented, with special interest in the information retrieval process, in contrast to the staff of computer centers, who are more concerned with data—their storage and manipulation.[103] Moreover, the difference in philosophy between computer centers and libraries on cost recovery for information remains a barrier to complete integration between them. Even some supporters of cooperation between computer centers and academic libraries are pessimistic that free service for basic activities will remain free.[104] These philosophical differences have been described as a "tension of different cultures," and they have to be overcome before there can be a successful merging of computer centers and libraries.[105] Finally, differences in salary, academic background, and even academic status would have to be resolved.[106]

The cost of new technology in academic libraries has been high, and it continues to grow. In the past, librarianship had been a labor-intensive profession, with a plentiful labor supply and low salaries. Even during the librarian shortage in the 1960s and early 1970s, salaries never adjusted to demand. Only in the last decade have librarians' salaries increased as more clerical functions have been shifted to the support staff. This trend was first noted in the middle 1950s, but the process has accelerated in the 1970s and 1980s under the impact of technology.[107] It has been the demonstration of the Veaner Theorem that once technology is used to handle routine mental tasks, work is driven downward in the work hierarchy, away from the professional to the nonprofessional support staff.[108] While support salaries have remained low, the reduction of clerical work has allowed the professional librarian to move toward the higher-paying management positions. Academic librarians' salaries are still lower than those of their colleagues in the teaching faculty, but they are higher than before this shift in job responsibility. These salaries comprise about 60 percent of the budget of any large or medium-size academic library.

At the same time that salaries began to rise, the costs for the new technology hit the library. One university librarian estimates that about 60 percent of his library's operating budget goes either to technology or to technologically related functions.[109] While this estimate appears high, these types of outlay will continue to grow as the academic library continues to adopt more sophisticated library technology and acquire new equipment. The limit will be less the library demand for library automation than the rate of funding allocated to the library for such operations.

The current rate of library funding is below what librarians feel is adequate to meet the demands on the academic library. Financial support for academic libraries has been determined by available revenues rather than by need.[110] Demand for research materials has exceeded the capacity of libraries to fulfill requests. Few libraries can produce more than half of the materials requested by patrons.[111] Scientific and technology-related materials have far outstripped the library budget's capacity to purchase them, and the proliferation of new programs and disciplines has only increased the problem. Libraries have attempted to alleviate their funding problems by looking for outside funding, and special attention has been given to attracting government and private funding. Most academic libraries have been active in grant-writing activities to raise funds for special projects. Preservation and retrospective conversion projects have been most popular with grant-funding agencies. Private funds have been solicited through increased activity in Friends of the Library organizations. Private donors have been most generous in donating collections and making special purchases of large or special collections. None of these sources, however, has helped to defray rising operating costs. Academic libraries have had to become participants in university endowment campaigns to find the funds to replace lost purchasing power. These campaigns are long-term projects that promise much in the future but provide little cash for the present.

A new cost in academic libraries is for replacing outdated computer systems, for which academic libraries are woefully undercapitalized.[112] Many libraries adopted parts of automated systems in the 1970s, and these libraries need to upgrade or purchase new systems. Funds to do this have been in short supply, so many academic librarians have been forced to work with yesterday's technology. They realize that the only money available will have to come from already existing funds in the library budget—but this budget lacks the flexibility to handle such expenditures.

The size and cost of an academic library have resulted in the study of ways to control future growth. Old ideas of a collection doubling or tripling its size in less than a decade have enough truth to scare library administrators who deal with budget and space problems. These individuals therefore attempt to replace the traditional (Alexandrian) model with a no-growth (or Phoenix) model. This no-growth model envisages a library's reducing its holdings around 30 percent, since this reduction would change availability by only 1 percent.[113] Regional centers of little-used materials, grouped around five or six libraries, would provide access to the unique title.[114] Advocates of this approach claim that this would ensure maximum usage of a collection at the lowest possible cost.

Another way to cut costs has been economies in personnel. University administrators have subscribed to adopting new library technology if a side benefit was reduction of personnel costs.[115] Experience has revealed that few personnel costs have been reduced by library automation, but an increase in productivity has in fact been achieved. The result is that the same number of librarians are administering and providing service for larger and larger collections.

A topic that reappears at frequent intervals as a potential cost cutter is resource sharing. These "frequent intervals" almost always coincide with an economic downturn that threatens library funding. Most of the large academic libraries have been reluctant to commit themselves to large-scale resource sharing for a variety of political reasons. Two of the most important reasons have been faculty resistance to not having research materials immediately available and loss of control by librarians over significant research collections. A major effort for resource sharing has been made by academic libraries in supporting the Center for Research Libraries (CRL) in Chicago, but it has been in the form of giving money rather than relinquishing control over existing collections. Duplication of collections is still widespread among the top research libraries, and few serious efforts to change this are apparent. In contrast, some of the small academic libraries have had little choice about resource sharing and have cancelled serials in cooperative ventures with other libraries of like size.[116] Despite this example, resource sharing is a good idea that is looking for implementation.

Librarians find college and university finances, and financial decision making, frustrating. Constant patron demand for services or materials that librarians are unable to satisfy lowers both patron and librarian morale. The result is a constant complaint about the reluctance of the institution to provide the necessary funding for books, journals, computers, equipment, and staff positions. Librarians know what kind of service they could provide with adequate financial support, but it is in the institution's political arena, where the decisions are made, that the librarians feel left out. Librarians, of course, are not the only members of the academic community who are outside the decision-making process. The teaching faculty expresses a similar powerlessness, because it also experiences decisions made by nameless administrators.

NOTES

1. Wesley W. Posvar, "The President Views the Campus Library," *Journal of Academic Librarianship* 3 (September 1977) 4:193.
2. David W. Adamany, "Research Libraries from a Presidential Perspective," in *Issues in Academic Librarianship: Views and Case Studies for the 1980s and 1990s*, edited by Peter Spyers-Duran and Thomas W. Mann (Westport, Conn.: Greenwood Press, 1985), p. 11.

3. Trevor Arnett, *College and University Finance* (New York: General Education Board, 1922), pp. 6–7.
4. Ibid., p. 7.
5. Roger L. Geiger, *To Advance Knowledge: The Growth of American Research Universities, 1900–1940* (New York: Oxford University Press, 1986), p. 41.
6. Ibid.
7. Ibid., p. 47., Arnett gives the collective wisdom of dealing with endowment income in the early 1920s (Arnett, *College and University Finance*, pp. 24–53).
8. J. Fredericks Volkwein, "State Financial Control of Public Universities and Its Relationship to Campus Administrative Elaborateness and Cost: Results of a National Study," *Review of Higher Education* 9 (1986) 3:268.
9. Howard R. Bowen, "What Determines the Costs of Higher Education?" in *ASHE Reader on Finance in Higher Education*, edited by Larry L. Leslie and Richard E. Anderson (Lexington, Mass.: Ginn Press, 1986), pp. 164–65.
10. J. Kent Caruthers and Melvin Orwig, *Budgeting in Higher Education* (Washington, D.C.: American Association for Higher Education, 1979), p. 1.
11. Ibid., p. 2.
12. Michael D. Cohen and James G. Marsh, *Leadership and Ambiguity: The American College President* (2d ed.; Boston: Harvard Business School Press, 1986), p. 95.
13. At least 90 percent of a state institution's budget derives from formulas based on student enrollments (Ibid., p. 97).
14. Ibid., p. 95.
15. *Universities, Information Technology, and Academic Libraries*, edited by Robert M. Hayes (Norwood, N.J.: Ablex, 1986), p. 15.
16. Cohen and Marsh, *Leadership and Ambiguity*, p. 95.
17. Ibid., p. 99.
18. Ibid., p. 95.
19. Gerald B. Robins, "From Understanding the College Budget," in *ASHE Reader on Finance in Higher Education*, edited by Larry L. Leslie and Richard E. Anderson (Lexington, Mass.: Ginn Press, 1986), pp. 27–28.
20. Caruthers and Orwig, *Budgeting in Higher Education*, p. 36.
21. Ibid., p. 37.
22. Ibid., p. 17.
23. Ibid., p. 18.
24. John M. Cooper, "Financing Academic Libraries: Making the Transition from Enrollment Growth to Quality Enhancement," *College and Research Libraries* 47 (July 1986) 4:354–55.
25. Francis M. Gross, "Formula Budgeting and the Financing of Public Higher Education: Panacea or Nemesis for the 1980's," *Association for Institutional Research Professional File* 3 (Fall 1979): 1–7.
26. Caruthers and Orwig, *Budgeting in Higher Education*, p. 43.
27. Michael E. D. Koenig and Victor Alperin, "ZBB and PPBS: What's Left

Now that the Trendiness Has Gone?" *Drexel Library Quarterly* 21 (Summer 1985) 3:22.

28. Robert J. Parden, "Planning, Programming and Budgeting Systems," in *Efficient College Management*, edited by William W. Jellema (San Francisco: Jossey-Bass, 1972), p. 11.
29. Ibid., pp. 17–18.
30. Michael L. Tierney, "Priority Setting and Resource Allocation," in *Evaluation of Management and Planning Systems*, edited by Nick L. Poulton (San Francisco: Jossey-Bass, 1981), p. 30.
31. Michael L. Tierney, "Administration: The Impact of Management Information Systems on Governance," in *Governing Academic Organizations: New Problems, New Perspectives*, edited by Gary L. Riley and J. Victor Baldridge (Berkeley, Calif.: McCutchan, 1977), p. 214.
32. L. James Harvey, *Zerobase Budgeting in Colleges and Universities* (Littleton, Colo.: Ireland Educational Corporation, 1977), p. 2.
33. Robins, "From Understanding the College Budget," p. 50.
34. L. James Harvey, *Managing Colleges and Universities by Objectives: A Concise Guide to Understanding and Implementing MBO in Higher Education* (Littleton, Colo.: Ireland Educational Corporation, 1976), p. 44.
35. Ibid.
36. Harvey, *Zerobase Budgeting in Colleges and Universities*, p. 2.
37. Tierney, "Priority Setting and Resource Allocation," p. 31.
38. Ibid.
39. Harvey, *Zerobase Budgeting in Colleges and Universities*, p. 3.
40. Koenig and Alperin, "ZBB and PPBS," pp. 22–23.
41. Caruthers and Orwig, *Budgeting in Higher Education*, p. 53.
42. Tierney, "Priority Setting and Resource Allocation," p. 33.
43. Robins, "From Understanding the College Budget," p. 50.
44. Frederick E. Balderston, *Managing Today's University* (San Francisco: Jossey-Bass, 1974), p. 47.
45. Roger N. Gaunt and Michael J. Haight, "Planning Models in Higher Education Administration," in *ASHE Reader on Finance in Higher Education*, edited by Larry L. Leslie and Richard E. Anderson (Lexington, Mass.: Ginn Press, 1986), p. 60.
46. Ibid., p. 62.
47. Ibid.
48. Ibid., p. 61.
49. Ibid.
50. Daniel A. Updegrove, "Using Computer-based Planning Models," in *Evaluation of Management and Planning Systems*, edited by Nick L. Poulton (San Francisco: Jossey-Bass, 1981), p. 64.
51. Ibid.
52. Ibid., pp. 64–65.
53. John Rohrbaugh, "Institutional Research as Decision Support," *New Directions for Institutional Research* 49 (March 1986) 1:6.
54. Richard G. Milter, "Resource Allocation Models and the Budgeting Process," *New Directions for Institutional Research* 49 (March 1986) 1:76.

55. Ibid., p. 77.

56. Ibid., p. 79.

57. Gaunt and Haight, "Planning Models in Higher Education Administration," p. 66.

58. Ibid., p. 68.

59. Shari Lohela and F. William Summers, "The Impact of Planning on Budgeting," *Journal of Library Administration* 2 (Summer–Fall–Winter 1981) 2,3,4:176.

60. Adamany, "Research Libraries from a Presidential Perspective," pp. 13–14.

61. Lohela and Summers, "Impact of Planning on Budgeting," p. 176.

62. Cooper lists the rate-per-student states: Alabama, Connecticut, Kentucky, Missouri, Ohio, Tennessee, and Texas; and the percentage-of-instruction states: Georgia, Louisiana, Mississippi, South Carolina, and West Virginia (Cooper, "Financing Academic Libraries," p. 355).

63. Koenig and Alperin, "ZBB and PPBS," p. 26.

64. Dennis C. Fields, "Library Management by Objectives: The Humane Way," *College and Research Libraries* 35 (September 1974) 5:344-49.

65. Koenig and Alperin, "ZBB and PPBS," p. 34.

66. Adamany, "Research Libraries from a Presidential Perspective," p. 13.

67. Ibid.

68. Lohela and Summers, "Impact of Planning on Budgeting," p. 182.

69. William A. Jenkins, "The Role of the Chief Financial Officer in Large Public Universities," *NACUBO Business Officer* 18 (January 1985) 7:29.

70. William G. Bowen, "The Role of the Business Officer in Managing Educational Resources," in *ASHE Reader on Finance in Higher Education*, edited by Larry L. Leslie and Richard E. Anderson (Lexington, Mass.: Ginn Press, 1986), p. 14.

71. Ibid., p. 17.

72. Robins, "From Understanding the College Budget," p. 46.

73. Thomas D. Snyder, *Digest of Education Statistics, 1989* (Washington, D.C.: Office of Educational Research and Improvement, U.S. Department of Education, 1989), p. 301.

74. Ibid., p. 302.

75. Ibid., p. 303.

76. Clark L. Bernard and Douglas Veaven, "Containing the Costs of Higher Education," *NACUBO Business Officer* 20 (August 1986) 2:29.

77. Ibid.

78. Ibid., pp. 29–30.

79. Martin M. Cummings, *The Economics of Research Libraries* (Washington, D.C.: Council on Library Resources, 1986), p. 14.

80. Statistics for this table have been gathered from two sources: Cummings, *Economics of Research Libraries*, p. 13; and Thomas D. Snyder, *Digest of Education Statistics, 1987* (Washington, D.C.: Center for Education Statistics, 1987) p. 238.

81. Snyder, *Digest of Education Statistics*, 1987, pp. 238–39.

82. Ibid.
83. Edward R. Johnson, "Financial Planning Needs of Publicly Supported Academic Libraries in the 1980s: Politics as Usual," *Journal of Library Administration* 3 (Fall–Winter 1982) 3,4:25.
84. Ibid.
85. Ibid.
86. Ibid., pp. 25–26.
87. John W. McCredie, "Introduction," in *Campus Computing Strategies*, edited by John W. McCredie (Bedford, Mass.: Digital Press, 1983), p. 4.
88. Linda H. Fleit, "Computerizing America's Campuses: How Technology Is Changing Higher Education," *Electronic Learning* 6 (March 1987) 6:19.
89. Ibid.
90. Mary Lee Shalvoy, "College Workstations: Vendors Line Up for a Multi-Billion Dollar Market," *Electronic Learning* 7 (November–December 1987) 3:27.
91. Fleit, "Computerizing America's Campuses," p. 21.
92. Ibid.
93. Ibid.
94. David C. Weber, "University Libraries and Campus Information Technology Organizations: Who Is in Charge Here?" *Journal of Library Administration* 9 (1988) 4:9.
95. Ibid., p. 7.
96. E. Gordon Gee and Patricia Senn Breivik, "Libraries and Learning," in *Libraries and the Search for Academic Excellence*, edited by Patricia Senn Breivik and Robert Wedgeworth (Metuchen, N.J.: Scarecrow Press, 1988), p. 26.
97. Clyde Hendrick, "The University Library in the Twenty-first Century," *College and Research Libraries* 47 (March 1986) 2:130.
98. Richard M. Dougherty, "Libraries and Computing Centers: A Blueprint for Collaboration," *College and Research Libraries* 48 (July 1987) 4:289–90.
99. D. Kay Gapen, "Myths and Realities: University Libraries," *College and Research Libraries* 45 (September 1984) 5:359.
100. *Universities, Information Technology, and Academic Libraries*, p. 75.
101. Anne Woodsworth, "Computing Centers and Libraries as Cohorts: Exploiting Mutual Strengths," *Journal of Library Administration* 9 (1988) 4:26.
102. Woodsworth quotes an unpublished study by J. R. Sack, entitled "Libraries and Technology Centers: Opportunities and Otherwise" (Ibid., p. 30).
103. Alan E. Guskin, Carla J. Stoffle, and Barbara E. Baruth, "Library Future Shock: The Microcomputer Revolution and the New Role of the Library," *College and Research Libraries* 45 (May 1984) 3:181–82.
104. Dougherty, "Libraries and Computing Centers," p. 294.
105. Woodsworth, "Computing Centers and Libraries as Cohorts," p. 30.
106. Diane J. Cimbala, "The Scholarly Information Center: An Organizational Model," *College and Research Libraries* 48 (September 1987) 5:395–96.

107. Archie L. McNeal, "Ratio of Professional to Clerical Staff," *College and Research Libraries* 17 (May 1956) 3:219–23.
108. Allen B. Veaner, "Librarians: The Next Generation," *Library Journal* 109 (April 1984): 623–24.
109. Isabelle Bruder, "The Library of the Future—Now," *Electronic Learning* 7 (March 1988) 6:22.
110. Barbara B. Moran, "The Unintended Revolution in Academic Libraries: 1939 to 1989 and Beyond," *College and Research Libraries* 50 (January 1989) 1:30.
111. Cummings, *Economics of Research Libraries*, p. 35.
112. Susan K. Martin, "Information Technology and Libraries: Toward the Year 2000," *College and Research Libraries* 50 (July 1989) 4:401.
113. Daniel Gore, "Zero Growth: When Is Not-Enough Enough? A Symposium," *Journal of Academic Librarianship* 1 (November 1975) 5:4–5.
114. Richard W. Trueswell, "Zero Growth: When Is Not-Enough Enough? A Symposium," *Journal of Academic Librarianship* 1 (November 1975) 5:6.
115. Robert MacVicar, "The President Views the Campus Library," *Journal of Academic Librarianship* 3 (September 1977) 4:197.
116. Bernard H. Holicky, "Collection Development vs. Resource Sharing: The View from the Small Academic Library," *Journal of Academic Librarianship* 10 (July 1984) 3:146–47.

CHAPTER FOUR

The University Administration and the Academic Library

THE RELATIONSHIP BETWEEN the university administration and the academic library has always been determined by the political environment of the institution. Every collegiate administration has the responsibility for the successful running of its institution, and the library is considered by the administrators as only a small part of this task. On the other hand, the library consumes a significant portion of the resources of any college or university budget, and at budget time the library seems like an uncontrollable drain on the university's resources.[1] Because of the other administrative demands of the institution, administrators lack the time, the opportunity, or the inclination to understand the functioning of the library. Consequently, the library is only rarely examined except during a budgetary or management crisis. Administrative insiders also see the library as an outsider in the university's power structure. This fact is reflected in the decisions made at the upper administrative levels that impact on the library without input from the library. The virtual isolation of the library from the policy councils of most institutions occurs at a time when the library is becoming increasingly important in providing information services on the local, regional, and national levels.[2] It therefore appears that this information role has not been translated into

increased prestige for academic libraries. An indication of the importance of the library within a college or university is the administrative
level at which the library director reports for evaluation of the library's
performance. Past experience has proven that the library director must
report to the academic vice-provost, or vice-chancellor level, before the
library can be considered a serious factor in academic decision making
on the campus.

Large college and university administrations grew very slowly in
the first two and a half centuries of American higher education. It was
not until the institutions became complex (in the early twentieth century) that bureaucratic structures were seen as necessary. Colonial and
most nineteenth-century colleges' administration consisted of a board
of trustees, a president, and a small faculty of professors and instructors. Almost all of the trustees were clergymen, as were the colleges'
presidents. Almost all the faculty and instructors were ministers, and
everyone had to meet reasonable standards of religious orthodoxy. In
such homogeneous institutions, diversity of moral or religious opinion
was rare, but dissension over educational policy was not uncommon.
Except for economic downturns, internal dissension closed the doors of
more colleges than any other cause. Another type of discord included
student rebellion, in the form of riots and strikes. All these difficulties
(among others) showed higher education leaders the necessity for special
officials to monitor college affairs.

The emergence of the university from the shadow of the liberal
arts college in the late nineteenth century resulted in the need for more
administrative layers in the academic structure. Division of the university into schools, divisions, and departments introduced the posts
of dean, division head, and department chairperson. New graduate programs also needed administrative heads. Federal funding mandated even
more posts by pushing for interdisciplinary centers and institutes. Larger
schools made budget and students' affairs more important, and a business staff became a necessity. Soon a bureaucratic staff with officers
and secretaries appeared, with the need for room and resources.

This growth pattern continues even today. Every time a new demand for services appears, more personnel are added.[3] The most common organizational structure now divides the university into academic
and administrative branches, with heads for each part. As the administrative apparatus has grown, faculty has become more and more distrustful
of the size and influence of the bureaucracy.[4] The U.S. Office of Education analysis reported in 1976–77 that there were 35.7 administrators for
every 100 faculty members in private institutions, and 19 per 100 in pub-

lic institutions.⁵ Faculty distrust in an expanding bureaucracy manifests itself more in complaining than in action, but these feelings reappear at intervals in faculty senates and committees as a desire to reduce the size of the bureaucracy.

The modern college and university have become so complex that it takes a large staff of administrators to run them. Besides the difficulty in finding the right people, problems from outside the academic world have made the administration of higher education institutions more difficult. Prosperity and increasing enrollments in the two decades after World War II made it easy for administrators to be successful, but this began to change in the more difficult 1970s, and it became serious in the period of fiscal restraint in the 1980s. Diminishing federal funding, tightening by state government of budgets, and an increasing emphasis on outside financial resources have combined to end the prosperity of the 1960s. These factors, which have caused college and university administrators to become more concerned about the efficient functioning of their institutions, have also made running an institution more burdensome. The average length of stay of an administrator in fifty-five types of line positions is between five and six years.⁶ While some of this movement is toward advancement to the next higher rank, much of it is out of administration and back to faculty ranks.

One difficulty in administering a college or university is that no consensus has developed on its mission. Thus the lack of goals, or "goal ambiguity," is a permanent feature of academic organizations.⁷ This lack of clearly defined goals means that each institution ends up defining its own goals and priorities. A change in campus leadership can reorient these priorities, and parts of the institution that are resistant to change, such as academic libraries, can be caught during the transition. Moreover, such academic goals that are advanced are highly contested, so that there is little agreement (but much rhetoric) on the mission of higher education.⁸ Because there is so little agreement on academic goals and because bureaucracy needs clear goals, the collegiate environment is cluttered with an amalgamation of differing types of bureaucratic behavior.

Organization theory gives insight into the organization and administration of modern colleges and universities. Although these theories are an outgrowth of thinking by management scholars on organizations in the profit sector, they also have relevance to higher education organizations. Current organizational research identifies six models on the nature of organizations: (1) scientific, (2) bureaucratic, (3) collegial, (4) political, (5) organized anarchy, and (6) economic self-interest. While each of

these organizational models has its proponents and adherents in higher
education, none is universally accepted.

The scientific is the oldest model of managing organizations still
used, with varying degrees of success. This model of organizational behavior is the outgrowth of research in the early twentieth century by
Frederick Taylor and his associates. Taylor was concerned with developing fair performance standards for organizations,[9] and motivation by
material reward was the key concept of this model. Time and motion
studies were relied upon to improve production and provide the basis
for rewards. This system worked better in the industrial world than in
higher education because of the difficulty of transferring time and motion studies into the academic environment. Moreover, the resistance of
the faculty toward standards of production has discouraged implementation. Only on the business side of university operations has it been
possible to use parts of this model.

The bureaucratic model is the second oldest, and in the present
climate in higher education, no more attractive than the scientific model.
This model is more or less identified with the writings of the German
sociologist Max Weber and the principles of scientific management. Two
principles, authority and hierarchy, form the basis of this organizational
model. *Authority* means both the power to command and the means to
enforce commands.[10] The principle of hierarchy is followed strictly, with
each lower office under the control and supervision of the higher one.[11]
Only those who demonstrate adequate technical training are allowed
to be members of the administration.[12] Conflict is managed through
bureaucratic channels, and is presumed to be temporary and resolvable.[13]
While most colleges and universities have at least some vestiges of the
bureaucratic system still in operation, especially on the business affairs
side, this model is less popular on the academic side. Because of its
lack of popularity and its inflexibility, most institutions have moved
away from the bureaucratic model, when possible. Yet the university
still retains vestiges of this model in appointments, tenure decisions,
and promotions.[14]

The most fashionable model in higher education is the collegial
model. This theory, which borrows heavily from the industrial human
relations school, emphasizes the interpersonal relationships of the individual rather than the needs of the organization. This model has colleges
and universities organized internally on the principle of a "community
of authority"—that is, four constituent groups: faculty, students, alumni,
and administration.[15] "Shared authority" is the basic characteristic of
this model, and in a perfect collegial system all members of the insti-

tution would participate in all relevant decisions.[16] The best description of this model is by one of its foremost proponents.

> At the departmental and at the college or school level the system for decision making is one of direct democracy. Every person of stated academic rank has an equal voice and vote in the realization of collective action. At the university level the system for decision making may be either direct or representative.[17]

Few institutions have totally adopted the preceding model, but most colleges and universities adhere to the collegial system in some fashion. The chief criticism of the collegial model is that it is too cumbersome and inefficient, because decision making must come from all interested parties.[18] It assumes, moreover, that conflict can be eliminated through consensus. This assumption has not been proven in actual practice.

The next model is the political, and it is gaining acceptance in higher education circles. This model comes from the works of Victor Baldridge, and it owes much to the organizational theories of conflict management.[19] Conflict theory postulates that conflict is endemic in any organization and only by bargaining among the political parties can these conflicts be resolved. While decision making in colleges and universities can be either bureaucratic or collegial, or both, political compromise is the key to making decisions.[20] This model appears to be becoming the most accepted among theorists on higher education.

A more recent model is that of organized anarchy. Again, this model owes its existence to organizational theory, but this time the two theorists, Michael D. Cohen and James G. Marsh, became frustrated with the failure of other organizational models to conform to the norms of organizational behavior in higher education. Consequently, they noted that, regardless of the prevailing organizational model, the underlying realities in colleges and universities cause the institution to react outside any organizational model. Because colleges and universities have problematic goals, unclear technology, and fluid participation the proponents of this theory classify their organizational behavior as "organized anarchies."[21] While this model is still under examination and acceptance is still questionable, it does explain certain aberrations of organizational behavior in higher education.

The last model, economic self-interest, is the most recent model in higher education organizational theory. Unlike the other models, this theory borrows heavily from the literature of economics. David A. Garvin advances this explanation of organization behavior because early models "focus exclusively on internal decision-making rules and procedures," lack details for testing the models, and fail to address the motivations of administration and faculty.[22] The motivating behavior guiding university policy for both administrators and faculty in this theory is self-interest rather than a formal organization model.[23] Economic self-interest is interpreted to resemble the profit motive in business, but in higher education it is the competitive environment, or the competition for resources, that shapes university behavior. While its creator confesses that this economic approach does not provide all the answers for students of higher education behavior, it adds insights unavailable in the other models.[24] This model is still under scrutiny by scholars in the field, and no decisions on its value have been decided by them.

The six organizational models outlined here have never been intended to be mutually exclusive. Organizational theory allows for mixtures of organizational systems, and it would be rare for any college or university to fit exactly into any one or two of these models. Different branches, departments, or subunits might have a different mix of the models, with the key depending on the administrative leadership of the individual unit. A better way of approaching these models is to use them as guides for further inquiry into the nature of the administrative structure of colleges and universities.[25]

The library participates in these organizational models to the extent that the library functions within the institution's administrative organizational structure. In the past, libraries have been allowed to develop their own organizational structures because college and university leaders have been unconcerned with the internal workings of the library. Consequently, libraries have adopted individual organizational models that may or may not be compatible with their parent institutions. Some aspects of the scientific model have been adapted for use in the library, but rarely with any success.[26] While many libraries have subscribed to the bureaucratic model, this appears to be changing. The collegial model appears to be increasing in popularity because it seems compatible with the needs of librarians to share in decision making as professionals. Rare is the library, however, that is immune from internal politics, but the political model is the one that seems the most unprofessional both to librarians and library administrators. Despite this distaste, the political model explains more about library operations than several of the other models. Conflict between departments and individuals in the library is more common than librarians like to think.[27] The organized anarchy model appears to be the least appropriate for libraries, but it may explain cases in which libraries function in the absence of strong administrative leadership. It does explain, however, the difficulty that the library has in securing increases in its percentage of the university's operating budget, because of the inability to locate the institution's power source.[28] Finally, the economic self-interest model seems to have only a limited impact on or appeal to libraries and librarians on the surface, but this model needs further study for its relevance to libraries. Internal competition for resources is a characteristic of most libraries, and considerable success accrues to the winners in this type of competition. Library independence in having administrative models different from those of its parent institution may be changing as more college and university administrators desire to incorporate the library into the institution's administrative superstructure.

Formal organizational structures are important in colleges and universities, but the key component becomes the decision-making process. In any academic organization, four types of decisions exist: (1) authority allocation, (2) research allocation, (3) resource acquisition, and (4) production.[29] *Authority allocation* is the decision on the individuals who should make policy decisions within the organization. *Resource allocation* is the decision on the distribution of tangible resources (i.e., funds, equipment, etc.) within the organization. *Resource acquisition* is the obtaining of resources for the use of the organization. Finally, *production* is the finished product of the decision process.

None of these types of decisions is made without reference to the other, or in isolation, and the decision-mode depiction (see figure 4.1) shows the variance within the decision structure.[30] Decisions on each of the eight systems and subsystems can be found on different planes of the decision-making process, according to the amount of participation involved. It is the degree of participation in decision making that establishes both the mode and the effectiveness of collegiate administration. The collegial mode of decision making is reflected in high participation and federated authority on this scale. In contrast, the bureaucratic way of decision making is expressed on the same scale as monarchical and corporate. This theory of decision making allows for a variety of administrative styles to produce decisions. It also ties the type of decision—authority allocation, resource allocation, resource acquisition, and production—to a specific decision-making mode. The issue then becomes the type of people recruited to become administrators.

Almost all college and university administrators are recruited from the academic world. Such recruitment, from presidents down to departmental chairpersons, has always been by promotion through faculty ranks. However, an exception has been the recent practice of appointing

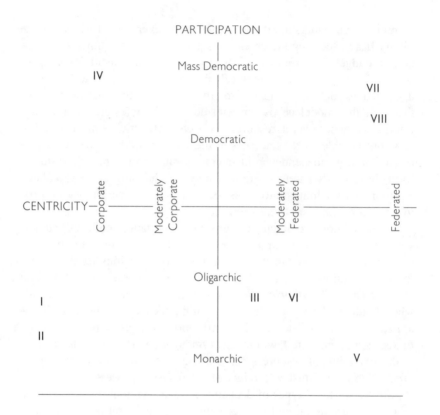

Codes

Type of Decision	Decision Making	
	System	Subsystem
Authority Allocation	I	V
Resource Allocation	II	VI
Resource Acquisition	III	VII
Production	IV	VIII

Source: Robert E. Helsabeck, *The Compound System: A Conceptual Framework for Effective Decisionmaking in Colleges* (Berkeley, Calif.: Center for Research and Development in Higher Education, 1973), p. 6.

Figure 4.1: Hypothetical Compound System Plotted by Amount of Participation and Degree of Centricity

presidents for political reasons, or from outside academia, to instill business practices in the institution. Outside of these exceptions, the normal chain of events starts with the identification of promising young faculty members for future entry into administrative ranks. Early promotions take place at the same institution, but at a certain level (most often at the dean level) this changes. A combination of ability and potential makes these administrators marketable for higher rank at other institutions. This movement from one institution to another creates a common outlook on academic management. Nonacademic administrators, who fall outside this promotion pattern, are recruited for their expertise at some nonacademic specialty, and promotions are more common at the original institution. While there is still recruitment of these specialists by other schools, nonacademic administrators rarely move beyond the vice-president rank.

Most academic administrators consider the academic library from the perspective of management, colored by personal experience. While no two university administrators view the library the same way, they all share a common experience in their past use of a library.[31] Regardless of the positive or negative aspects of this contact, this experience gives administrators insight into the function of the library. Their knowledge of the actual operation of the library is a different matter, and they rarely intervene in library matters. It is the constant demand for funding which brings the library into conflict with other, equally valuable programs, projects, or centers and attracts the attention of administrators. The university computer center is the one agency that offers the most competition to the library.[32] Until the early 1970s, this threat was more apparent than real, but in the 1980s computer centers have become a serious rival to the library for funding. This fact has become apparent to academic administrators as the computer centers assume more importance in the academic world.

Despite efforts to understand the college and university environment in traditional organization terms, the collegiate world is best understood as a mixture of complementary and competing parts. At the top is the board of trustees, or regents, and at the bottom is the faculty. Students are a complementary partner, but they remain outside the decision-making chain. While students can cause difficulties by their behavior or lobbying, they serve only as an irritant to others involved in collegial decision making. It is the trustees, the administrators, and the faculty who determine policy in all colleges and universities. An understanding of the role and functions of each of these bodies is necessary before we turn to how they interrelate.

The boards of trustees have an oversight function in the governance of the university. An estimated 48,000 trustees and regents, on 2,300 governing boards, are responsible for the more than 3,000 colleges and universities in the United States.[33] While trustees in the modern university serve as intermediaries between the university and the general public, the statutory authority still resides with them. In constitutional authority, the American university is subject to government by an oligarchy of laypersons, but in practical usage this government is delegated to the university's administration.[34] Trustees tend to take a proprietary interest in the affairs of their institutions. They are, by nature of their backgrounds, conservative, and this conservatism makes them less receptive to faculty and student pressures. Consequently, they expect the faculty to be contented, or at least not radical, and the students well behaved.[35] A breakdown of the primary occupations of board members reflects the conservative orientation of governing boards (see table 4.1).[36] Fifty-five percent of the total number of board members are active in or retired from business or the professions.

Trustees play an active role in decision making, often with mixed results, when basic changes in the orientation of the university are considered. This occurs most often in the selection of a new president or a decision on curriculum reform. A famous case is the refusal of the Princeton trustees to back the reforms of Woodrow Wilson in 1910, leading to his resignation as president.[37] Another function of the board of trustees is to serve as a court of last appeal on all matters of importance to the university. Most boards of trustees also have standing committees to assist them in their duties. The major criticism of the trustee system has been that the trustees are concerned almost exclusively with the fiscal affairs of the institution rather than its overall educational mission.[38]

The trustees of private and public institutions differ in several important respects. Public boards are usually smaller, with an average of nine persons in comparison to the twenty-five to fifty members on private boards. Trustees of public institutions are appointed by the governor, subject to legislative approval, or are elected by the public on an at-large basis. These individuals serve staggered terms to ensure continuity. Despite the appearance of independence, in almost every state there is little doubt that on the really important decisions the governor and the state legislature play the dominant role.[39] Private institutions have a range of options, but most select boards by election. Usually a committee on nominations will first select and then persuade a prospective board member to serve for a fixed number of years.[40] Often the boards

Table 4.1: Primary Occupation of Governing Board Members

Occupations	Percentages	
Business	37	
Large corporations		14
Small businesses		12
Banking and financial services		10
Other		1
Other Occupations	28	
Clergy		13
Homemakers		5
Other		5
Executives of nonprofit companies		4
Government officials		2
Professions	14	
Lawyers		7
Health professionals		4
Other		3
Education	11	
Higher education		7
Elementary/secondary education		4
Retired	10	
Corporation/financial officers		4
Other		4
Professionals		2

Source: Association of Governing Boards, *Composition of Governing Boards, 1985* (Washington, D.C.: Association of Governing Boards of Universities and Colleges, 1986), p. 10.

are elected by the previous board, but sometimes alumni or church bodies elect or appoint members. Either way, the new board member is appointed to support the broad objectives of the institution. Regardless of methods of selection, both public and private boards of trustees are composed of prominent alumni interested in the welfare of the institution. Despite differences in size and composition, private institutions have had a better record of trustee noninterference in routine university business than the public schools.[41]

Most contact between the board of trustees and the university comes through the office of president. The trustees expect that the president will be able to administer the college or university so that a minimum of trouble or criticism will reach them.[42] A time of close contact between trustees and the university administration is during the annual budgetary process and hearings before the legislature. This contact is of special importance during periods of financial crisis at the state level or in the university. Then "the quality of board decisions is in direct ratio to that of the staff work provided by the president through his office and other administrative offices under his direction." [43] It is in the aftermath of the budgetary process that the president is most vulnerable to dissatisfaction by the governing board. Many institutions have "lost" a president because of a governing board's unhappiness in the aftermath of a political or economic crisis.

[The academic library is too low in the collegiate power structure for the board of trustees to be concerned about its policies. Rarely does a library issue reach the trustees, unless it concerns the hiring of a head of the library or a new library building. An exception is when a controversy involves a conflict over library personnel or an unpopular decision on library service. On these occasions, trustees are apprised about the severity of the problem, without direct intervention. Another arena where trustees may come into contact with the library is through Friends of the Library activities. While most of these contacts are part of fund-raising campaigns, these contacts can be an opportunity for the library to make friends who can come in handy later. This type of contact is more common among private than public institutions, but it occurs in both types of schools.

The president of the institution has always had the responsibility for providing leadership. In colonial times and continuing into the nineteenth century, presidents had broad powers. Many dynamic presidents of the early days of higher education were entrepreneurial types who tended to behave autocratically. Among the duties of the president were the appointment, promotion, and salary level of each member of the faculty. Beginning in the 1890s, the academic department assumed the task of handling faculty selection because the presidents were no longer able to cope with the large turnover of junior-level faculty and conduct the evaluative tasks necessary to build strong faculties.[44] The rapid expansion of universities in the twentieth century has made the president less able to control even the general administration of the institution as the role of the president has expanded to include affairs both on and beyond the campus. Two former university presidents have described the characteristics of the president this way: "The American college president is supposed to be a scholar, a good speaker, a financial wizard, all things to all men, and a good fellow." [45]

The president is a product of the academic environment. Most presidents have had ten to fifteen years' teaching experience before their elevation to an administrative position, but few have achieved interna-

tional renown as scholars or scientists.[46] A majority of the presidents
have educational backgrounds in the humanities, social sciences, and
education, but this may be changing as other disciplines are becoming
better represented.[47] Since the average age of a newly chosen president is in the mid-forties, his or her former career as a teacher and
researcher was in the midcareer cycle before administrative duties were
undertaken.[48] Nearly all presidents have had experience as academic administrators before assuming their presidency. An early study indicates
that 51 percent of presidents have held a position at least at the dean
level, and the percentage increases to 71 for all administrative levels.[49]
Rare is the president who has not had experience at more than one institution. Presidents have been full-time teachers or administrators at an
average of three institutions.[50] It is in this constant contact and interaction in the collegiate setting that the presidents have developed personal
ties and attitudinal affiliation with the academic establishment.

The president makes the most significant contribution in the setting
of institutional goals. These goals are important both to the president
and the future of the institution because success is measured in relationship to achievement of these goals. A survey in the academic year
1986–87 indicates that more than 80 percent of the university presidents
were concerned with the quantitative goals of maintaining or increasing
resources (facilities and equipment or financial support).[51] Qualitative
and educational goals were next in importance.[52] The problem with goal
setting is the relatively short tenure of presidents. Recent research shows
that presidents last only about four and a half years,[53] and such a short
tenure makes it difficult to implement institutional change. Part of the
problem is that most presidents come to their posts as outsiders—but the
majority of the institutions' corps of administrators are insiders.[54] By
the time the presidents learn their way in the administrative corridors of
power, they become vulnerable to a host of problems, many of them not
of their making. Too often, the president is held accountable for activities over which he or she has had only token authority.[55] Finally, most
presidents have been selected in a process filled with representatives of
vested interests, so that the new appointee is a compromise candidate
who lacks the authority to make significant changes.[56]

The increasing burdens of office have placed restrictions on the
ability of the president to accomplish all the tasks necessary for the
office. Recent studies show that outsiders, constituents, and administrators consume nearly a third of the president's daily routine.[57] Rather
than curtailing these contacts, the president has delegated some of the
routine tasks to subordinates. Consequently, most universities have de-

veloped an administrative bureaucracy to handle these burdens. It is
in the selection of key personnel that the president develops the most
leverage on the direction of the institution.[58] This opportunity to influence institutional policy lasts approximately ten years (sometimes
well beyond the term of office), with the period somewhat below this
figure for large institutions.[59] Because of time and energy constraints,
many university presidents have become interested in the lessons of
corporate management.[60] Any attempt to impose these management
principles, however, has created unease among the faculty and some
administrators.[61] Several university presidents have resigned their posts
in the last decade because of entrenched opposition to an emphasis on
managerial rather than collegial principles of administration.

The president of the modern college and university is too busy
with administrative details to bother much with the library except for
specific problems. One president has described his relationship with the
library in these terms:

> The president is involved in four different ways: first, in recruiting a
> director or dean of the library; second, in reviewing and approving the
> library's long-term plan; third, in establishing the library's overall budget
> and goals for accomplishments that are to be derived from the budget;
> fourth, in reviewing the evaluations which are made of the library and its
> director.[62]

The key factor in the relationship of the president and the library is
whether the president has confidence in the library's leadership.[63] Without this confidence, both the library director and (indirectly) the library
will suffer in the political infighting that is always waged in academic
life. Another way that the president can influence the direction of the
library is by outlining priorities, such as interinstitutional cooperation,
new technologies, preservation, and curriculum orientation.[64]

Over the course of history, most of the great academic libraries
have been products of the intervention of great presidents. Harvard University has had a long history as an educational institution, but from
colonial days to the present the library has benefited from attention by
the university president. In the late nineteenth century, the friendship
and support of the president of Harvard, Charles William Eliot, for the
long-time librarian at Harvard, Justin Winsor, is a case in point. Winsor
was able to expand the library collection and, at the same time, improve
library service with the active support of Eliot.[65]

Another good example of this type of interaction has been at the
University of Illinois. Because of its founding in 1867, the university

started much later than other established universities in building a large library collection. Thus a series of strong university presidents have worked in concert with equally talented university librarians to build a world-class library at Illinois. The guiding principle behind both Harvard and the University of Illinois has been the belief that a great university needs a great library.

Many presidents have wanted to leave a lasting legacy of their tenure in office for the university, and the library has sometimes benefited from this desire. Three types of presidential aid to the library have been the most beneficial: good will toward the library, financial resources, and a willingness to hire talented administrators. Of the three types of aid, the most significant have been the hiring (and retaining) of good administrators and the consistent allocation of sufficient funds to build library collections. Conversely, financial neglect and the appointment and retention of weak administrators has caused more than one library to stagnate.

As universities expand, another type of administrative officer, the vice-president, has become an important figure on campus. This officer did not exist until the twentieth century, but now all colleges and universities have vice-presidents, or their equivalent in rank, for academic and administrative affairs. Several of the large institutions have as many as five or six vice-presidents. While the president is busy with "outside" responsibilities, these individuals act as the "inside president" in their respective spheres.[66] The vice-president for academic affairs deals, say, with faculty and curriculum problems, and has administrative responsibility for all academic divisions and departments. He or she should also be a faculty member with experience and training to cope with the stressful demands of the position.[67] This person must also have a good professional relationship with the university president, which means that the vice-president should have almost daily interaction with him or her, as well as a scheduled time to establish this type of relationship.[68]

The vice-president for administrative affairs is meanwhile responsible for the business or financial affairs and orientation of the institution. This person must also keep the other officers of the institution apprised of the college or university's current financial status. A 1983 survey of chief financial officers (CFOs) indicates that most CFOs were selected on the basis of previous university experience, and most admitted that the chief academic officer was at a higher organizational level than the CFO.[69] These individuals are committed to seeking effectiveness and efficiency, and they tend to be analytical and quantitatively oriented.[70] They believe that faculty members are short-sighted in understanding short- and long-range cost and administrative implications of policy decisions.[71] Furthermore, administrators believe that they are "under-valued and regarded as second-class citizens."[72] A series of business offices is under this vice-president's administrative control.

Together, these and other designated vice-presidents serve as the cabinet for the president. This branch of the university has expanded as functions have been added to the mission of the institution, and most employees under these administrators in public institutions are civil service personnel.

The vice-president to whom the library director reports determines the place of the library in the institution's power structure. While in theory each of the vice-presidents has equal access to and influence on the president, in actuality the vice-president for academic affairs has the lion's share of advantages. After all, the university's justification for existence is its educational mission. Thus, the vice-president for academic affairs has contact with the deans and faculty leaders, and this constituency has the greatest power to influence the success or failure of the president—more than the constituency of the business vice-president. Again, this authority is relative to the effectiveness of the vice-president for academic affairs in performing his or her duties. The closer the library is to the academic functions of the institution, the more influence it has in the administration. Consequently, library directors who report to the vice-president for academic affairs have an initial advantage over those who don't, but this advantage can be nullified unless the library director can develop a close working relationship with the vice-president. This close working relationship is important because the vice-president for academic affairs usually takes an active role in evaluating the job performance of the library director.[73]

Another important administrative officer in the university bureau-cracy is the dean. Deans occupy the middle ground between the aca-demic department and the upper levels of administration, so they can be classified as middle management. Large institutions may have several deans with responsibilities covering all aspects of academic life. Smaller schools have few deans, but they have broader responsibilities. The dean of a college within a large university has two major responsibilities: recommending and allocating the annual budget and recommending the appointments and promotions of the college faculty.[74] An overwhelm-ing majority of the deans have backgrounds of advancement through the academic hierarchy. These deans, who serve as the president's admin-istrative cabinet, advise the president on educational matters and carry out collective decisions. While these officers are subservient to the will of the president and serve at the president's pleasure, a strong dean has the potential to become a power broker in the university. Most deans use a consultative management style, but final decision making remains with the dean.[75] Talented deans are often recruited by other institutions for higher administrative positions.

Library directors at the large academic libraries are often one of these deans, and at the smaller libraries the director reports to a dean. Either way, the relationship between the library and the university is determined by the relationship of these deans to the library. A "pecking order" is established among these deans through force of personality or by the strength of the dean's department. It is in this pecking order that the library finds itself at risk, because so much depends on the personality of the library director. Even if the library director is a dean, the perceptions of the other deans toward the library director are important in determining the status of the library.

At the bottom of the hierarchical scale is the department. Its faculty consists of senior professors and a mix of junior professors and instructors. Power tends to be concentrated among the senior professors, and on occasion a famous professor can become influential in the affairs of the university without holding any administrative rank. These professors have become influential by their ability to attract external sources of funding and build fiefdoms of political power.[76] The faculty plays the most significant role in institutional policymaking in curriculum and program issues, but it does so through the academic department and the university committee. Yet the faculty is always distrustful of administrators, and it opposes what it considers alien concepts of management being imposed on it.[77] Academic departments have retained authority in the university because they constitute a number of decentralized power centers that can veto university administrative initiatives.[78]

The chairperson is the faculty member who has the most advantageous position in determining policy in the academic department. Early in the century, prominent professors became so powerful as chairmen of departments that they formed "departmental dictatorships."[79] Nowadays it is rare for a department chairperson to accumulate enough power to be dictatorial and still be able to keep the position, but a chairperson *does* bear the responsibility for the college's instructional and research programs. Again, it is important whether the departmental chairperson is selected by the administration, or by members of the department, or on a rotating basis. In most institutions, certain prestige departments have more "clout" than others with the university administration. An example is the prestige of chemistry departments at the major research institutions. The quality of their scholarship combined with the aggressiveness of their faculty has made chemistry departments more powerful than their size warrants.[80] This prestige factor often accounts for fluctuations in the influence of these departments.

The academic department and the library interact through representatives from the department, and it is common for departments to appoint a liaison from their faculty to represent a department in its dealings with the library. Among smaller libraries, this professor may also participate in selection of materials, but this contribution is made less frequently as more librarians assume this responsibility. This liaison function is among the many given out in the department, and the success of communication depends on the interest and energy of the faculty representatives and the encouragement of the librarians. Consequently, it is not surprising that some departments have more influence with the library than other departments with less prestige or less-active liaison activities.

The faculty senate is the forum for the interchange of ideas by the faculty. Often this representative body has other names, such as Faculty Council or Advisory Board, but it still has the duty of advising the president or chancellor on faculty concerns. Lack of such a body has resulted in faculties forming into union-type organizations, hostile to the institution's administration.[81] Early in the history of the university, administrators found that a senate served several useful functions as a sounding board. A senate was a place where the administration "could sound out opinion, detect discontent so as better to cope with it, and further the posture of official solidarity by giving everyone parliamentary 'rights.' "[82] Faculty senates were especially valuable for administrators during the depression, when salary reductions were necessary.[83] Modern university senates still provide the same setting, but they also serve as a forum for the faculty to propose and to help implement change. An ongoing problem is that only a minority of the faculty ever participates in the business of the senate. Only full professors have the prestige necessary to exert influence at the university level.[84] While faculty senates recognize the importance of libraries, they are often unable to favor library allocations over demands for larger faculty salaries and departmental programs.[85]

Most of the serious work of the faculty senate is done in committees, and three types of committees are common in colleges and universities: administration appointed; faculty elected; and mixed, with faculty-elected representatives and administrative appointees.[86] These committees can be advisory or have delegated powers.[87] Advisory committees serve as a receptacle for opinions or they can provide an over-

sight function. Committees with delegated powers assume complete
authority over a subject or problem. Less scholarly faculty members
and senior professors tend to participate more on committees, because
the more productive scholars consider committee work a low-status and
low-reward activity.[88]

Most of the contact between the faculty senate and the library
is between the senate library committee and the library administration.
These committees tend to be advisory rather than have delegated powers.
Opinion varies on whether librarians should be active on this committee.
Some library administrators prefer that only teaching faculty be members. Others allow a limited number of librarians to participate on such a
committee. Either way, this committee is important in dealing with routine problems of interest to the teaching faculty. Special effort should
be given to this committee because it can be a good friend in crisis
situations, or a liability if the members have been alienated. Another
important function of this committee is that in many institutions it plays
an important role in the hiring and firing of library directors.

The outline of the administrative structure of the college and university organization is incomplete without an understanding of its underlying power structure. Two surveys of perceived power in sixty-eight
universities were undertaken in, 1964 and again in 1971, and both show
the political facts of life in a university in a composite form. The results
of these surveys are reproduced in table 4.2.[89] Perhaps the least surprising finding is the importance given in the surveys to the president, and a
fascinating factor is the political significance attributed to the regents or
trustees. This perception appears to be more a case of potential power
than actual use, but memories of intrusion by trustees linger in any
institution.[90] Vice-presidents, various deans, and the faculty follow in
rank order, with departmental chairpersons below legislators. Students
are farther down on the list, even after the disturbances of the 1960s. The
relative low-power status of the faculty goes counter to the conventional
wisdom that "the locus of real 'academic power' is in the faculty."[91]

Comparison of private and public institutions indicates differences
between their power structures. The major difference is that legislators are as important to public universities as grants are to private
universities.[92] Such a difference is easily explained by the differing
nature of the two types of institutions.

These studies found an external cluster of power (legislators, regents, and state and federal governments) and an internal cluster (vice-
presidents, deans, faculty, and chairpersons),[93] but the most significant
finding was declared in the following terms:

Table 4.2: Power Structure of American Universities, 1964 and 1971

| | 1964 | | | 1971 | | |
Power Holder	Rank	Mean	Stand. Dev.	Rank	Mean	Stand. Dev.
President	1	4.65	.62	1	4.52	.69
Regents or trustees	2	4.37	.82	2	4.36	.81
Vice-presidents	3	4.12	.82	3	4.06	.81
Deans (prof. schools)	4	3.62	.84	4	3.50	.80
Deans (grad.)	5	3.59	.89	6	3.35	.89
Deans (lib. arts)	6	3.56	.89	5	3.41	.83
Faculty	7	3.31	.97	7	3.35	.92
Chairpersons	8	3.19	.93	9	3.10	.88
Legislators	9	2.94	1.37	8	3.20	1.35
Federal govt.	10	2.79	1.06	10	2.89	.95
State govt.	11	2.72	1.21	11	2.80	1.09
Grants	12	2.69	1.06	13	2.68	.93
Alumni	13	2.61	.90	14	2.58	.79
Students	14	2.37	.82	12	2.77	.79
Citizens	15	2.08	1.02	15	2.11	.94
Parents	16	1.91	.87	16	1.94	.73

Source: Edward Gross and Paul V. Grambsch, "Power Structures in Universities and Colleges," in *Governing Academic Organizations: New Problems, New Perspectives*, edited by Gary L. Riley and J. Victor Baldridge (Berkeley, Calif.: McCutchan, 1977), p. 28.

> Powerful deans are not found in universities with weak faculties: quite the reverse. A powerful set of deans is usually found along with a powerful faculty, as a powerful dean of library arts is found along with a powerful set of departmental chairmen. One conclusion is that faculties may well maintain their power only when deans and chairmen have the power to provide proper consideration and they may require that deans and chairmen have a great deal of power indeed.[94]

While this study is nearly two decades old, it is still the best analysis of the collegiate power structure available. Several of the categories may have changed somewhat, particularly the federal government and legislators, but the main outline of power still remains.

Colleges and universities are a complex social organization, filled with special-interest groups jockeying for influence. When resources are plentiful, these groups coexist, but during financial crises they mobilize for action.[95] Most final decisions are negotiated compromises between competing groups, and the participants in this process share the gains or losses.[96] This process takes place regardless of the size of the institution, but the stakes are always higher in the large universities.

The library participates in the power process regardless of its appearance as a neutral. Decisions are made on the direction of the institution, say, or on the closing of programs that impact directly on the library. Budget allocations are decided that promote growth or cutbacks in operations. These decisions are taken in upper-level administrative circles, but the cumulative effect determines the future role of the library, whose prestige determines much of the administration's view of the library. Low reputation and poor service guarantee that the library will have little chance of escaping budget cutting. On the other hand, a prestigious and efficient library can present a good case for exceptions to fund reductions. The weakness of the library in this scenario is that too often the library is left to the interpersonal skills of the library director. Frequent openings of library directors' positions attest to the fragile nature of the relationship between the director and the administration. Several well-publicized incidents in the recent past have shown that the library is not faring well in such tenuous relationships. In what is becoming a familiar scene, a new vice-chancellor or vice-provost assumes office, and one of the first steps is to remove the library director. Sometimes the removal is the result of a long-standing feud between the two, but the result is nevertheless harmful to the library and to the career of its director.

Another factor in the administrative organization of the university is unionism. Unionization has been interpreted either as "a breakdown of the traditional approach to managing academic organizations" or as a "natural progression" of the conflict between competing forces.[97] Another explanation for unionization is that as trustees and administrators have insisted upon greater faculty accountability, the faculty has turned to collective measures for self-protection.[98] Collective bargaining for the academic community has almost always been a response to deteriorating economic conditions. Research indicates, however, that—despite early evidence to the contrary—salary increases now differ very little between union and nonunion institutions.[99]

A factor that has retarded the growth of faculty unions has been the United States Supreme Court's 1980 decision in the case of the *National Labor Relations Board* versus *Yeshiva University*. In this decision, a narrow majority ruled that the entire faculty at Yeshiva University was managerial and therefore not entitled to bargain collectively under the protection of the National Labor Relations Act.[100] Nevertheless, uncertainty remained, and this uncertainty over the managerial status of the faculty has retarded further attempts to unionize institutions in higher education (but mostly at private colleges). At first, only a few colleges attempted to apply this principle to existing union contracts, at renewal time.[101] Recently, however, a statement by the director of collective bargaining for the American Association of University Professors (AAUP) has characterized the *Yeshiva* decision as effectively ending collective bargaining and organizing at private colleges and universities.[102] Moreover, the movement has grown in private colleges and universities for nonrecognition or decertification of collective bargaining units.[103] The response of faculty unions has been to band together to pursue legislative remedies.

Collective bargaining has set procedures of operation, and researchers identify three stages in this bargaining process: (1) unionization, (2) negotiation, and (3) administration of a contract.[104] The academic administration has the responsibility to administer the provisions of the union contract. While an adversarial rather than collegial atmosphere is prevalent, each side has its rights and privileges in the contract. This adversarial relationship may be the result of conflict long before collective bargaining or it may be the product of the system. Either way, administrators must abide by the contract or suffer a flurry of formal grievances that reflect on their job performance.[105]

Unionization has been less dramatic in changing governance patterns than theory would suppose. Faculty governance has remained in the form of faculty senates, and decision making is shared between the senate and union in what is known as *dual-track governance*.[106] The faculty senate handles academic matters, and the union restricts itself to faculty welfare issues.[107] This partnership works as long as senate and union responsibilities are carefully delineated and kept separate.[108] The future of this type of partnership is still uncertain, and the big drive for unionization seems to have cooled in the 1980s.

The library participates in collective bargaining in institutions that have adopted this form of governance. Librarians may be treated as part of the faculty or with other technical staff because they comprise too narrow a political base to stand alone in collective bargaining.[109] Either way, the library is treated the same as any other segment of the university community. Librarians and the faculty are interested in the same bargaining issues: salary and fringe benefits, grievance procedures and a dispute-resolution mechanism, rights and privileges for the union, and employment conditions.[110] Librarians have the right to initiate grievances, but otherwise the library is outside the institution's decision-making system. While the library is protected by rules and regulations, it still depends heavily on its director for input into the higher decision-making circles. Isolation of librarians is just as dangerous for them in a unionized environment as in a traditional one. In a union environment, the academic library suffers if union bargaining tends to take as large a share of institutional resources as possible for faculty compensation and to leave little for other institutional needs, such as the library.[111]

The relationship between the university administration and the academic library is complex because it involves so many potential communication problems. College and university administrators find the library an integral but fringe responsibility. Because they have little understanding of the functioning of the library, these administrators leave its control to library administrators. Invariably, they place the library in the context of the ideal institution. The common thesis is that a good library and a productive faculty mean a quality institution. Again, the library is thought of in the context of the institution rather than as a separate entity. In contrast, librarians have difficulty comprehending the nature of the collegiate environment. Although library administrators and librarians have experience in the collegial environment as students and sometimes as teachers, they nevertheless find the institution's politics and power structure bewildering. The result is that librarians tend to develop an "us and them" mentality and, in this kind of scenario, feel that the institution is unappreciative of the accomplishments of the library and its staff. It is this incompatibility of viewpoints which produces much of the misunderstanding between administrators of the institution and the professional staff of the library. Despite good will on both sides, in crisis situations the lack of communication and understanding becomes crucial in the library's success or failure.

NOTES

1. Robert M. O'Neil, "The University Administrator's View of the University Library," *New Directions for Higher Education* 39 (1982): 5.
2. Patricia Battin, "The Library: Center of the Restructured University," *College and Research Libraries* 45 (May 1984) 3:172.
3. Kathryn M. Moore, "The Structure of Administrative Careers: A Prose Poem in Four Parts," *Review of Higher Education* 8 (Fall 1984) 1:7.
4. Laurence R. Veyser, *The Emergence of the American University* (Chicago: University of Chicago Press, 1965), pp. 308–9.
5. Logan Wilson, *American Academics: Then and Now* (New York: Oxford University Press, 1979), pp. 81–82.

6. Moore, "Structure of Administrative Careers," p. 3.
7. J. Victor Baldridge, "Alternative Models of Governance in Higher Education," in *Governing Academic Organizations: New Problems, New Perspectives*, edited by Gary L. Riley and J. Victor Baldridge (Berkeley, Calif.: McCutchan, 1977), p. 3.
8. Ibid.
9. Fred J. Heinritz, "Quantitative Management in Libraries," *College and Research Libraries* 31 (July 1970) 4:232.
10. Max Weber, *The Theory of Social and Economic Organization* (New York: Free Press, 1964), pp. 324-30.
11. Ibid., p. 331.
12. Ibid.
13. James L. Bess, *Collegiality and Bureaucracy in the Modern University* (New York: Teachers College Press, 1988), p. 3.
14. C. James Schmidt, "Faculty Status in Academic Libraries: Retrospective and Prospect," in *New Horizons for Academic Libraries*, edited by Robert D. Stueart and Richard D. Johnson (New York: K. G. Saur, 1979), p. 414.
15. John D. Millet, *The Academic Community: An Organizational Essay* (New York: McGraw-Hill, 1962), p. 62.
16. Bess, *Collegiality and Bureaucracy*, p. 3.
17. Millet, *Academic Community*, p. 75.
18. Bess, *Collegiality and Bureaucracy*, pp. 3–4.
19. Ibid., p. 4.
20. Ibid.
21. Michael D. Cohen and James G. Marsh, *Leadership and Ambiguity: The American College President* (2d ed.; Boston: Harvard Business School Press, 1986), pp. 2–3.
22. David A. Garvin, *The Economics of University Behavior* (New York: Academic Press, 1980), p. 4.
23. Ibid., p. 5.
24. Ibid.
25. Ibid., p. 4.
26. Tai Keun Oh, "New Dimensions of Management Theory," *College and Research Libraries* 27 (November 1966) 6:433.
27. Mary Lee Bundy, "Conflict in Libraries," *College and Research Libraries* 4 (July 1966) 4:253–60.
28. Dennis P. Carrigan, "The Political Economy of the Academic Library," *College and Research Libraries* 49 (July 1988) 4:329–30.
29. Robert E. Helsabeck, *The Compound System: A Conceptual Framework for Effective Decisionmaking in Colleges* (Berkeley, Calif.: Center for Research and Development in Higher Education, 1973), pp. 4–5.
30. Ibid., p. 6.
31. O'Neil, "University Administrator's View of the University Library," p. 5.
32. Ibid., p. 8.
33. Association of Governing Boards, *Composition of Governing Boards, 1985* (Washington, D.C.: Association of Governing Boards of Universities and Colleges, 1986), p. 3.

34. Hofstadter remarks on the incongruity of the academic profession under the constitutional authority of outsiders. Richard Hofstadter and C. DeWitt Hardy, *The Development and Scope of Higher Education in the United States* (New York: Columbia University Press, 1952), p. 129.

35. Frank L. McVey and Raymond M. Hughes, *Problems of College and University Administration* (Ames: Iowa State College Press, 1952), p. 53.

36. Association of Governing Boards, *Composition of Governing Boards, 1985*, p. 10.

37. Veyser, *Emergence of the American University*, pp. 246–47.

38. Frederic W. Ness, "Campus Governance and Fiscal Stability," in *Efficient College Management*, edited by William W. Jellema (San Francisco: Jossey-Bass, 1972), p. 42.

39. Millet uses his experience both at the presidential level and as chief executive officer of the Board of Regents in Ohio to come to this conclusion. John D. Millet, *Politics and Higher Education* (University: University of Alabama Press, 1974), pp. 61–62.

40. Henry L. Bowden, *Boards of Trustees: Their Organization and Operation at Private Colleges and Universities* (Macon, Ga.: Mercer University Press, 1982), pp. 2–3.

41. Hofstadter and Hardy, *Development and Scope of Higher Education*, p. 131.

42. McVey and Hughes, *Problems of College and University Administration*, p. 6.

43. Samuel B. Gould, "Trustees and the University Community," in *The University as an Organization*, edited by James A. Perkins (New York: McGraw-Hill, 1983), p. 221.

44. Roger L. Geiger, *To Advance Knowledge: The Growth of American Research Universities, 1900–1940* (New York: Oxford University Press, 1986), p. 16.

45. McVey and Hughes, *Problems of College and University Administration*, p. 6.

46. Wilson, *American Academics*, p. 90.

47. A breakdown of the totals in 1969 shows that 58 percent of the presidents had backgrounds in the humanities, compared with only 17 percent in the social sciences and 17 percent in education. The remainder was only 8 percent for the other fields. Cohen and Marsh, *Leadership and Ambiguity*, p. 15.

48. This midcareer cycle translates into an average teaching career of around eleven years before one starts on administrative responsibilities. Michael R. Ferrari, *Profiles of American College Presidents* (East Lansing, Mich.: Michigan State University Graduate School of Business Administration, 1970), p. 95.

49. Ibid., p. 101.

50. Cohen and Marsh, *Leadership and Ambiguity*, p. 15.

51. Robert Birnbaum, "Consistency and Diversity in the Goals of Campus Leaders," *Review of Higher Education* 12 (Fall 1988) 1:21–22.

52. Ibid., p. 22.

53. Moore, "Structure of Administrative Careers," p. 3.
54. Moore states that less than 20 percent of the presidents were promoted from positions within their institutions, but a majority of administrators are promoted from within. (Ibid., p. 6.)
55. Ness, "Campus Governance and Fiscal Stability," p. 44.
56. James L. Fisher, "Presidents Will Lead—If We Let Them," *NACUBO Business Officer* 18 (March 1985) 9:38.
57. Cohen and Marsh, *Leadership and Ambiguity*, p. 130.
58. Frederick E. Balderston, *Managing Today's University* (San Francisco: Jossey-Bass, 1974), p. 44.
59. Cohen and Marsh, *Leadership and Ambiguity*, pp. 161–63.
60. Daniel T. Seymour, "Higher Education as a Corporate Enterprise," *College Board Review* 147 (Spring 1988): 2.
61. The author was president of Wayne State University at the time he wrote this chapter. See David W. Adamany, "Research Libraries from a Presidential Perspective," in *Issues in Academic Librarianship: Views and Case Studies for the 1980s and 1990s*, edited by Peter Spyers-Duran and Thomas W. Mann (Westport, Conn.: Greenwood Press, 1985), p. 7.
62. Seymour, "Higher Education as a Corporate Enterprise," pp. 2–3.
63. Adamany, "Research Libraries from a Presidential Perspective," p. 12.
64. Robert M. O'Neil, "Academic Libraries and the Future: A President's View," *College and Research Libraries* 45 (May 1984) 3:185–86.
65. Kenneth J. Brough, *Scholar's Workshop: Evolving Conceptions of Library Service* (Urbana: University of Illinois Press, 1953), p. 28. Winsor was both a scholar and a library administrator. See Robert E. Brundin, "Justin Winsor of Harvard and the Liberalizing of the College Library," *Journal of Library History* 10 (January 1975): 67.
66. Edward Gross and Paul V. Grambsch, "Power Structures in Universities and Colleges," in *Governing Academic Organizations: New Problems, New Perspectives*, edited by Gary L. Riley and J. Victor Baldridge (Berkeley, Calif.: McCutchan, 1977), p. 31.
67. McVey and Hughes, *Problems of College and University Administration*, p. 86.
68. Robert E. Wolverton, "The Chief Academic Officer: Argus on the Campus," in *Leadership Roles of Chief Academic Officers*, edited by David G. Brown (San Francisco: Jossey-Bass, 1984), pp. 8–9.
69. William A. Jenkins, "The Role of the Chief Financial Officer in the Large Public Universities," *NACUBO Business Officer* 18 (January 1985) 7:28.
70. Sigmund G. Ginsburg, "Understanding Administrators," *NACUBO Business Officer* 17 (June 1984) 12:26.
71. Ibid., p. 27.
72. Ibid., p. 28.
73. Adamany, "Research Libraries from a Presidential Perspective," pp. 18–19.
74. Doris W. Ryan, "Deans as Individuals-in-Organizations," in *The Dilemma of the Deanship*, edited by Daniel E. Griffiths and Donald J. McCarty (Danville, Ill.: Interstate, 1980), p. 141.

75. Allan Tucker and Robert A. Bryan, *The Academic Dean: Dove, Dragon, and Diplomat* (New York: Macmillan, 1988), pp. 9–11.

76. Burton R. Clark, "Faculty Organization and Authority," in *Governing Academic Organizations*, edited by Gary L. Riley and J. Victor Baldridge (Berkeley, Calif.: McCutchan, 1977), pp. 74–75.

77. William R. Brown, *Academic Politics* (University: University of Alabama Press, 1982), p. 6.

78. Irving J. Spitzberg, "It's Academic: The Politics of the Curriculum in American Higher Education," in *Libraries and the Search for Academic Excellence*, edited by Patricia Senn Breivik and Robert Wedgeworth (Metuchen, N.J.: Scarecrow Press, 1988), p. 158.

79. Veyser, *Emergence of the American University*, p. 322.

80. Tucker and Bryan, *Academic Dean*, p. 6.

81. Deane G. Bornheimer, Gerald P. Burns, and Glenn S. Dumke, *The Faculty in Higher Education* (Danville, Ill.: Interstate, 1973), p. 154.

82. Veyser, *Emergence of the American University*, p. 342.

83. McVey and Hughes, *Problems of College and University Administration*, p. 86.

84. Paul L. Dressel, Craig F. Johnson, and Philip M. Marcus, *The Confidence Crisis* (San Francisco: Jossey-Bass, 1970), p. 78.

85. Adamany, "Research Libraries from a Presidential Perspective," p. 11.

86. Bornheimer, Burns, and Dumke, *Faculty in Higher Education*, p. 66.

87. Ibid., p. 70.

88. Clyde J. Wingfield, "Campus Conflict and Constitutional Maintenance," in *The American University: A Public Administration Perspective*, edited by Clyde J. Wingfield (Dallas: Southern Methodist University Press, 1970), p. 9.

89. Gross and Grambsch, "Power Structures," p. 28.

90. Ibid., p. 30.

91. Wingfield, "Campus Conflict and Constitutional Maintenance," p. 8.

92. Gross and Grambsch, "Power Structures," p. 32–33.

93. Ibid., p. 39.

94. Ibid.

95. J. Victor Baldridge and Frank R. Kemerer, "Images of Governance: Collective Bargaining versus Traditional Models," in *Governing Academic Organizations: New Problems, New Perspectives*, edited by Gary L. Riley and J. Victor Baldridge (Berkeley, Calif.: McCutchan, 1977), p. 257.

96. Ibid.

97. Ibid., p. 258.

98. Joel M. Douglas, "Faculty Collective Bargaining in the Aftermath of Yeshiva," *Change* 13 (March 1981) 2:36–37.

99. Ibid., p. 38.

100. Ness, "Campus Governance and Fiscal Stability," p. 47.

101. Joan C. Marshall, "The Effects of Collective Bargaining on Faculty Salaries in Higher Education," *Journal of Higher Education* 50 (May–June 1979) 3:318.

102. Norman J. Kopmeyer, "Yeshiva Revisited: Alternative Remedies," *Footnotes* (Spring 1989), p. 1.
103. Ibid.
104. Baldridge and Kemerer, "Images of Governance," p. 259.
105. Tucker and Bryan, *Academic Dean*, p. 28.
106. Barbara A. Lee, "Contractually Protected Governance Systems at Unionized Colleges," *Review of Higher Education* 5 (Winter 1982) 2:70.
107. Ibid.
108. Ibid., p. 81.
109. Robert C. O'Reilly and Marjorie I. O'Reilly, *Librarians and Labor Relations: Employment under Union Contracts* (Westport, Conn.: Greenwood Press, 1981), p. 70.
110. Ibid.
111. Adamany, "Research Libraries from a Presidential Perspective," p. 11.

CHAPTER FIVE

The Teaching Faculty and the Academic Library

THE TEACHING FACULTY of colleges and universities has a vested interest in the fate of academic libraries. Faculty members need to use the library because professional success in the academic world is tied to research and teaching, and libraries have the materials to help the faculty achieve renown in both of these endeavors. Because of the necessity for this contact, the teaching faculty is inclined to favor the library unless conditioned to do otherwise. Conditioning occurs as a collective experience of a professor during his or her collegiate days as an undergraduate and graduate student or as a young faculty member working for advancement. These experiences may give the professor an orientation toward the library that is neither wholly positive nor negative, but which may conflict with reality. The intellectual baggage that the faculty member carries makes the library a source of either pleasure or disappointment, for expectations among the faculty are so high that librarians have difficulty coping with them. Yet no part of the college or university can be more loyal to the library in a crisis than the faculty. It is this kind of conflicting interaction that makes the relationship between the faculty and the library so complex.

The teaching faculty is by nature conservative in its approach to the university. Most of the innovative reforms in higher education have been proposed and implemented from the office of the university president and the administration or else from outside forces, often over the protests of the faculty.[1] While individual professors may favor educational reforms, most of the faculty finds comfort in the status quo. This need for stability is in part because of confusion among faculty members over their roles in society and in higher education. Interviews with five hundred faculty members in the early 1970s at a wide range of universities found "a pervasive unease and confusion, and, most strikingly, a lack of professional identity."[2] The interviewers were particularly disturbed that faculty members "do not seem to have a sense of belonging to a body of professionals with shared goals, shared procedures for attaining them, and agreed ways of estimating their realization."[3] Only in research and publication did the faculty show agreement, but even on these subjects the consensus was slight.[4] Too much specialization and too divergent an outlook among academic disciplines have resulted in a fragmented faculty, uncertain of its present and future roles in the university. A more recent study of professors, in the mid-1980s, reinforces the view that the teaching faculty is deeply troubled about trends in its profession.[5] Nearly 40 percent of faculty say that they may leave the profession within the next five years.[6] They are concerned most about job security, advancement, and salaries, but also about falling morale in their academic departments.[7] A study of faculty with more positive attitudes indicates that participation in institutional decision making is one of the top factors in its satisfaction.[8]

Despite uncertainty over other aspects of its educational role, the academic faculty *does* belong to a professional group. Sociological theory of professional employees has identified characteristics of professions, and these include a demand for autonomy, divided loyalties between peers and parent organization, tension between professional values and bureaucratic expectations, and peer evaluation of their work.[9] Another definition lists the characteristics of a profession as "a high degree of knowledge and technical skill" and a code of ethics.[10] A final definition is that university teaching is "an occupation the practice of which requires more than ordinary amounts of complex knowledge, acquired by persistent and systematic study and authoritatively certified."[11] In the sense of these definitions, university teaching is similar in practice to the legal, medical, and engineering professions. Faculty members, regardless of the size or type of institution, subscribe in varying degrees to all of these definitions of a professional group.

Despite common professional characteristics, the faculties of colleges and universities are far from homogeneous. Differences in orientation between faculty in the traditional disciplines and those in the more practical professions have haunted institutions of higher education both in the past and now.[12] The traditional disciplines are those with broad subject matter in areas from the liberal arts to science. Professional disciplines are those with the task of instructing students in the more practical arts—agriculture, law, medicine, nursing, theology, etc. Rare is the institution that does not have some discord between the two factions. Often the debate revolves around applied versus pure research, and the faculty can tear itself apart in arguments over these issues.

Despite differences between disciplines and personal orientations, the faculty shares several characteristics, and these characteristics have been described by one scholar as the Cartesian approach.[13] He identifies the following six principles:

1. Intellectual activity should be pursued individually and independently.
2. There can be no limit on inquiry.
3. Rational consideration is universal.
4. The scholar should have objectivity—a certain detachment from the situation to which he is applying his reason.
5. Personal calculations of a scholar must always be made to amplify the time for scholarship.
6. A secure and stable environment is essential to the cultivation of reason.[14]

The academic world accepts these principles as a matter of fact, and the faculty, regardless of discipline, will defend them to the bitter end.

Individual faculty members have a variety of ways to gain status, but all of the ways concern their relationship with their institution. Professors derive satisfaction from association with institutions with a reputation for quality.[15] This tie to quality is important because the reputation of an individual faculty member comes from the recognition accorded to his or her personal research by peers in the discipline and by the shared, collective reputation and visibility of the academic department.[16] Rank and salary are tied together as symbols of prestige and status, but these issues also provide constant sources of disagreement. Personal relationships are especially important among faculty members in the same department because of the close contact with each other. Among the many possible causes of dissatisfaction among the faculty, the promotion of a supposed equal to greater rank or responsibility can weaken an otherwise strong department.[17]

The faculty has a dual role in the operations of colleges and universities, as each professor carries out not only his or her responsibilities for teaching and research but also collegial duties.[18] The faculty's collegial responsibilities are to share in the decision-making processes on matters of academic policy at the three levels of department, college, and university. Most faculty members participate directly only in departmental decision making, and responsibility for the other levels is delegated to departmental representatives. Few of the more productive researchers are active in decision making higher than the departmental level because there is evidence of a negative relationship between faculty influence in institutional decision making and research productivity.[19] The more productive researchers avoid collegial responsibilities to concentrate on research because success in the academic world is guaranteed by research accomplishments. These productive scholars, however, devote some attention to governance issues at the departmental level or to activities that influence their life as a scholar, if only out of self-interest. Senior faculty members are more likely to be engaged in governance activities than junior faculty because junior faculty are too involved in tenure and promotion activities.[20] Current research indicates that senior faculty's increased interest in governance activities coincides with a drop in research productivity.[21]

Much of faculty politics resides within the academic department. These departments are autonomous because the historical development of the university promoted decentralization.[22] Early in the history of the university, faculty appointments were made by the president with some guidance from other administrators, but by the first decades of the twentieth century this task was delegated to the individual departments. Now departments select faculty and determine academic policy with only occasional dissent from the upper echelons of the institution. It is in selection of faculty that the department makes its important contribution to the quality of the institution. A survey of 1,200 faculty members in the late 1960s verified that the department receives the basic loyalty of the faculty.[23] After all, the department handles the recruitment, rewards, and communications of the faculty.[24]

The role of the departmental chairperson is to provide leadership for the department. Resource allocation is the most important management tool available to departmental chairpersons, and this tool is used in varying fashion by successful chairpersons.[25] Various methods of selecting a departmental chairperson are used, but most often it is by appointment by the president upon nomination by a dean or by election by members of the department.[26] The mode of selection is important because it determines the source of authority. Chairpersons appointed by higher administration have more authority over the department than those elected by colleagues. The rotating method of appointing a chairperson is sometimes used because the office is viewed by the professors as so heavy a burden that it is almost impossible to fill otherwise.[27] While most departments use some variation of the collegial model of shared decision making, this type of decision making is imperative for the chairperson elected by peers. Moreover, the collegial model works best when the members subscribe to the same value systems. The political and ideological turmoil surrounding the Vietnam War was one occasion when academic and political value systems clashed. Even several decades later, many departments, particularly among the humanities and social sciences, still bear the ideological scars from this debate.[28]

Often the activities of the department are disturbed by the policies of the chairperson. Personality conflicts are always a possibility in peer relationships, and interdepartmental psychological warfare has hurt more than one department. Often academic leaders from outside the department have to intervene, much to the discomfort of both sides in the dispute. Apathy remains the greatest threat to the effective operation of the department because a smooth-running department depends on the faculty's sharing goals and participation in departmental and university affairs.[29] Rather than academic issues, the deteriorating economic base of the faculty has turned many faculty members toward collective bargaining. The collegial model depends on a community of academic interests, but unionization is predicated on an adversarial relationship between the faculty union and the administration.

Much of the routine faculty business takes place in the departments. Two of the more important functions are curriculum decision making and student counseling. Both tasks are time consuming but necessary for the health of the department. It is also in the department that senior professors have the obligation to mentor junior faculty members in research, teaching, and professional conduct.[30] Despite this obligation, an adversarial relationship between department members sometimes develops over personality, resources, or scholarship that hinders the mentoring process. Too often, the denial of tenure is the result of the failure of departmental mentoring. Women faculty have been especially bitter over this failure.

The faculty has a number of collegial responsibilities. Research, teaching, and service are the triad upon which the faculty is judged.

The standard academic philosophy is that "research receives, assimilates and discovers knowledge and teaching interprets and transmits knowledge." [31] In theory, research and teaching responsibilities are equal, but in practice in the modern university research has assumed primacy. Teaching is still considered an important function in all institutions, but research is where the national reputations are made. In the smaller liberal arts colleges, however, teaching is still regarded as the primary responsibility, but even here faculty has to publish to advance in the profession. The conflict between the research and teaching roles is in evidence in all but the largest institutions, and it surfaces even in these institutions on occasion. In an ideal world, research and teaching should be complementary, but sometimes they have become contradictory.

Research is the most prestigious of the faculty responsibilities. A definition of research is "the methodical acquisition of knowledge, hitherto unknown." [32] Because of the thrill of finding the unknown, the researcher tends to be more interested in ideas than people, in the laboratory and the library than the classroom, and in grants than university budgets.[33] Moreover, interviews with faculty at research universities have found that professors in these institutions like to do research.[34] In theory, research and the resulting publications ought to result from commitment to the advancement of a discipline, but enlightened self-interest is as important a motivation. Rarely does the product of research transform the nature of a discipline, but a discipline's progress is measured by the scholarly contributions of its scholars.[35] This process also leads to interaction among scholars at conferences and informal gatherings. The criterion of success for the researcher is in the collective judgments of peers in his or her discipline. Scholarship is assessed by peer evaluations because there is no other way to judge scholarly attainment. Despite some weaknesses because of bias (both pro and con), no other system has worked as well. Finally, it is this loyalty to a discipline or professional field of knowledge, rather than to the college or university, that promotes faculty mobility.[36] Renown in research is the avenue for advancement for a professor, whether it is within the institution or in the form of job offers from other research institutions.

The amount of time devoted by the faculty to research varies according to the type of institution. A 1984 faculty survey shows the extent to which it devotes its time to research (see table 5.1).[37] Only in the research universities and the doctoral-granting universities is research a major focus of activity, and the higher the quality of the institution, the more that time is spent in research. Table 5.2 is a breakdown of faculty who spend eleven or more hours a week on research.[38] The results suggest that the bulk of research is conducted at the large research universities, but even in these institutions a significant number of faculty is involved in little or no research.

Table 5.1: Faculty Research by Type of Institution and Percentage of Time

Type of Institution	None	1–4	5–10	11–15	Over 20	Total
			Hours per Week Spent in Research			
Research univ. I	7	13	22	25	33	100
Research univ. II	9	14	27	26	24	100
Doctoral-granting univ. I	11	23	30	19	17	100
Doctoral-granting univ. II	10	37	27	14	12	100
Comprehensive univ. and coll. I	22	32	28	12	6	100
Comprehensive univ. and coll. II	26	32	24	12	6	100
Liberal arts coll. I	17	30	30	18	5	100
Liberal arts coll. II	42	39	13	5	1	100
Two-year colleges and institutions	46	33	15	5	1	100
All institutions	23	27	23	15	12	100

Total respondents 4,426

Sources: Carnegie Foundation for the Advancement of Teaching, "The Faculty: Deeply Troubled," *Change* (September–October 1985), p. 33; Burton R. Clark, *The Academic Life: Small Worlds, Different Worlds* (Princeton, N.J.: Carnegie Foundation for the Advancement of Teaching, 1987), p. 84.

Publishing the results of research can be frustrating. Faculty members have the option of writing journal articles or book-length manuscripts, and both have their pitfalls. A conservative estimate of the number of scholarly journals published in the United States in 1990 was about 10,000.[39] The worldwide production is approximately 140,000 serials of all types. Most of the prestigious scholarly activity is reported in these 10,000 or so refereed journals, and the rewards of reputation, promotion, and salary are given to those who are successful in having their research published in them. Most complaints about the "journal system" concern the pressures to publish, fairness of peer reviews, and delays in publication.[40] Of these complaints, the most serious is the widespread belief that the editorial peer review system is biased.[41] Because of delays in publication, many scholars, especially in the sciences,

Table 5.2: Faculty Research Time under and over Eleven Hours a Week

	Hours per Week Spent in Research		
Type of Institution	0-10	11 or More	Total
Research univ. I	42	58	100
Research univ. II	50	50	100
Doctoral-granting univ. I	64	36	100
Doctoral-granting univ. II	74	26	100
Comprehensive univ. and coll. I	82	18	100
Comprehensive univ. and coll. II	82	18	100
Liberal arts coll. I	77	23	100
Liberal arts coll. II	94	6	100
Two-year colleges and institutions	94	6	100
All institutions	73	27	100

Total respondents 4,426

Source: Burton R. Clark, *The Academic Life: Small Worlds, Different Worlds* (Princeton, N.J.: Carnegie Foundation for the Advancement of Teaching, 1987), p. 78.

have turned to preprints and working papers rather than depend upon the journal process.[42]

Some of the same complaints appear vis-à-vis scholarly monographs, but the problems seem less serious. Humanities and social science researchers average two or more submissions of manuscripts to publishers before their manuscripts are accepted for publication,[43] and 20 percent of these scholars fail to find a publisher for a completed book-length manuscript.[44] Despite these difficulties, professors are less unhappy about book publishing than journal publishing.[45]

Teaching has its own sets of standards and rewards, and the committed teacher is concerned about the two central facets of teaching: the stimulation of thinking and the transmission of knowledge.[46] Research is not a priority because it is not what the teacher considers a primary responsibility. Service to students, both undergraduates and graduate students, rather than discovery, is such a person's obsession. Teaching is also time consuming, with the norm being two hours of lecture preparation for each hour of class time. Nevertheless, the conscientious teacher often exceeds this norm in an effort to broaden the educational experience of students. One test of teaching effectiveness is a study of how often and at what level a teacher assigns students to use the library.[47] Another characteristic of the good teacher is a commitment to excellence.[48] Yet even the proponents of rewards for good teachers admit that teaching is difficult to evaluate fairly.[49] However, few faculty members advocate more stringent evaluations of teaching because such measurements infringe on the autonomy of the professor.[50]

The close tie between teaching and service makes it difficult to distinguish between the traditional teaching role of the faculty and the service instruction of academic librarians. In both cases a body of information is passed from the expert to the student for the educational enhancement of the student. The only difference is that the faculty provides information on a subject discipline, and the academic librarian makes available information for bibliographical uses. Both types of teaching take place in a formal educational setting, and, as the information age makes more information available, the importance of the academic librarian as a teacher will grow.

The amount of time spent by faculty on teaching varies according to the type of institution, and this variation obtains in both undergraduate and graduate education. A breakdown of faculty work loads shows the range of teaching loads at each type of institution (see table 5.3).[51] A subsequent restructuring of the data indicates that undergraduate teaching loads at the top research universities are considerably lower than those at the other types of institutions (see table 5.4).[52] Teaching loads at the graduate level are reflected in a comparison of the teaching at the undergraduate and graduate levels. While the data reflect a concentration on graduate teaching, undergraduate instruction constitutes an important part of the workload (see table 5.5).[53] The data reinforce the contention, however, that in the top seventy research universities in the United States graduate teaching is emphasized over undergraduate teaching. Moreover, faculties in institutions just below these elite schools are more involved in undergraduate teaching.

Many adherents of teaching, feeling that teaching is deteriorating in higher education, argue that the emphasis on research, as well as departmental neglect, loyalty to individual disciplines, faculty control of the curriculum, and general institutional neglect, have all contributed to the decline of teaching.[54] Critics of higher education feel that deterioration of undergraduate teaching comes about in part because the research scholar is more interested in the graduate student than in the undergraduate, and in individual research above everything.[55] These critics of

Table 5.3: Workload for Teaching Undergraduates by Type of Institution and Percentage of Faculty Time

Type of Institution	Hours per Week Spent Teaching					
	None	1–4	5–10	11–15	Over 20	Total
Research univ. I	31	35	28	6	0	100
Research univ. II	19	35	33	11	2	100
Doctoral-granting univ. I	14	27	40	18	1	100
Doctoral-granting univ. II	13	17	42	28	2	100
Comprehensive univ. and coll. I	8	13	41	36	2	100
Comprehensive univ. and coll. II	5	13	42	38	2	100
Liberal arts coll. I.	3	9	53	32	3	100
Liberal arts coll. II	4	14	36	43	3	100
Two-year colleges and institutions	3	9	13	65	10	100
All institutions	11	18	32	35	4	100

Total respondents 4,932

Source: Burton R. Clark, *The Academic Life: Small Worlds, Different Worlds* (Princeton, N.J.: Carnegie Foundation for the Advancement of Teaching, 1987), p. 77.

the academic world have been campaigning for renewed emphasis on teaching for decades, and the debate resurfaced in the late 1980s at the national level. Despite more attention, reforms in teaching have been slow to develop.

Service is the least appreciated of the faculty's responsibilities. Colleges and universities encourage service as a payback to the community and the nation for society's support for higher education. Also, service provides a "testing ground for practical application of the lessons learned on a theoretical basis in the institution."[56] Two requirements are necessary, however: that the service be related to the regular curriculum and that it be needed and desired by the community.[57] The faculty gets involved because community programs often need the type of experts that the university can provide. Rewards to the faculty come in acknowledgments from both the community and the institution. National service brings the added benefit of a better national reputation for the institution.

To successfully combine research and teaching requires a commitment of large blocks of time. Self-reports of faculty work weeks indicate

5.7: Faculty Research versus Teaching by Type of Institution and ntage

of Institution	Heavily in Research	Both: Toward Research	Both: Toward Teaching	Heavily in Teaching	Total
earch univ. I	16	49	23	12	100
earch univ. II	15	40	27	18	100
ctoral-granting univ. I	8	34	36	22	100
octoral-granting univ. II	6	18	45	31	100
Comprehensive univ. and coll. I	3	22	34	41	100
Comprehensive univ. and coll. II	3	22	35	40	100
Liberal arts coll. I	4	22	44	30	100
Liberal arts coll. II	1	9	27	63	100
Two-year colleges and institutions	1	7	23	69	100
All institutions	6	24	30	40	100

Total respondents 2,896

Source: Burton R. Clark, *The Academic Life: Small Worlds, Different Worlds* (Princeton, N.J.: Carnegie Foundation for the Advancement of Teaching, 1987), p. 86.

Table 5.4: Faculty Teaching Workload under and over Five Hours a Week by Type of Institution

Type of Institution	Hours per Week Spent Teaching		
	0–4	5 and More	Total
Research univ. I	66	34	100
Research univ. II	54	46	100
Doctoral-granting univ. I	41	59	100
Doctoral-granting univ. II	30	70	100
Comprehensive univ. and coll. I	20	80	100
Comprehensive univ. and coll. II	18	82	100
Liberal arts coll. I	12	88	100
Liberal arts coll. II	18	82	100
Two-year colleges and institutions	12	88	100
All institutions	29	71	100

Total respondents 4,932

Source: Burton R. Clark, *The Academic Life: Small Worlds, Different Worlds* (Princeton, N.J.: Carnegie Foundation for the Advancement of Teaching, 1987), p. 77.

trast, the faculty of other types of institutions accept the standards of their schools and opt to emphasize teaching.

Teaching loads also differ between disciplines. Humanities faculties have heavier teaching loads than their colleagues in the sciences, and they are also more involved in undergraduate teaching.[68] Social science faculties fall somewhere between the work loads of the humanities and science faculties, with a tendency to lean toward the humanities. The best explanation for this difference is the availability of resources. In the resource-rich fields, such as physics, biology, and engineering, more time is apportioned for research than in the resource-poor humanities.[69]

Success for the faculty is measured by the obtaining of tenure or promotion to a higher rank. Tenure is ranked only behind salary as the most significant factor to be considered when one is job hunting.[70] Despite recent steps to incorporate teaching skills as an integral part of the tenure process, successful research is the proven way to gain tenure.

that the 60-hour week is standard.[58] Even if this figure is biased in favor of faculty, the average academic work week is at least 55 hours. The expectation is that the faculty members will spend 40 percent of their time in teaching, 40 percent in research, and 20 percent in service.[59] However, this breakdown ignores the fact that the division between research and teaching is never that neat. A university president estimated that each published research paper represented approximately 1,500 hours of preparation.[60] This same individual described the production of a competent academic researcher in these terms:

> If he is teaching classes six or eight hours a week, we may regard him as devoting part time to research, let us say 900 to 1,000 hours in the college year. He might reasonably be expected to supervise six to eight research workers and produce, with his student, two papers a year, two students graduating with the doctor of philosophy degree. This is a conservative estimate, and many able men would produce more. The value of a research man who was doing less than half as much should be questioned.[61]

Table 5.5: Faculty Teaching at Undergraduate and Graduate Levels by Type of Institution and Percentage at Each Level

| | Levels of Instruction | | | | |
Type of Institution	Entirely Undergrad.	Both Levels	Entirely Grad.	Not Teaching	Total
Research univ. I	16	56	23	5	100
Research univ. II	28	54	14	4	100
Doctoral-granting univ. I	31	57	9	3	100
Doctoral-granting univ. II	39	52	6	3	100
Comprehensive univ. and coll. I	52	38	7	3	100
Comprehensive univ. and coll. II	65	30	3	2	100
Liberal arts coll. I	94	4	1	1	100
Liberal arts coll. II	79	14	5	2	100
Two-year colleges and institutions	94	2	1	3	100
All institutions	56	33	8	3	100

Source: Burton R. Clark, *The Academic Life: Small Worlds, Different Worlds* (Princeton, N.J.: Carnegie Foundation for the Advancement of Teaching, 1987), p. 77.

The 1984 faculty survey by the Carnegie Foundation for the Advancement of Teaching further details faculty responsibilities (see table 5.6).[62] Moreover, it distinguishes between the faculty tasks of the four-year and two-year institutions. The most notable difference is between the number of working hours for the faculty in two-year institutions (43.9) and in four-year institutions (36.4). These figures slightly modify the 55-hour standard, but the absence of a service component leaves out a significant part of a faculty member's responsibilities at the four-year institutions. Although service is rarely 20 percent of faculty members' time, committee work and national societies constitute a considerable drain on time. Finally, the different emphasis toward undergraduate teaching is clearly shown. While these survey data mask the considerable difference between faculties at the four-year institutions, they give considerable insight into faculty responsibilities at the two-year institutions.

Regardless of the average faculty work load, the individual faculty member has to juggle a variety of responsibilities to be successful. It

Table 5.6: Working Hours per Week at 2- and Median Hours for Each Task)

Type of Institutions	Task
Four-year institutions	Course preparation
	Undergraduate instruct
	Research
	Office hours
	Administration
	Advising and counseling
	Graduate instruction
	Consulting
Totals	
Two-year institutions	Undergraduate instruction
	Advising and counseling
	Course preparation
	Office hours
	Administration
	Research
Totals	

Source: Carnegie Foundation for the Advancement of Teaching, "The Faculty: Deeply Tro (September–October 1985), p. 33.

has been noted that, on the department level, teaching is usually sized and valued, but publication is given more weight by uppe administration.[63] Despite the delicate balancing act between res and teaching, the life of a professor has some advantages. In the s that the professor determines his or her professional priorities, job formance is holistic.[64] Moreover, the academician can have a ser of creativity, because he or she controls the "product" from beginnir to end.[65]

The research-teaching load differs according to the type of institution. Professors believe that time spent teaching is time diverted from research, so the teaching load issue becomes extremely important to them.[66] The Carnegie Foundation for the Advancement of Teaching's 1984 faculty survey found considerable difference between types of institutions in the ways faculties balance research and teaching responsibilities (see table 5.7).[67] The majority of the faculty of a research university leans toward balancing its research-teaching responsibilities in the direction of research. These professors have adapted to their academic environment by accepting the necessity to do research. In con-

A study of the tenure process in 1978–79 indicates that 67 percent of all faculty are tenured, but differences appear on tenure rates between disciplines (see table 5.8).[71] A more recent study confirms this figure, but shows that the tenure rate differs between public institutions, 68.1 percent, and private ones, 55.7 percent.[72] Although this figure seems to be not especially high, academic leaders have long worried about departments with nothing but tenured faculty. Enough disquiet has resulted that some institutions have set limits to the number of tenured faculty or have tightened requirements to restrict the number of successful tenure cases. Most faculty realize that it is much more difficult to secure tenure in the present academic environment than in the past.[73]

Nearly half of all assistant professor departures are the result of dismissal or denial of reappointment prior to tenure consideration.[74] The threat of a tenure denial is also important in the high number of resignations. The tenure approval rate of all institutions for the 1978–79 academic year was 58.3 (see table 5.9)[75] Even with this figure there were significant differences between types of public and private universities and colleges (see table 5.10).[76] The tenure rate was lowest at private four-year colleges (49.2), followed in order by public universities (59.5), by public four-year colleges (64.3), and finally by private universities (73.5). Another study of the tenure process indicates that

Table 5.8: Tenure Status of Full-Time Faculty by Field and Percentage in 1978–1979

Field	Tenured No.	%	Tenure Track No.	%	Nontenured No.	%	Total No.	%
Physical sciences	15,896	75.2	4,132	19.6	1,108	5.2	21,136	100
Engineering	10,508	69.9	3,651	24.3	872	5.8	15,031	100
Mathematical sciences	11,233	67.8	4,006	24.2	1,330	8.0	16,569	100
Life sciences	17,433	65.5	7,282	27.4	1,884	7.1	26,599	100
Social sciences	27,917	63.4	13,018	29.6	3,087	7.0	44,022	100
Humanities	43,129	69.4	14,747	23.7	4,310	6.9	62,186	100
Education	23,667	64.5	9,730	26.5	3,281	8.9	36,678	100
Total	149,783	67.4	56,566	25.5	15,872	7.1	222,21	100

Source: Frank J. Atelsek and Irene L. Gomberg, *Tenure Practices at Four-Year Colleges and Universities* (Washington, D.C.: American Council on Education, 1980), p. 19.

Table 5.9: Tenure Approval Rates at All Institutions by Selected Fields, 1978–1979

Field	Number	Percentage Approved
Physical sciences	516	66.0
Engineering	485	70.0
Mathematical sciences	511	64.0
Life sciences	849	57.4
Social sciences	1,391	53.3
Humanities	2,126	55.7
Education	1,384	60.7
Total All Fields	7,262	58.3

Source: Frank J. Atelsek and Irene L. Gomberg, *Tenure Practices at Four-Year Colleges and Universities* (Washington, D.C.: American Council on Education, 1980), p. 23.

Table 5.10: Faculty Approved for Tenure by Field and Type of Institution, 1978–1979

Field	Public Univ.	Private Univ.	Public 4-Yr. Colleges	Private 4-Yr. Colleges
Physical sciences	74.0	96.5	71.0	45.6
Engineering	66.4	75.8	70.7	n/a
Mathematical sciences	65.9	73.2	69.4	54.1
Life sciences	59.0	62.3	60.9	49.5
Social sciences	56.2	76.4	55.2	42.8
Humanities	52.4	67.5	63.3	51.7
Education	60.6	78.4	72.3	47.3
Total All Fields	59.5	73.5	64.3	49.2

Source: Frank J. Atelsek and Irene L. Gomberg, *Tenure Practices at Four-Year Colleges and Universities* (Washington, D.C.: American Council on Education, 1980), pp. 28–29.

teaching is second in importance to research, but it is not ignored in faculty evaluation for tenure.[77] Outstanding teaching cannot save an indifferent scholar, but it has an impact on tenure when the research record of the candidate is adequate but not brilliant.[78] Service plays little or no role in tenure decisions.[79] Research is less important at small institutions, where teaching has always had a strong constituency, but it still plays a role. Teaching rather than research assumes primacy, but a good publishing record can make the difference in the final tenure decision.

Many faculty members have become critics of the tenure system. Some of the newer faculty members resent the fact that older faculty had an easier time gaining tenure—so much so that polarization has occurred between senior faculty members and younger assistant professors.[80] A survey of terminated faculty in 1984 shows that they viewed themselves as committed teachers and were critical of the "publish or perish" syndrome.[81] Others have claimed that tenure shelters deadwood in the upper faculty ranks.[82] Finally, tenure has loopholes in that institutions can discharge faculty members for incompetence and in financial emergencies.

Research rewards faculty with salary increases more than teaching does, and merit raises are closely tied to the production of publications.[83] Only a small number of excellent teachers, an estimated 10 percent, is correspondingly rewarded for teaching.[84] Teaching is rewarded better at the comprehensive, liberal arts, and two-year colleges, but teachers' salaries never reach the levels of salaries at the research- and doctoral-level institutions. Therefore, the best way for faculty from any other type of institution to make significant salary advances is to become involved in administration, either as a department chairperson or in a higher administrative position.[85] Besides salary, other ways to reward productive scholars are sabbaticals, decreased teaching loads, and institutional support for research activities.

Faculty members have always had a privileged position vis-à-vis the library. From the beginning of academic libraries, the faculty have had greater access to the book collection than others and also have had extended borrowing privileges. (These privileges have always been defended by professors, and any extension of them is seized upon eagerly.)[86] Once the faculty accepts an improvement in service, any attempt to dilute this new "right" will be met with determined resistance. Faculty, however, has a restricted view of the functions of a library: it believes that every library function should be oriented toward scholarship. This single-minded preoccupation with scholarship caused one observer to conclude that if "left to themselves, most scholars would ruin a library in short order." [87] Part of this problem has been the growing specialization of disciplines. Virtually every large research field has been subdivided into a wide variety of subdisciplines, each of which has created an increasing demand for library materials; however, the slowness of curriculum changes has moderated some of this demand.[88] Academic libraries, on the other hand, have difficulty keeping up with even the moderate expansion of these subdisciplines. Every new field means that the library has to cut back on the acquisition of materials from the established disciplines, and supporters of these "old" disciplines react negatively to such cutbacks.

Certain disciplines lend themselves to dependency on the library and librarians for service. The 1984 Carnegie national faculty survey gave a breakdown of faculty distribution by discipline (see table 5.11)[89] that shows that of the six broad discipline categories, the "soft" professions have the largest percentage of faculty, with 30 percent. "Hard" professions follow with 20 percent. Humanities faculty has 17 percent, physical and social sciences faculties have 13 percent each, and the biological sciences faculty has only 7 percent. In the past, however, academic libraries have not collected materials to correspond to the above distribution of these disciplines. Most of the explanation for this failure derives from historical collecting policies, but part of the reason today is that different disciplines require differing kinds of support from libraries. The traditional collecting priorities have been humanities, social sciences, sciences, and then the applied professions.

A test of these priorities indicates that this traditional approach may be changing. An examination of one of the large Big Ten universities in FY1988 shows that its materials acquisitions come remarkably close to the distribution of the professoriat (see table 5.12).[90] The distribution of acquisitions is 27.4 percent for the "soft" professions, 18.0 percent for the humanities, 17.1 percent for the "hard" professions, 17.2 percent for physical sciences, 12.2 for social sciences, and 8.1 for biological sciences. Categories above the average for the representation of professors were the physical sciences, the humanities, and biological sciences, and those below were the social sciences and the "soft" and "hard" professions.

The library is recognized by the humanities faculty as essential to humanistic scholarship. Humanities faculties have long considered themselves the "transmitters of the cultural heritage of mankind," but since World War II they have been unable to respond to the challenges presented by the popularity of the sciences and the social sciences,[91] whose faculties in turn have considered the library "the organic and functioning center of the campus."[92] Large library collections with diverse holdings are held to be necessary to promote humanities research because humanities scholars consider the library a "center for learning, not just a support for the educational activity that takes place in the classroom."[93] They also believe that it supports the central mission of the university in promoting a liberal education and provides the resources so that this liberal education can take place. Perhaps the most eloquent spokesperson for this viewpoint states the goal in these terms:

Table 5.11: Distribution of Faculty by Discipline

Discipline or Professional Area	Percent of Professoriat	Discipline or Professional Area	Percent of Professoriat
BIOLOGICAL SCIENCES	7	PHYSICAL SCIENCES	13
Biology		Mathematics and statistics	
Physiology and anatomy		Chemistry	
Bacteriology, molecular virology, microbiology		Physics	
Biochemistry		Earth sciences	
Botany		General/other	
Zoology		SOCIAL SCIENCES	13
General/other		Psychology	
		Sociology	
"HARD" PROFESSIONAL	20	Economics	
Engineering and industrial arts		Political science	
Agriculture and forestry		Anthropology and archaeology	
Medicine		Geography	
Nursing		General/other	
Dentistry			
Other health fields		"SOFT" PROFESSIONAL	30
Architecture and design		Education	
Vocational and technical		Business, commerce, management	
		Arts	
HUMANITIES	17	Physical and health education	
English language and literature		Home economics	
Foreign language and literature		Law	
History		Journalism	
Philosophy		Religion and theology	
Other		Social work	
		Library science	
		Total	100

Source: Burton R. Clark, *The Academic Life: Small Worlds, Different Worlds* (Princeton, N.J.: Carnegie Foundation for the Advancement of Teaching, 1987), pp. 38–41.

True liberal education requires that the student's whole life be radically changed by it, that what he learns may affect his action, his tastes, his choices, that no previous attachment be immune to examination and hence re-evaluation.[94]

Reorientation of the educational curriculum away from "the basics" and the decline in language competency during the last twenty

Table 5.12: Breakdown of University of Illinois FY 1988 Materials Budget, Comparing Categories with Professoriat

Discipline or Profession	Percent of Professoriat	Funds	Percent of Budget
Biological sciences	7	$ 358,117	8.1
"Hard" professional	20	755,547	17.1
Humanities	17	809,776	18.0
Physical sciences	13	755,831	17.2
Social sciences	13	536,893	12.2
"Soft" professional	30	1,210,661	27.4
Totals	100	$4,416,825	100.0

Source: Unpublished manuscript by Carl Deal, head of collection development at the University of Illinois at Urbana-Champaign, on the allocation of materials budget funds for the fiscal year 1988 at the University of Illinois Library in 1989.

years have had a negative impact on humanities research and the need for foreign-language resources.[95] The result has been that supporters of humanities scholarship have felt themselves under attack, and it has been difficult for them to accept the success of the sciences and social sciences in gaining funds and fame. Consequently, competition between the humanities and the other disciplines has become part of the political scene in many of the large research universities. A critic of this relationship has even insisted that "the relations between natural science, social science, and humanities are purely administrative and have no substantial intellectual content." [96] An even harsher assessment has been made by Steven Muller, president of Johns Hopkins University, at a 1981 conference on future changes in the relationship of the university and the academic library:

> If you think about the library . . . it is still the heart and soul of the university, but only in terms of the arts and sciences. It's not the heart and soul of the modern university, because the arts and sciences are no longer the core of the modern university.[97]

Humanities scholars have an affection for the library, but, as with other scholarly groups, they have a distinct approach to using it. They utilize the resources of the library heavily, but they prefer to select materials at their leisure, without interference. Although seeking help only as a last resort, these scholars find the atmosphere of the library invigorating. They read current literature to be aware of trends and potential research topics, but they use older or archival literature for research and writing.[98] Citation studies indicate that humanities researchers rely more on books than on journal articles for their research.[99] While these professors have fewer resources for research assistants and others forms of support than those in the sciences, they enjoy working in the library. Much of their activity is in the rare-book room or special collections as they look for primary resources, often unavailable anywhere else.[100] They tend, however, to be nonreceptive toward any type of library change, especially automation. The card catalog is an "old friend," and online catalogs are strange and forbidding. As more libraries adopt automated systems, much of the resistance is slowly giving way as it appears that only a small fraction of scholars is dead set against computer technology.[101] Humanities professors still complain about computers and long for the "good old days," but outright resistance is beginning to abate. These scholars have also been less receptive to alternative types of research formats (microfiche, microfilm, etc.) because "paper is a three dimensional object that carries sensory weight" and can be touched, carried, folded, and always remains familiar.[102] Librarians have long noted patrons' resistance to microform products, and a survey of microfiche users in 1968 revealed that less than 9 percent of them had a positive attitude toward microfiche.[103]

Humanities scholars believe that the academic library should be a depository for research collections rather than an information-dispensing organization. A study of humanities faculty library-information-seeking behavior reinforces the serendipity of humanist scholars, but it also notes their reluctance to use computer-assisted reference. This study, at the University of Utah in 1975,[104] indicates that the humanities faculty takes many approaches to information gathering (see table 5.13).[105] Five types of information gathering have almost equal standing, with references in monographs and journals at the top and word of mouth from colleagues at the bottom. Computer-assisted reference is so little used as to be insignificant, but it should be remembered that this type of reference service was in its infancy as a bibliographical reference tool in the mid-1970s. The slowness of humanities databases to be marketed in any type of format has meant that the process of information gathering for the humanities has not progressed much since the 1975 study. More recent research shows that computer-assisted reference activities still rank low in faculties' information-seeking behavior.[106]

Faculty in the scientific disciplines has different information needs than either the humanities or the social sciences faculty. For a long time scientists have wanted to be "liberated from the increasing drudgery

Table 5.13: Results of Survey on Information Seeking in Humanities

Information Types	Number	Percentage
References in printed sources	80	23.0
Subject catalog	69	19.8
Printed bibliographies	64	16.4
Browsing	62	17.8
Word of mouth	47	13.5
Others	14	4.0
Computer-assisted reference	12	3.5
Totals	348	100.0

Source: Elaine Broadbent, "A Study of Humanities Faculty Library Information Seeking Behavior," *Cataloging and Classification Quarterly* 6 (Spring 1976) 3:23–37.

of literature searching."[107] Scientists have also suffered from "library phobia," or fear of confronting all the seemingly strange services offered by the library. Consequently, scientists fill their information needs from a variety of informal channels before turning to the library, such as preprints, meetings with colleagues, and personal subscriptions to journals.[108] Personal recommendations remain the preferred medium, followed by chance, and only as a last resort does the scientist turn to index sources in the library.[109] In this sense the scientist is less a scholar than a researcher who pieces together bits of information, acquired by whatever means are fastest and most efficient, and applies them to a theory and methodology of his or her creation.[110] Journals, therefore, assume much more importance than books.

Books are used in reserve readings as background material, but the leading edge of research is in unpublished research papers and conference presentations. This type of interchange is important in science because of the social group which forms around research and is sometimes called the "invisible college."[111] The publishing scheme for scientists starts with the technical report, the preprint, the periodical, and finally the monograph.[112] Those resources that provide access to these types of materials are in great demand among scientists and engineers. Scientists of course like having resources readily available, and they prefer departmental libraries over centralized collections.[113] This preference has led to political problems for library administrators who insist upon centralized collections. Finally, many scientists have nothing to do with the library because, for them, the laboratory is the only place where they do their research.[114]

Scientists also have access to more financial resources than professors in either the humanities or the social sciences. A survey of federally sponsored research in universities in the 1960–61 academic year showed that 76 percent of scientists received federal research funds, compared with 30 percent of social scientists and 5 percent of humanists.[115] More recent data on federal academic research money, for 1983–84, show that the imbalance has worsened: 77 percent for physical and biological sciences, 18 percent for engineering, and 5 percent for social science.[116] Efforts to increase funding for social sciences and the humanities were attempted in the 1970s, but these initiatives were abandoned in the 1980s. Federal support for the social sciences dropped from 5.8 percent in 1975 to 2.8 in 1985.[117]

Because of their financial assets, scientists have research grants and student assistants to help them seek out library resources. Student assistants have helped the scientists counter their library phobia, and at the same time these students help compile the bibliographies and supporting documents necessary for grant applications. Also, the scientists' dependency on current publications makes them more receptive to new technology. CD-ROM products, especially those with full text, are popular with scientists because these databases give them access to more information more quickly. Despite considerable interaction between scientists and librarians, some scientists have little or no contact with the library because their research is confined to the laboratory (or the computer). Since these scientists have such limited contact with the library, they are neither pro nor con the library. It is this mix of competing needs that makes the library so important to the faculty concerned with teaching and research.

Social scientists have another distinct approach to research. As social science broke away from the humanities in the late nineteenth and early twentieth centuries, its research orientation changed from library-based research to the collection of data in the field.[118] Fieldwork meant that field methods and methodology became the crucial issues for the discipline. While the results of this fieldwork were usually published in monograph format, the overriding concern was exactitude in research methods. Studies of social scientists since the 1960s indicate that they rely mostly on English-language materials, and they use journals far more than books.[119] They also are interested in currency of information rather than a narrative approach. While social scientists use the library as a research tool, they consider the computer center to be of equal or even more value than the library.[120] Some of the traditional social science disciplines, however, still find the library the focus for much of their research, but as new subdisciplines emerge this dependency may lessen. For these varied reasons, social scientists use the library more than the physical scientists but less than the humanists.

The interests of the applied professions have been ignored because none of these fields fits into the traditional categories. Collecting materials for art and architecture, business, home economics, journalism, law, library science, physical education, religion, and social work has been a routine function of academic libraries, but, unlike other discipline areas, no overall collection-development plan has been devised. The faculties of these subjects or disciplines have been more concerned with gaining access to information by whatever means possible than with large library collections. Because of a combination of government support and financial resources, business, education, and law have been blessed with an assortment of databases available for use by their faculties. Business, education, and law professors have availed themselves of these databases and reference sources, and at the same time they have demanded more and better service. The other fields have been less fortunate in acquiring resources, but their faculties are appreciative of the library services available. Because of the diversity among these disciplines, the applied professions (except business and law) have not been able to acquire the political clout within the university, or in the library, that their numerical strength might indicate.

Recent research gives some guidelines to the types of materials available to scholarly researchers at a large academic library. A 1982 citation analysis and faculty survey at Pennsylvania State University concluded that most of the demand for book and journal articles can be met by a large university library.[121] However, the data indicate differences between the disciplines (see table 5.14).[122] Availability of books for the social sciences and of articles for the sciences is high in comparison to their availability for the humanities. The result of this study indicates that humanities faculties have to depend on interlibrary loans much more frequently than the other disciplines or fields. Another significant factor is that nearly one in five faculty members admitted that they had modified or given up research projects because of the lack of resources at the library.[123] Less satisfaction is shown, however, by scholars for research materials at small academic libraries.[124] On the whole, scholars find it difficult to locate all the materials that they need—83 percent find at least one book a month that is not listed in the circulation system and 84 percent find that one or more books are unavailable because these books are checked out or lost.[125]

Table 5.14: Book and Article Titles Available in Pennsylvania State University Collections

Disciplines	Books			Articles		
	Cited	Available	Percent	Cited	Available	Percent
Humanities	228	156	68.4	80	59	73.8
Sciences	239	175	73.2	792	728	92.0
Social sciences	239	187	78.2	258	207	80.2
Totals	706	518	73.3	1,130	994	88.2

Source: James G. Neal and Barbara J. Smith, "Library Support of Faculty Research at the Branch Campuses of a Multi-Campus University," *Journal of Academic Librarianship* 9 (November 1983) 5:277–79.

The demands of research and scholarly pursuits have led to the creation of a scholarly communications system. This system allows the faculty to communicate its research findings for the broadest distribution possible. The academic library plays a prominent role in the scholarly communication system, whose objectives should be:

1. *Access.* Readers should have access to a comprehensive bibliographic system that allows them to identify and locate material and to obtain it at a reasonable cost and without excessive delay.

2. *Entry.* Authors should find a variety of book publishers and journal editors willing to give a manuscript a fair reading and committed to a decision based on scholarly merit.

3. *Quality control.* The system should have the capacity to differentiate between works of greater and lesser quality, of greater and lesser importance, and to match the form of publication to these differences.

4. *Timeliness.* Manuscripts should be accepted or rejected promptly, and works should be published on schedule. Advance announcements should keep scholars apprised of forthcoming books and articles, and distribution systems should make completed work available rapidly.

5. *Coordination.* The participants in the communications venture— scholars, publishers, technologists, scholarly societies, government and foundations, and libraries—should be mindful of their obligations and their interdependence, and pursue their goals in light of the effects their actions have on others and on the entire system.

6. *Adaptability.* Since the needs of scholars, the tools of scholarship, the uses of knowledge, and the economic and social environment are constantly changing, the scholarly community should maintain a responsive attitude toward the elimination of obsolete methods and materials and toward possibilities of productive innovation.

7. *Financial viability*. Financing arrangements should ensure the economic viability of each function essential to the system of scholarly
communication.[126]

Research libraries are involved mostly with access, timeliness, coordination, and financial viability. Of special concern from the viewpoint
of academic libraries, however, is access to research materials. Without
access, scholars would find the communication system useless.

Computers and the attitudes of the teaching faculty toward computer applications have long-range implications for scholarly communications and academic libraries. A 1986 survey of scholarly computer use
showed that its use is increasing among the teaching faculty, with more
than 90 percent having some access to a computer and 45 percent having
exclusive use of a personal computer.[127] This total, especially faculty
gaining exclusive access to a microcomputer, is expanding at an accelerating rate, and by the early 1990s the number may reach nearly 100
percent. Younger professors tend to approach computers more readily
than older ones, but both age groups use them for more than the word
processing function.[128] Computers tend to be used more for research
than teaching, since computer-aided instruction is used less than other
ways.[129] Although most faculty acquire personal computers to help them
in their writing of journal articles and book manuscripts, they are receptive to using them for other purposes.[130] Finally, only a small percentage
of faculty members has negative perceptions of the computer and its effect on their disciplines.[131] This survey is important in understanding
faculty perceptions of the automated academic library.

Regardless of the scholarly emphasis, sooner or later the teaching and research role of the faculty brings professors into direct contact
with the library and the library staff. Research projects, classroom assignments, reserve reading, and the student research assignments make
the faculty aware of the strengths and deficiencies of a library. But of all
these ways, it is always research that draws the faculty to the library. Assistance in research is the function performed by librarians that is most
appreciated by the faculty.[132] Scholars are primarily interested in two
things: convenience of research materials and reliability of sources.[133]
Of the two, however, convenience has the higher value.[134] Any regulation that the faculty member interprets as a "restraint of research" will
result in the librarian's being considered a "hostile agent."[135] Much of
the contact of the faculty with the library is as user, but despite some
familiarity with library functions, the faculty is poorly informed about
the needs, staffing patterns, and other activities of the library.[136] In fact,

most scholars profess a revulsion for administrative activity, as well as for the routine housekeeping tasks so important to the functioning of the library.[137] The faculty may support the library, but it is dedicated to preserving the materials budget. The view of a political science professor at the University of Illinois in the mid-1940s expresses this sentiment in these words: "In the abstract, it would seem that the scholar would prefer savings in every branch of library cost before the actual purchase of books and documents is curtailed." [138] Another professor suggests that to the extent the library staff demonstrates that it shares the faculty's concern for the growth of the collection, librarians will be accepted by the teaching faculty as equals.[139]

The contact between the faculty and librarians is also important in determining faculty perceptions of the competence of the library staff. Rarely is every book on a reading list available or on the shelf in correct call-number order, but the way the staff responds to this problem makes a lasting impression on a professor. A hostile subordinate staff member can sometimes undo the good work of an entire library staff by an uncooperative attitude.[140] Often the faculty member has expectations that few librarians can match.[141] In general, the teaching faculty wants books returned to the shelves with the least amount of delay and a reduction of the time that periodicals are unavailable at binding.[142] The unavailability of a book or journal issue at time of need is considered by scholars to be the research library's most serious shortcoming.[143] Any type of remote storage is unpopular with the faculty if the retrieval of material is slow.[144] It is here, in dealing with the faculty, that the departmental library has the advantage over the centralized library. Professors respond better to smaller units. Subject specialists are also useful, because this individual, especially if a personal relationship has already been established, has a good chance of placating an unhappy or dissatisfied professor. Moreover, subject expertise allows the librarian to respond by communicating in terms familiar to the professor.[145] Faculty places such a high value on subject specialization that librarians with subject expertise are accepted more readily by them.[146] A professor of English at Ohio State University made the following suggestion:

> On the staff of every large research library there should be at least a few persons whose major training has been, not in library science, but in the various fields of the humanities and social sciences. These people should not only have had extensive personal experience in research, but even more important, they should be expected to keep up with all the latest

developments in their fields, such as the appearance of new reference works and bibliographies.[147]

Nevertheless, evidence shows that faculty utilization of the library is not high. Most faculty members tend to build their own collections, and often their contacts with the library are through graduate assistants.[148] Part of the reason for this reluctance by faculty members to use the library is the difficulty of understanding the library's bibliographic apparatus. They have to be aware of a multiplicity of bibliographic sources that must be consulted before research materials can be found.[149] It is far easier for professors to send graduate students into the library than go themselves.

Bibliographical instruction is another factor that promotes interaction between faculty and the library. While most professors do not utilize this service, those who do value bibliographic instruction highly. Some faculty members subscribe to the belief that "faculty members as well as students need constant instruction in the use of the library, especially as the field of interest shifts from familiar to unfamiliar bodies of material." [150] Help for new students in orienting them to the library and assistance on term papers are equally appreciated. Every librarian has experienced the anguish of hearing a nonlibrarian give bibliographic instruction, so it is important for librarians to assume these duties.

Other services also provide positive contact between the library and the faculty. The two most common faculty-librarian contacts are reference assistance and computerized literature searching.[151] A faculty survey reveals that the teaching faculty is generally satisfied with reference service.[152] Computerized literature searching is used by only 41 percent, although 80 percent have such searching available.[153] Lists of new materials received by the library and tutorials on CD-ROM databases are other services that the faculty can appreciate. Similar tutorials on library automation systems are also a good investment in time by librarians. More of these service activities will become necessary as libraries continue to automate.

Faculty members respond to services provided by the library through their activities on university committees. By membership on committees, boards, and commissions, the faculty participates in the governance of the library. Most often, the senate library committee is the most important of these committees. Library committees usually play only an advisory role, but in weak organizations they may fill the void by actually doing library administrative work.[154]

A survey of these committees in the late 1960s indicated that the university library committee averages thirteen faculty members and serves largely in an advisory capacity.[155] Another survey, in the early 1980s, indicated a difference between the faculty members and the librarians in the perceived success rates of these committees.[156] Part of the problem was the low status of the library committee in the hierarchy of academic committee work.[157] Library input, especially from the library director, on the nominations or appointments to the library committee should be required.[158] Moreover, the chairperson of this committee should be sympathetic toward and familiar with the operations of the library.[159] While these bodies serve in an advisory capacity, in times of crisis they can assume a more significant role. Key periods are in the hiring or firing of a library director, or during periods of faculty or university administration unrest over library policies or personnel issues. Because of the sensitive nature of the evaluation of library personnel and services, many of the senate library committees are restricted to nonlibrarians. Other such committees have only token librarian participation.

On the national and regional scene, various cooperative schemes have been attempted by librarians to solve the problems of expense and space by resource sharing, but teaching faculties have been less than enthusiastic about most of them. Faculties like having materials accessible for their use or for their graduate assistants. Cooperatives or resource sharing have two disadvantages for the faculty: (1) bibliographic expertise in finding the citation and (2) delay in receiving materials.[160] This is why many faculty members consider interlibrary loans both "time-consuming and frustrating."[161] These problems make the faculty insist that library materials be readily accessible even at the cost of duplication of materials. Only by providing large networks of libraries with fast and efficient delivery systems can this problem be solved. Unless material can be made available within four days, the faculty will remain dissatisfied with resource-sharing efforts. Faculty, however, still depends heavily on interlibrary borrowing, despite some reluctance to take full advantage of interlibrary lending possibilities.[162]

The debate over the accessibility of research materials has landed the teaching faculty in the middle of the controversy among librarians over centralized versus decentralized collections. Libraries became decentralized into branch libraries for two historical reasons: collections grew faster than space could be provided and faculties demanded that collections in their specialties be housed near them. Most library administrators, especially just after World War II, felt that centralized col-

lections could be administered more efficiently in one large building.[163]
Part of the drive for centralized libraries was because many of the departmental and professional school libraries had been outside the administrative control of the university librarian. The reorganization of
the Stanford University Library in 1949 was a direct response to this
type of problem.[164] Other considerations in favor of centralization were
improved communications, duplication of materials, and the difficulty
of administering standard rules and regulations.[165] Consequently, collections were centralized as soon as the necessary building could be built.
The movement gathered momentum at the same time that the specialized academic departments (especially among the sciences) demanded
that the branch libraries be preserved. Despite library administrators'
still believing in the virtues of a centralized library, faculty resistance
on many campuses was often strong enough to preserve the branch
libraries. This issue is still a political hot potato, and more than one
library administrator has incurred the wrath of the teaching faculty in
an attempt to close a branch library.

More recently, the debate over centralized and decentralized libraries has changed from one of politics and space needs to a philosophical controversy over the nature of *information flow*. Proponents of
centralization suggest that the growing interdependence of knowledge,
inconvenience to the user, and expense are major reasons in favor of
centralized library collections.[166] Critics of centralized collections have
countered that the development of new technologies has invalidated
these arguments, and decentralized libraries are no more expensive than
centralized ones.[167] Regardless of the merits of this new turn in the debate, the fact remains that politics determines the fate of branch libraries,
not philosophical discussions over information flow. The teaching faculty wants branch libraries, and it will fight to attain or maintain them.

Faculty members also are concerned about library hours. Conve-
nient and longer hours are desired both by the faculty and its graduate
students. Humanities professors are especially interested in greater accessibility of special collection materials.[168] Undergraduate students and
their instructors also lobby for extended hours. Reducing library hours
is guaranteed to promote a major crisis between the library and the rest
of the campus.

Another way the library and faculty interact is in the recruitment
of academic "stars." Many of the large universities recruit outstanding
research scholars, and the library can be a determining factor in attracting these individuals.[169] Many departments make a library tour part of
the interviewing process, and the attitude of the library staff may be

as important to the prospective scholar as the collection itself.[170] These tours are a good opportunity for librarians to orient a prospective professor to the ways the library operates and to establish a future working relationship between the faculty and the librarian.

The teaching faculty remains a staunch supporter of the academic library only as long as the library and its staff respond to its needs. In general, scholars give academic libraries a favorable rating, but newer professors are less satisfied than older ones.[171] Anything viewed as a threat to a faculty's concept of the research library is looked upon with distaste because individual faculty members view the library in the light of personal self-interest. Because of this self-interest, professors become upset at what they interpret as the library's emphasis on nonessentials, which to them include everything not involved in the building of a collection of materials for scholarship. Humanities faculties are especially notorious for wanting the library to be a depository for scholarship, but many social science faculties, and some science faculties, also subscribe to this viewpoint. Other researchers want the academic library to adjust to new research priorities.[172] New technology, equipment, and staffing problems may be important to library administrators and librarians, but most faculty members consider these developments unsettling—or worse, in competition with what to them are the more important collection-building functions. Librarians have a difficult task in convincing the teaching faculty that these housekeeping functions improve the service to them.

Librarians have a difficult job in dealing with the teaching faculty, but no task is more important for the future of the academic library. It is a full-time effort to interact with the teaching faculty to build a constructive working relationship, but no working relationship can be established unless librarians are treated as coequals in the pursuit of scholarship. Academic librarians have the bibliographic expertise that many scholars lack, and a close working relationship can be established by librarians using this expertise in the interest of scholarship. At the same time, librarians need to appreciate that the teaching faculty is a mix of competing disciplines and subdisciplines. Faculty members are allied loosely around the institutional priorities of research, teaching, and service. The closer librarians come to identifying with these institutional priorities, the better it is for the academic library. This means that librarians have to be participants, not spectators, in research. Participation in research and in publishing are important ways for librarians to bond with the institution. Working with the teaching faculty to build library collections is another part of the job. Collection development is time consuming, but it is a service that the teaching faculty can appreciate. Few members of the teaching faculty have either the time or the expertise to select materials in their disciplines, much less in related disciplines. Collection development is one of several areas where librarians have the opportunity to work with the teaching faculty, for the benefit of both the library and the scholar. The academic library has a symbiotic relationship with the university, and the librarian should have the same type of relationship with the teaching faculty.

𝒩OTES

1. Paul L. Dressel, *Administrative Leadership: Effective and Responsible Decision Making in Higher Education* (San Francisco: Jossey-Bass, 1981), pp. 17–18.
2. Mervin Freedman and Nevitt Sanford, "The Faculty Member Yesterday and Today," *New Directions for Higher Education* 1 (Spring 1973): 3
3. Ibid.
4. Ibid.
5. Carnegie Foundation for the Advancement of Teaching, "The Faculty: Deeply Troubled," *Change* (September–October 1985), pp. 31–34.
6. Ibid., pp. 32–33.
7. Ibid., pp. 32–34.
8. Carnegie Foundation for the Advancement of Teaching, "The Satisfied Faculty," *Change* (March–April 1986), p. 33.
9. J. Victor Baldridge, "Alternative Models of Governance in Higher Education," in *Governing Academic Organizations: New Problems, New Perspectives*, edited by Gary L. Riley and J. Victor Baldridge (Berkeley, Calif.: McCutchan, 1977), pp. 5–6.
10. John D. Millet, *The Academic Community: An Essay on Organization* (New York: McGraw-Hill, 1962), p. 72.
11. Edward Shils, *The Academic Ethic* (Chicago: University of Chicago Press, 1983), p. 8.
12. Millet, *Academic Community*, p. 97.
13. William R. Brown, *Academic Politics* (University: University of Alabama Press, 1982), p. 18.
14. Ibid., pp. 18–19.
15. Laurence R. Veyser, *The Emergence of the American University* (Chicago: University of Chicago Press, 1965), p. 320.
16. Millet, *Academic Community*, p. 54.
17. Frederick E. Balderston, *Managing Today's University* (San Francisco: Jossey-Bass, 1974), p. 49.
18. Gail W. McGee and Robert C. Ford, "Faculty Research Productivity and Intention to Change Positions," *Review of Higher Education* 11 (Autumn 1987) 1:14.
19. Millet, *Academic Community*, pp. 74–75.

20. Brown, *Academic Politics*, pp. 58–59
21. Marvin W. Peterson and Robert Blackburn, "Faculty Effectiveness: Meeting Institutional Needs and Expectations," *Review of Higher Education* 9 (1985) 1:128.
22. E. E. Duryea, "Evolution of University Organization," in *The University as an Organization*, edited by James A. Perkins (New York: McGraw-Hill, 1983), p. 31.
23. Paul L. Dressel, F. Craig Johnson, and Philip M. Marcus, *The Confidence Crisis* (San Francisco: Jossey-Bass, 1970), p. 48.
24. Brown, *Academic Politics*, p. 58.
25. Mary B. Mitchell, "The Process of Department Leadership," *Review of Higher Education* 11 (Winter 1987) 2:173–74.
26. John D. Millet, a political scientist and a former president of Miami University (Ohio), recommended appointment rather than election. Millet, *Academic Community*, p. 89.
27. Brown, *Academic Politics*, p. 61.
28. Both the bitterness and the lasting impact of the disturbances of the late 1960s and early 1970s can be seen most starkly in Allan Bloom's chapter on the sixties. See Allan Bloom, *The Closing of the American Mind: How Higher Education Has Failed Democracy and Impoverished the Souls of Today's Students* (New York: Simon and Schuster, 1987), pp. 313–35.
29. J. Victor Baldridge and Frank R. Kemerer, "Images of Governance: Collective Bargaining versus Traditional Models," in *Governing Academic Organizations: New Problems, New Perspectives*, edited by Gary L. Riley and J. Victor Baldridge (Berkeley, Calif.: McCutchan, 1977), p. 262.
30. Steven M. Cahn, *Saints and Scamps: Ethics in Academia* (Totowa, N.J.: Rowman and Littlefield, 1986), pp. 52–53.
31. Shils, *Academic Ethic*, pp. 8–9.
32. Ibid., p. 9.
33. James A. Perkins, "Organization and Functions of the University," in *The University as an Organization*, edited by James A. Perkins (New York: McGraw-Hill, 1983), p. 7.
34. Burton R. Clark, *The Academic Life: Small Worlds, Different Worlds* (Princeton, N.J.: Carnegie Foundation for the Advancement of Teaching, 1987), p. 84.
35. Cahn, *Saints and Scamps*, p. 44.
36. Millet, *Academic Community*, pp. 70–71.
37. Carnegie Foundation for the Advancement of Teaching, "The Faculty," p. 33; Clark, *Academic Life*, p. 78.
38. This table is a reformulation of the table created by the Carnegie Foundation for the Advancement of Teaching study. (Clark, *Academic Life*, p. 78.)
39. This figure is based on growth patterns slightly above those calculated on the 1977 figures. (*Scholarly Communication: The Report of the National Enquiry* (Baltimore: Johns Hopkins Press, 1979), pp. 37–38.)
40. *Scholarly Communication*, pp. 40–50.
41. Herbert C. Morton and Anne J. Price, *The ACLS Survey of Scholars: Fi-

nal Report of Views on Publications, Computers, and Libraries (Washington, D.C.: Office of Scholarly Communication and Technology, American Council of Learned Societies, 1989), pp. 7–9.

42. David W. Lewis, "Inventing the Electronic University," College and Research Libraries 49 (July 1988) 4:294.

43. Scholarly Communication, p. 93.

44. Ibid.

45. Ibid., p. 94.

46. Deane G. Bornheimer, Gerald P. Burns, and Glenn S. Dumke, The Faculty in Higher Education (Danville, Ill.: Interstate, 1973), pp. 10–11.

47. Peterson and Blackburn, "Faculty Effectiveness," p. 30.

48. Cahn, Saints and Scamps, p. 13.

49. Bornheimer, Burns, and Dumke, Faculty in Higher Education, pp. 179–80.

50. Brown, Academic Politics, pp. 23–25.

51. Clark, Academic Life, p. 75.

52. This table is a reformulation of a table created by the Carnegie Foundation for the Advancement of Teaching study. (Clark, Academic Life, p. 75.)

53. Ibid., p. 77.

54. Bornheimer, Burns, and Dumke, Faculty in Higher Education, pp. 5–9.

55. Perkins, "Organization and Functions of the University," p. 7.

56. Bornheimer, Burns, and Dumke, Faculty in Higher Education, p. 46.

57. Ibid., p. 47.

58. Michael D. Cohen and James G. Marsh, Leadership and Ambiguity: The American College President (2d ed.; Boston: Harvard Business School Press, 1986), p. 126.

59. Peterson and Blackburn, "Faculty Effectiveness," p. 28.

60. Frank L. McVey and Raymond M. Hughes, Problems of College and University Administration (Ames: Iowa State College Press, 1952), p. 274.

61. Ibid.

62. Carnegie Foundation for the Advancement of Teaching, "The Faculty," p. 33.

63. Aden Ross, "Tenure, or the Great Chain of Being: Academic Life and the Wheel of Fortune," Change 19 (July–August 1987) 4:55.

64. Brown, Academic Politics, p. 11.

65. Ibid.

66. Clark, Academic Life, pp. 72–73.

67. Ibid., p. 86.

68. Ibid., p. 93.

69. Ibid.

70. James B. O'Toole, "Tenure: A Conscientious Objection," Change 10 (June–July 1978): 24.

71. Frank J. Atelsek and Irene L. Gomberg, Tenure Practices at Four-Year Colleges and Universities (Washington, D.C.: American Council on Education, 1980), p. 19.

72. Howard R. Bowen and Jack H. Schuster, American Professors: A National Resource Imperiled (New York: Oxford University Press, 1986), p. 45.

73. Joyce E. Williams and Elinor Johansen, "Career Disruption in Higher Education," *Journal of Higher Education* 56 (March–April 1985) 2:146.
74. Dolores L. Burke, "The Academic Marketplace in the 1980s: Appointment and Termination of Assistant Professors," *Review of Higher Education* 10 (Spring 1987) 3:208.
75. Atelsek and Gomberg, *Tenure Practices*, p. 23.
76. Ibid., pp. 28–29.
77. Katherine Lewellan Kasten, "Tenure and Merit Pay as Rewards for Research, Teaching, and Service at a Research University," *Journal of Higher Education* 55 (July–August 1984) 4:506–7.
78. Ibid., p. 507.
79. Ibid.
80. Donald E. Miller, "Genteel Poverty: Reflections of an Assistant Professor," *Change* 11 (May–June 1979): 11.
81. Williams and Johansen, "Career Disruption in Higher Education," p. 150.
82. Logan Wilson, *American Academics: Then and Now* (New York: Oxford University Press, 1979), p. 75.
83. Kasten, "Tenure and Merit Pay," p. 508.
84. Ibid., p. 509.
85. Ibid., p. 510.
86. Dressel, *Administrative Leadership*, p. 17.
87. John E. Burchad, "The Library's Function in Education," in *The Library in the University*, edited by John David Marshall (Hamden, Conn.: Shoe String Press, 1967), p. 51.
88. Robert B. Downs, "Development of Research Collections in University Libraries," in *The Library in the University*, edited by John David Marshall (Hamden, Conn.: Shoe String Press, 1967), pp. 69–70.
89. Clark, *Academic Life*, pp. 38–41.
90. Unpublished manuscript by Carl Deal, head of collection development at the University of Illinois (Urbana), on the allocation of materials budget funds for FY1988 at the University of Illinois Library in 1989.
91. Charles B. Osburn, *Academic Research and Library Resources: Changing Patterns in America* (Westport, Conn.: Greenwood Press, 1979), p. 69.
92. Francis G. Wilson, "The Library Catalog and the Scholar," *College and Research Libraries* 3 (June 1942) 3:201.
93. Francis G. Wilson, "Zero Growth: When Is Not-Enough Enough? A Symposium," *Journal of Academic Librarianship* 1 (November 1975) 5:5.
94. Bloom, *Closing of the American Mind*, p. 370.
95. Osburn, *Academic Research and Library Resources*, p. 85.
96. Bloom, *Closing of the American Mind*, p. 350.
97. *Universities, Information Technology, and Academic Libraries*, edited by Robert M. Hayes (Norwood, N.J.: Ablex, 1986), p. 70.
98. *Scholarly Communication*, p. 45.
99. Ibid.
100. James D. Hunt, "Search and Research: The Librarian and the Scholar," *College and Research Libraries* 19 (September 1958) 5:369–74.

101. Morton and Price, *ACLS Survey of Scholars*, p. 41.
102. Shoshana Zuboff, *In the Age of the Smart Machine: The Future of Work and Power* (New York: Basic Books, 1988), p. 130.
103. Ralph W. Lewis, "User's Reaction to Microfiche, A Preliminary Study," *College and Research Libraries* 31 (July 1970) 4:265.
104. Elaine Broadbent, "A Study of Humanities Faculty Library Information Seeking Behavior," *Cataloging and Classification Quarterly* 6 (Spring 1976) 3:23–37.
105. Ibid., p. 26.
106. Morton and Price, *ACLS Survey of Scholars*, pp. 46–49.
107. Henry Gilman, "What the Scientist Expects of the Librarian," *College and Research Libraries* 8 (July 1947) 3:331.
108. Gerald Jahoda, "Planning Improved Library Service for Scientists in Universities," *College and Research Libraries* 28 (September 1967) 5:343.
109. Osburn, *Academic Research and Library Resources*, p. 49.
110. Ibid.
111. Diana Crane, "Social Structure in a Group of Scientists: A Test of the 'Invisible College' Hypothesis," in *Key Papers in Information Science*, edited by Belver C. Griffith (White Plains, N.Y.: Knowledge Industry Publications, 1980), pp. 10–25. "Invisible College" refers to an elite of interacting and productive scientists within a research area.
112. David C. Weber, "A Quagmire of Scientific Literature," *College and Research Libraries* 18 (March 1957) 2:103.
113. Gilman, "What the Scientist Expects of the Librarian," pp. 331–32.
114. J. R. Blanchard, "Departmental Libraries in Divisional Plan University Libraries," *College and Research Libraries* 14 (July 1954) 3:244.
115. Harold Orlans, *The Effects of Federal Programs on Higher Education: A Study of 36 Universities and Colleges* (Washington, D.C.: Brookings Institution, 1962), p. 99.
116. Thomas D. Snyder, *Digest of Education Statistics, 1987* (Washington, D.C.: Center for Education Statistics, 1987), p. 275.
117. Carnegie Foundation for the Advancement of Teaching, "The Ups and Downs of Federal Funding for R&D," *Change* (November–December 1987) 6:36.
118. Osburn, *Academic Research and Library Resources*, p. 60.
119. Ibid., pp. 60–61.
120. Ibid., p. 61.
121. James G. Neal and Barbara J. Smith, "Library Support of Faculty Research at the Branch Campuses of a Multi-Campus University," *Journal of Academic Librarianship* 9 (November 1983) 5:277.
122. Ibid., pp. 277–79.
123. Ibid., p. 279.
124. Morton and Price, *ACLS Survey of Scholars*, pp. 45–46.
125. *Scholarly Communication*, p. 133.
126. Ibid., p. 7.
127. Morton and Price, *ACLS Survey of Scholars*, p. 33.

128. Ibid., pp. 36–37.
129. Ibid., p. 38.
130. Ibid., p. 40.
131. Ibid., p. 41.
132. Gaby Divay, Ada M. Ducas, and Nicole Michaud-Oystryk, "Faculty Perceptions of Librarians at the University of Manitoba," *College and Research Libraries* 48 (January 1987) 1:28.
133. Eldred Smith, *The Librarians, the Scholar, and the Future of the Research Library* (New York: Greenwood Press, 1990), p. 19.
134. Ibid.
135. John Van Erde, "The Library and the Researcher," *College and Research Libraries* 19 (March 1958) 2:106.
136. Robert M. O'Neil, "The President Views the Campus Library," *Journal of Academic Librarianship* 3 (September 1977) 4:195.
137. Robert S. Runyon, "Power and Conflict in Academic Libraries," *Journal of Academic Librarianship* 3 (September 1977) 4:200.
138. Wilson, "Library Catalog and the Scholar," p. 203.
139. Felix Reichmann, "Hercules and Antaeus," *College and Research Libraries* 14 (January 1953) 1:23.
140. Richard D. Altick, "The Scholar's Paradise," *College and Research Libraries* 15 (October 1954) 4:377–78.
141. Jacques Barzun, "The Scholar Looks at the Library," *College and Research Libraries* 7 (April 1946) 2:113–17.
142. Altick, "Scholar's Paradise," pp. 378–79.
143. Smith, *Librarians, the Scholar, and the Future of the Research Library*, p. 25.
144. Walter Rundell, "Relations between Historical Researchers and Custodians of Source Materials," *College and Research Libraries* 29 (November 1968) 6:471.
145. A good overview of the relationship between the subject specialist and the faculty is in Thomas J. Michalak, "Library Services to the Graduate Community: The Role of the Subject Specialist Librarian," *College and Research Libraries* 37 (May 1976) 3:257–65.
146. Divay, Ducas, and Michaud-Oystryk, "Faculty Perceptions of Librarians," p. 32.
147. Altick, "Scholar's Paradise," p. 377.
148. James D. Culley, Denis F. Healy, and Kermit G. Cudd, "Business Students and the University Library: An Overlooked Element in the Business Curriculum," *Journal of Academic Librarianship* 2 (January 1977) 6:296. This has been confirmed by others. See Smith, *Librarians, the Scholar, and the Future of the Research Library*, pp. 24–25.
149. Smith, *Librarians, the Scholar, and the Future of the Research Library*, pp. 11–12.
150. Wilson, "Library Catalog and the Scholar," p. 205.
151. Divay, Ducas, and Michaud-Oystryk, "Faculty Perceptions of Librarians," p. 32.

152. Morton and Price, *ACLS Survey of Scholars*, p. 46.

153. Ibid., p. 47.

154. Mary Sellen and Dana Anderson, "Faculty Library Committees: Evaluations from the Librarians' Perspective," *Journal of Library Administration* 5 (Summer 1984) 2:79.

X 155. Raymond Kilpela, "The University Library Committee," *College and Research Libraries* 29 (March 1968) 2:141–43.

156. Sellen and Anderson, "Faculty Library Committees," p. 85.

157. Ibid., p. 84.

158. Robert M. O'Neil, "The University Administrator's View of the University Library," *New Directions for Higher Education* 39 (1982): 8.

159. Ibid.

160. Herman H. Fussler, "The Research Librarian in Transition," in *The Library in the University*, edited by John David Marshall (Hamden, Conn.: Shoe String Press, 1967), p. 139.

161. Van Erde, "Library and the Researcher," p. 105.

162. Morton and Price, *ACLS Survey of Scholars*, p. 49.

163. Edward G. Holley, "Reaction to 'A Brief for Centralized Library Collections,'" *Journal of Academic Librarianship* 9 (September 1983) 4:201.

164. Elmer M. Grieder, "The Reorganization of the Stanford University Libraries," *College and Research Libraries* 13 (July 1952) 3:246–52.

165. Douglas W. Bryant, "Centralization and Decentralization in Academic Libraries: A Symposium," *College and Research Libraries* 22 (September 1961) 5:332–33.

166. Thomas D. Watts, "A Brief for Centralized Library Collections," *Journal of Academic Librarianship* 9 (September 1983) 4:196–97.

167. Hugh C. Atkinson, "A Brief for the Other Side," *Journal of Academic Librarianship* 9 (September 1983) 4:200–201; Michael K. Buckland, "Foundations of Academic Librarianship," *College and Research Libraries* 50 (July 1989) 4:392.

168. Rundell, "Relations between Historical Researchers and Custodians of Source Materials," p. 471.

169. Richard A. Bartlett, "The College Library and the Recruiting Process," *Journal of Library History* 4 (January 1969) 1:253–55.

170. Ibid., pp. 254–55.

171. Morton and Price, *ACLS Survey of Scholars*, p. 45.

172. Peter S. Graham, "Research Patterns and Research Libraries: What Should Change?" *College and Research Libraries* 50 (July 1989) 4:433–34.

CHAPTER SIX

Academic Librarians and the University

$\mathcal{L}$*IBRARIANS HAVE BEEN* dedicated to the goals of the academic library, but they have displayed little understanding of the university environment in which they have to operate. This ignorance of both the academic and political environments is not surprising since most librarians have had little direct contact with the university beyond that of serving the needs of faculty and students in the relative isolation of the library. Contact between the teaching faculty and librarians is both of a personal nature and in the special relationship of the librarian-patron context. Decisions are sometimes made at the university administration level that librarians misunderstand and find disturbing, so that librarians have difficulty mobilizing themselves to operate effectively in the collegiate political arena. Thus librarians need to be aware of the social, economic, and political environment in which the academic library operates.[1] Most often, contact with the central administration is left in the hands of the library director, whose success depends on an ability to interact on a professional and social level with administrative superiors and peers. In many cases this scenario resembles a general fighting a battle without benefit of an army. Finally, librarians lack comprehension of the rules of conduct which govern and assure success in the academic arena.[2] All these factors place librarians at risk in the highly politicized atmosphere of the university.

Part of the difficulty of librarians' operating successfully in the university political environment is their lack of professional identity. Librarians consider themselves professionals without ever realizing the ramifications of the term. To most librarians, *professionalism* denotes an attitude toward the library profession and a commitment to high standards of patron service. Most other professions operate under a different standard. Perhaps the most famous definition of a profession is by the American philosopher Alfred North Whitehead: "The term profession means an avocation whose activities are subjected to theoretical analysis, and are modified by theoretical conclusions derived from that analysis."[3] This definition requires that a profession must lend itself to rigorous and objective self-examination. In this sense, librarianship resembles the college teaching profession and the definitions given to it in chapter 5. Especially relevant is the theory that defines the characteristics of a profession as the demand for autonomy, divided loyalties between peers and parent organization, tension between professional values and bureaucratic expectations, and peer evaluation.[4] Some confusion over librarianship as a profession is tied to the fact that women constitute a majority of librarians in academic libraries. Woman-dominated professions have historically suffered in terms of status and salary in comparison with man-dominated professions, and discrimination in American higher education, among librarians and faculty, has been a persistent and pressing problem.[5]

Other efforts to list the requirements of a profession include a requirement that a profession has to have a code of ethical conduct. After several decades of debate and changing of minds, the American Library Association (ALA) finally adopted a code of ethics, in 1981, that reflects on the commitment of librarians to high ethical standards in dealing with the acquisition and dispensing of information.[6] Another requirement is that a profession should "limit its own freedom and control its own training."[7] Library and information science schools have been busy fulfilling this requirement since early in the twentieth century. A corollary is that these professionals "must be devoted to the service of others, not to self-interest."[8] Librarianship subscribes to each of these professional definitions without reservations, but a new study of professions places librarianship in a more critical light.

A recent study of professions by a professor of sociology classifies academic librarians as part of the professions involved with qualitative information. Other professions in this grouping are professions (i.e., academics, advertisers, journalists) specializing in some aspect of providing qualitative information for the use of others.[9] Librarians have had in the past and still have in the present "physical custody of cultural capital" in the form of books and journals, and they have utilized this control by emphasizing access to information and, to a lesser extent, education of users and entertainment.[10] Academic librarians, however, have emphasized access to information almost to the exclusion of the other functions. This theory claims that a profession's ability to sustain its control over its domain (or jurisdiction) lies partly in its control of academic knowledge.[11] The academic knowledge system accomplishes three tasks that further the profession: legitimation, research, and instruction.[12] Legitimation is acceptance of the existence of the profession as a value to society. Research produces the practical results of the interests and energies of the members of the profession. Finally, instruction is the way the profession educates itself to accept the burdens of the profession. Each profession has its jurisdictional claims for professional status furthered or retarded by public opinion and by the actions of its members in the workplace.[13]

The most significant part of this theory of professionalism for academic librarians is in the analysis of the competition for jurisdictions. This theory suggests that every successful profession has had to withstand challenges to its professional status from rival professions. An example is the medical profession in the United States, which has been able to weather competition from a variety of outsiders. Such challenges have made the medical profession so unified in protecting its jurisdiction that it is unrivaled by other professions. This type of analysis advances a thesis that academic librarians have suffered in status because of the lack of jurisdictional competition from professions outside the library world.[14] Academic librarians have had a monopoly in the library because no other profession considered the activities there worthwhile enough to challenge the librarians. This lack of competition for jurisdiction may be changing due to the widening gap between the librarian and the information scientists, but at present the jurisdictional competition is insufficient to uplift the status of either academic librarians or information scientists. While this theory is suggestive, it is still only a theory; yet it *does* give some insight into the complex world of professions and the bewildering place where librarianship finds itself at present.

Regardless of all the theories on librarians as professionals, the debate is still far from being decided among academic librarians. The debate about professionalism was particularly lively in library literature during the 1970s, but much of the intellectual steam went out of the debate in the middle 1980s as the issue changed to one of academic status for librarians. Many librarians found the debate over professionalism sophomoric, until they were faced in the workplace with the problems of salaries, working conditions, and organizational chaos.[15] Professional status issues, however, appealed to academic librarians. After all, the difference between a discussion of professionalism and professional status was a shift in the emphasis from the profession as a whole to the relationship between the librarian and institution. Even this more personal orientation was soon displaced by other types of issues. The concern now is less with these issues than with coping with the daily problems of dealing with fewer financial resources and facing the demands of new technology. Yet, the uncertainty over professionalism, professional status, and the need to deal with an uncertain financial future have combined to create growing tensions among academic librarians.

The academic library has always had an identity separate from that of the rest of the university. Sometimes this has been beneficial, but more often it has hurt the cause of the library. Often the library is the most monumental building on the campus and the focus of much of the scholarly activities of the institution. Yet, more than any other academic or administrative unit in the college or university, the library has resisted change in form and structure.[16] This has been despite warnings from prominent librarians on the dangers of the library's isolation from the academic mission of the university.[17] Such a warning was given as far back as the early 1950s, but little has been done to prevent the consequences of this isolation. This isolation has been most obvious in the lack of involvement of library administrators in the campus decision-making process. Left out of long-range campus planning, they have been involved in decision making only at a superficial level on even library-related topics such as campus automation, expansion, and building plans.

Part of the problem of library isolation has been the slowness of academic librarians to adapt to newer administrative modes of operation. While other academic units in colleges and universities have adopted various structures of administration and decision making—most of them resembling the more democratic collegial models, the academic library has retained its basic hierarchical form. It consists of a director and assistant directors administering departments (which are based on traditional library functions).[18] This incompatability between collegial and hierarchical governance structures has caused some difficulty between the university and the library in the past because both have had trouble adjusting to it. The most obvious difficulty has been an ineffectual response by the library to various university priorities.[19] In most library hierarchical structure, communication goes up and down the chain of command, with any bypassing of regular channels discouraged. The hierarchical type of administrative organization in the library has been difficult to equate with the types in other academic departments, and this system has made efforts to introduce a collegial style of management into the library difficult. Because of the hierarchical nature of most libraries, the library director has retained more administrative prerogatives than other academic officers. The use of these administrative prerogatives has often been a source of contention among academic librarians. These librarians contrast their treatment with the more collegial atmosphere of the teaching faculty and note the difference.

Only recently, as technological changes have had a direct influence on library operations, have academic libraries considered alternative organizational structures. Efforts by librarians to become involved in a more participatory environment in the library have had mixed results. Despite encouragement from ACRL's "Standards for Faculty Status for College and University Librarians" (1975), which calls for libraries to adopt an academic form of government, academic libraries have been slow to adjust to such governance procedures. The reason has been a combination of historical development in some of the older, prestigious private university libraries and reluctance to recognize academic librarians as part of the academic environment by both private and public universities. Examples of academic libraries that have adopted faculty governance show that it is a slow and laborious task, full of political pitfalls.[20] Yet, despite these pitfalls, full faculty governance in libraries is popular among academic librarians. It has been adopted in libraries that are otherwise reluctant to move toward other forms of faculty status. Finally, faculty governance brings the library closer to governance practices in the university, and this fact allows librarians more freedom in their dealings with the faculty.

The library director serves as the chief administrative officer of the academic library. Early library directors tended to be autocratic types, and this has changed slowly over time.[21] A study of the functions of the head of a library suggests that the position should combine the skills of an administrator, an educator, and a scholar.[22] This mixture of skills has been the traditional picture of a library director, but more recently the ideal has been the library director as a leader or manager. The difference between these concepts has been defined in the following fashion:

> Leadership is knowing where to go; management is knowing how to get there. Leadership is setting desirable objectives; management is dis-

covering efficient methods of achieving these objectives. Leadership is charismatic, qualitative, idealistic; management is analytical, quantitative, politically demonstrable; leadership is unique, innate, and amorphous.[23]

Little attempt has been made to pick library directors in relation to the distinction between leadership and management characteristics. Consequently, the overwhelming majority of university librarians have been selected in the last twenty years for their management rather than their leadership skills. Leadership-oriented library directors are concerned with library goals, and they tend to delegate authority in the running of the library. They hire capable subordinates and allow them the freedom to do their jobs. On the other hand, management-oriented library directors involve themselves in the daily operations of the library in the name of efficiency. These directors recruit subordinates that share their zeal for efficient library operations. Both types of directors can be successful in certain situations and unsuccessful in others, according to the type of institution and the type of library. Yet rarely do search committees for library directors pose the job search in this light. Instead, future library directors are interviewed and offered positions for any number of reasons, from previous administrative experience to personality. Some institutions prefer the traditional mixture of scholar-administrator, and too often these institutions end up hiring a nonlibrarian. This trend will probably continue until the library profession responds by producing this type of candidate from its ranks.

The type of library director finding favor with search committees goes in cycles. Leadership types were in vogue during the post–World War II library boom. These directors had lengthy and successful careers until most of them retired by the mid-1970s. Difficulties with library budgets and other types of political problems in the mid-1970s produced a new crop of directors. More often than not, these directors were management rather than leadership types. They had a less lengthy and successful stay as directors. The growing instability in job tenure among directors led to concern within the library profession about the nature of the position. Much of this talk has quieted, but the increasing dominance of director positions by managers rather than leaders is still a source of concern. By the late 1980s, most library directors were manager types, with an occasional director displaying leadership tendencies. The library profession needs more leadership-type directors to provide balance and to help the profession enter the information age.

The majority of library directors of academic libraries have always been men. While women have always outnumbered men in the library profession, this advantage has never been translated into equal access to top management positions. A 1930 survey of seventy-four large academic libraries showed that men held fifty-five head librarian positions and women nineteen, but in 1966–67 not one of the seventy-four Association of Research Libraries (ARL) was directed by a woman.[24] A survey of head librarians of American colleges in the mid-1960s (over 3,000 libraries) concluded that men tended to become head librarians at an earlier age than women, and they were more likely to be head librarians of large colleges.[25] Although men were only slightly more numerous than women, women were underrepresented in terms of the total percentage of women in the profession.[26] Only in the last decade have more women been appointed to upper-level administrative positions. A recent study of library directors showed that in 1981 twelve ARL directors were women.[27] The present trend is for women administrators to succeed or fail without the added burden of "pioneering."

The impact of these changes on the tenure of university library directors is uncertain. A 1973 article suggested that the dramatic replacement of ARL directors in the early 1970s meant that the future tenure of these directors would average only five to six years.[28] Another study, in the mid-1980s, challenged this prediction by showing that the average tenure period for university librarians of both ARL and non-ARL libraries has been slowly rising since the mid-1970s.[29] Evidence from other sources, however, indicates that library directors were finding their positions increasingly complex, risky, and difficult.[30] This issue of library-director turnover is significant because turnovers that are too frequent can weaken the working relationship between the academic library and the university.

The library director has several constituencies to which he or she is responsible. Selection of a new director is recognized as a decision affecting all academic disciplines, and for this reason the search is more complex than the searches for deans or directors of academic or support units.[31] Vacancies at this level are filled after a lengthy search, and the candidate is exposed to a wide range of people, from the president of the institution down to representatives from the library. Also, the better the position, the longer the search. Search committees are appointed with the task of weeding the candidates to a "long list" of at least ten. Recommendations are necessary at this level because personal applications are a sign of lack of status. Since almost anyone can persuade a friend to nominate the initiator, the failure to do so is an indication of weakness on the part of the candidate. A "short list" of three to five candidates is finally interviewed, with a secondary list of another two to three candidates as a backup list. While most successful candidates come from the initial list, some institutions will extend a search if none of the original candidates is acceptable. Once a director has been hired, this new person has to decide who, among all those whom he or she met during the interviewing process, are the power brokers. Inability to focus on the power brokers can result in a very difficult career for the new director. Some of the selectors may be librarians, but most will be from other parts of the institution.

A new library director has only a limited number of years to succeed. Hugh Atkinson, the former university librarian at the University of Illinois at Urbana-Champaign, laughed at the three-envelope joke, but he also said that it contains a good deal of truth. Every new library director should write three letters, to be placed into three envelopes to be opened in event of three crises. In the midst of the first big crisis the first envelope is opened and says: "Blame your predecessor." Surviving the first crisis, only to be hurled into the next crisis, the second envelope is opened and it says: "Reorganize." If the director survives the first two crises but a third one appears, the third message will instruct the director to write three new letters to prepare for the next position.

Behind this tale is the story of more than one success and failure. Blaming one's predecessor is almost a tradition in American politics and is a common expedient in any organization, even an academic one. Unless the former director was universally despised, however, this tactic has its dangers in alienating the supporters of the previous regime.

Reorganization is an expedient that a library director has to use sparingly. Some reorganization may be necessary to adapt the organization to new technology and methods, but most often it is used to bypass individuals rather than to fire, retire, or discipline them.[32] Moreover, reorganization works only if an organization is clear in its mission and objectives.[33] Almost every new library director will make some changes, but the wise ones will wait for at least a year before making major alterations to operations or procedures. Sometimes a director is hired by the university administration to implement major reforms, and reorganization is a part of these reforms. Such a director is at risk almost immediately, because the administration will look for reforms before the director has been able to prepare the library for changes. More than one director has left after only a short stay, because of the political fallout of such a situation.

All too often the success of the library director is tied to the director's relationship with his or her superior. In most cases, the library director reports directly to the chief academic officer, a vice-provost or -president for academic affairs. It is rare that a director succeeds unless his or her relationship with this person is good. Two prerequisites are necessary for a good working relationship: accessibility and time. Chief academic officers are always busy, so a scheduled meeting time is the best strategy. Hugh Atkinson invested considerable energy in working with his vice-president for academic affairs at the University of Illinois at Urbana-Champaign. Atkinson, who made certain that he had an hour-long session once a week during the academic year, wanted the vice-president to hear good news about the library as well as its problem areas. This technique worked well for Atkinson, and it differs considerably from the story of an ARL library director who was not on speaking terms with his chief academic officer for several years. Almost yearly, news stories surface about a library director resigning because of an inability to get along with the chief academic officer.

The library director has external as well as internal responsibilities. While most of a director's attention is directed toward the internal workings of the library, outside duties impinge directly on the director's time and energy. In part, this is because the director's responsibilities are similar to those of the university president in having a broad service mission.[34] Directors have the responsibility to participate in national and regional library activities. These activities can be time consuming, but a library administrator must depend on subordinates to cover for him or her in these eventualities. If the library is fortunate enough to be in a regional or local network, the director should provide leadership and guidance for the network. Finally, the director has a multitude of social engagements, from Friends of the Library gatherings to social events, that he or she *must* attend.

The role of the library director has been analyzed in depth because for most librarians this person is their contact with the university at large. Budget and personnel decisions made by the university administration filter down through the library administration. Below the library director, however, is at least one more layer of library administration. Assistant directors have the responsibility to advise the library director and to implement library policies. They are also in training as candidates for future openings at the library-director level. Below the assistant directors is a host of heads of departments and other divisions. While librarians have more contact with these midlevel administrators than with the directors or assistant directors, these administrators merely implement decisions made at a higher level. It is how well this system operates that makes life easy or difficult for the working librarian.

The role of librarians has been examined ever since librarianship became a profession in the late nineteenth century. In most cases, librarians were seen as the custodians of the resources necessary for scholarship, but beyond this contention there was little consensus. Most of the librarians were concerned with housekeeping tasks—ordering, cataloging, and classifying books and journals.[35] Little distinction was made between the clerical and professional functions, and this has continued to hurt the image of librarianship. The need to move away from these housekeeping duties caused library leaders to suggest reforming hiring practices. Too often librarians had been hired at the lowest wages possible, without regard to their talents.[36] In this light, the president of Wellesley College, Mildred H. McAfee, suggested in the 1940s that "librarians should become increasingly professional, scholarly, and executive, learning to delegate enough routine business to clerically trained non-professional assistants so that the routine services essential to the library may not preclude the rendering of the service essential to the academic community."[37] Part of the solution was to recruit more men into the library profession, but this had the unfortunate side effect of reducing promotional opportunities for woman librarians. Another way was to separate librarians from clerical work by hiring more clerical staff (proportionally) than librarians.[38] This approach has been more successful as librarians have assumed a leadership rather than a clerical role, but this policy has also reduced the demand for librarians.

Librarians have become less certain over their role in the library and in the university as a result of these reforms. One viewpoint is that "the academic librarian has as his aim the maintenance and enrichment of organized knowledge for the 'education of scholars.'"[39] Pressures on librarians from the faculty to be "bookmen," or specialists in subject fields, and a corresponding demand within the profession for librarians to be efficient managers have resulted in confusion over the nature of librarianship. Even the recent emphasis on librarians as information scientists has promoted confusion. Then, university requirements that librarians either function as academic faculty or be classified as a separate professional group have made academic librarians uncertain in their role and status. Complicating this confusing scenario is the belief, expressed most clearly by Robert B. Downs, formerly the university librarian at the University of Illinois at Urbana-Champaign, that the status of librarians is an indicator of the status of the library in the university.[40] It is no wonder that academic librarians have been so uncertain about their role in the collegiate life.

The debate over faculty status for librarians has had a lengthy history. While some confusion exists over where, at what university, and when the first grant of faculty status took place—at the University of Montana (1902) or Columbia University (1911)—the idea came out of a demand that academic librarianship should not be an impediment to a professorship but be itself a professorship.[41] Most of the arguments pro and con back in 1940 resemble those in the debate today.[42] Librarians have also debated the merits of faculty status and academic status. *Faculty status* is defined as possession of all the prerogatives and responsibilities of the teaching faculty, including faculty rank.[43] *Academic status* is a kind of reduced faculty status, because those holding it have some, but not all, of the usual faculty privileges.[44] The most notable absence is faculty rank. Most of the original drive for faculty status was the result of the unsatisfactory position of librarians in the structure of the university.

When Robert Bingham Downs assumed his position as university librarian at the University of Illinois in 1944, librarians were classified in civil service. Besides the difficulty of hiring qualified librarians in this system, Downs found "a certain stigma felt by the library staff in being classified as civil service workers."[45] After a thorough study of job performance, Downs was able to persuade the university administration to reclassify librarians as faculty. Frank Lundy, the university librarian at the University of Nebraska, also maintained that academic rank enabled "the director of libraries to recruit and retain staff members with better educational background and greater ability than would otherwise be available."[46] The pursuit of faculty status has meant "official recognition by the institutions that librarians are part of the instructional and research staff."[47] This recognition has been slow in coming from the institutions because of the difficulty of identifying library service with teaching and the reluctance of librarians to accept research responsibilities.

Academic librarians have not presented a united front on either faculty status or academic status issues. Part of the problem has been that academic librarians have experienced a variety of systems in the workplace, from civil service to full faculty status. Librarians, not unlike the teaching faculty, are reluctant to exchange the known for the unknown, even if a new system promises more advantages in the future. A survey of 115 academic libraries in 1957 indicated that 35 institutions gave professional librarians faculty status with rank and about 27 with academic status.[48] Another 43 universities regarded librarians as belonging to a separate professional group,[49] and 11 institutions classified libraries in civil service or a similar type of system.[50] The wide range of

views by university librarians in the Downs article revealed the intensity of feelings on the faculty status debate in the late 1950s.[51] While
fewer libraries remained in civil service in the 1980s, more libraries
have been unionized since the mid-1960s. A 1982 survey of librarians'
status among members of the Association of Research Libraries (ARL)
showed that, of 89 libraries, 41 had faculty status and 48 had professional status.[52] The key finding was that major private institutions were
much less likely to grant faculty status to librarians than were comparable state institutions.[53] Finally, the movement was away from faculty
status in the last decade, as six institutions had either abolished faculty status for librarians or were modifying requirements.[54] Librarians
in these cases were not meeting academic standards, or they were opting
out of the process. These findings indicate that librarians still have reservations about a total commitment to faculty or academic status, despite
the apparent benefits in personal prestige and salary.

The official Association of College and Research Libraries
(ACRL) stance is in favor of faculty status for librarians, but this has
not stilled agitation for other forms of professional status. A major step
forward was the acceptance by the American Association of University
Professors (AAUP) in 1956 of academic librarians as members. This
acceptance gave impetus for leaders in academic libraries to launch a
drive for full faculty status for academic librarians. Beginning in 1959,
ACRL advanced faculty status as a right for academic librarians, but
nothing concrete came of this claim for almost a decade. A 1968 ACRL
resolution calling for full faculty status for academic librarians was implemented by ACRL leadership over the opposition of the American
Library Association (ALA) Council, but it was a document of intent
rather than a statement of fact. Faculty status was defined in this document to mean faculty rank and equality in salary and benefits with
the teaching faculty. It was not until 1971, however, that ACRL's Academic Status Committee drafted standards, and an official statement on
faculty status for librarians was adopted. The American Library Association lists nine criteria for complete faculty status in its "Standards for
Faculty Status for College and University Librarians":

1. Assignment of professional responsibilities only, and review by a
   committee of peers.
2. Governance by a "library faculty."
3. Membership in college governing bodies.
4. Equal compensation for equal education and experience; academic
   year appointment; salary adjusted upward for extra contact days.

5. Eligibility for tenure.
6. Eligibility for promotion, with titles and ranks identical to those of other faculty.
7. Eligibility for leaves on equal basis with other faculty.
8. Equal access to research grants.
9. Academic freedom.[55]

Academic librarians who have some form of faculty status are estimated at 79 percent.[56] Although this figure is on the high side, a majority of academic librarians have some form of faculty rights and responsibilities.

While faculty status demands have had only a limited impact on the finances of colleges and universities, they have caused some of the teaching faculty to question the issue of librarians as faculty. Only a minority of the teaching faculty is openly hostile to librarians' acquiring faculty status, but these hostile individuals can be a vocal element on any campus. Much of their hostility is because faculty rank is recognized by the teaching faculty as a "jealously guarded" status symbol.[57] Equal rank and status also require that librarians meet the same professional standards as the rest of the teaching faculty, and these requirements have frightened many librarians away from the ACRL position. Increased job stress is advanced by critics as one of the major problems of faculty status, but the evidence is inconclusive whether faculty status causes more or less job satisfaction and stress.[58] Some librarians have advocated a retreat from faculty status to a vocational civil service type of status, depending on possible unionization to improve salaries and benefits.[59] But the evidence is that academic librarians lack "the clout and the community of interest to secure the recognition for themselves as a unique group" which must precede union bargaining.[60]

Other efforts have resulted in the establishment of a separate category of academic professionals, usually with scientific and technical staff.[61] One critic of faculty status goes so far as to describe it as "an unnecessary burden which results in an artificial force-fitting of activities into an inappropriate mold," but at the same time the author admits that he enjoys "being a professor and is oriented toward professorial activities." [62] Often these critics argue that a better solution would be a dual track system.[63] Some librarians, such as reference librarians and subject bibliographers, would be in tenure track positions, and others, such as technical services librarians, would have a different status.[64] Most librarians are aware, however, that dual track systems rarely work because they create bad feelings and divisions (or worse) among librarians. Finally, two colleges, Evergreen State College and St. Cloud

University, have experimented with a system in which librarians rotate assignments with faculty from other departments.[65] In this way librarians become teaching faculty on a part-time basis, and they have the responsibility of meeting tenure requirements on equal terms with the other faculty.

Supporters of faculty status for librarians counter the argument of their foes by citing the benefits of faculty status. Besides higher professional status and better salaries, they argue that faculty status helps them in their daily interactions with faculty and students. The benefit of faculty status for the university is, as statistics show, that these libraries tend to be more efficient, as the example of the University of Illinois at Urbana-Champaign Library shows.[66] Other benefits, both personal and for the institution, are described as including: "job advancement, personal recognition when no advancement is possible, improved relationships with teaching faculty as a result of better understanding of the research process, increased responsiveness to change and openness to innovation, and better library service through shared knowledge and experience." [67] These benefits to the institution, however, are not always apparent, as a 1984 study of university administrators shows.[68]

Supporters of faculty status discount the argument about the lack of higher academic qualifications for library staff by citing the examples of university faculty members without doctoral degrees.[69] Despite these arguments, fears are expressed in the library profession about the requirement for research behind faculty status. These fears also concern whether or not a "caste system" is in the process of formation between research and nonresearch librarians.[70] It is true that leaders in the library profession publish more often than their colleagues. A 1982/1983 study of library leaders at the UCLA Senior Fellows Program confirmed that these leaders published much more than a control group of academic librarians.[71]

The requirement for librarians to conduct research is controversial despite the argument that no profession can survive without a critical professional literature. Many librarians fight research requirements, either because they lack confidence in their research skills or they resent the intrusion of research on what they consider more important, service to patrons. Back in the 1950s, cogent arguments were made for a research program on library problems, and these arguments still have relevance today. Daine maintained that "the fact that there has been, relatively, so little research into library problems undoubtedly explains the confused status of librarianship as a profession." [72] While the picture for research has improved since the middle 1950s, only a tiny percentage of librarians conducts research—but other disciplines also experience low research productivity without a crippling effect.[73] Advocates of research claim that "research is also one of the traditional measures of faculty competence—indeed, the only tangible evidence of originality, continuing scholarly interest, and professional dedication."[74] A 1972 British survey of academics, investigating the reasons for doing research,[75] gave the following reasons: one enjoys doing it (91.9%), to advance knowledge (54.3%), to aid promotion (50.0%), personal prestige (49.5%), duty as a university teacher (40.9%), and financial reward (10.2%).[76]

Various criticisms of library research are expressed in the library profession. One of the major criticisms is that no adequate theoretical framework for a particular methodology has ever been established.[77] Two types of research have predominated among librarians: a vague type of social science methodology and how-my-library-did-it-good studies. Many library educators and some librarians have attacked both types of research without substituting anything worthwhile in their place. The lack of rigorous inferential statistical methodology has been documented, but the reasons for it are still uncertain.[78] Critics of the quality of library research only need to consult journals in other disciplines to see that "pedestrian" and "dull" can be applied to them as well.[79]

Publishing research findings is also a daunting task, and many librarians fear rejection of their research contributions. This fear of the rejection of manuscripts, however, is also shared by other disciplines. A 1979 survey of humanities and social science scholars reported that 56 percent of respondents had a rejected article that remained unpublished.[80] The rejection rate for librarians, moreover, is within the average of other disciplines. One study placed the rejection rate as high as 77.3 percent for library journals.[81] A more recent study revises this estimate, to approximately 60 to 70 percent, which is in line with the social sciences and humanities rejection rate.[82]

The major complaint among librarians at faculty status libraries is the lack of release time for research. A 1977 survey of ARL libraries showed that 97 percent of the faculty status librarians incorporated evidence of research and publication into their promotion and tenure requirement, but only 9 percent of the libraries provided release time on a regular basis.[83] This survey also revealed that 76 percent of non–faculty status libraries use evidence of research and publication for promotion and tenure purposes.[84] Such information indicates that librarians are held to a high standard of professional achievement, whether or not they want to participate. A more recent survey of libraries with faculty status (comparable, that is, to other faculties on their campuses) indicates that 76.3 percent of the institutions' librarians are eligible for sabbaticals and 50 percent for release time.[85] Finally, a 1987 study of librarians and teaching faculty indicates that the times available for research were remarkably similar, and the reasons given to avoid research were much the same.[86]

An atmosphere that is conducive to research is almost as important as acquiring research skills. Evidence from other disciplines shows that scholars who perceive colleagues to be supportive are more likely than others to seek the advice of and to collaborate with colleagues on research projects of common interest.[87] Success in a research project will depend upon the degree of help the researchers receive from colleagues when encountering research problems.[88] Intense competition and little collegial interaction among colleagues hinders research.[89] Involvement in professional associations is another way to encourage research.[90] A profile of personality traits of the prolific scholar identified the following characteristics: (1) high standards for productivity, (2) task orientation, (3) curiosity, (4) need for recognition, and (5) adaptability.[91] Few libraries would knowingly turn away people with these qualities, but some libraries refuse to hire librarians with strong research interests.

Another factor is the benefit of a mentor or sponsor in developing research interests and skills. The majority of mentors for other disciplines are faculty members from their doctoral program, but others are acquired from subsequent work experience.[92] Librarians lack the exposure of the traditional mentor process, but it can be developed from library colleagues. Other professions have developed mentoring traditions, and in some, such as business, the manager is responsible for developing talent.[93] The most common type of mentorship is the mentor-protégé relation, in which the experienced librarian develops the skills of the younger librarian. This type of mentorship helps not only the organization but also the profession, by producing active librarians who are self-confident and knowledgeable.[94] Mentoring also can be used to help young librarians meet tenure requirements of research or to publish for professional advancement. Gender has been a difficulty for mentoring in other professions, as men have traditionally mentored men and women have mentored women, but in librarianship this trend must be ended as talent is more important than artificial distinctions. Perhaps the most successful mentor in the library profession was Hugh Atkinson of the University of Illinois Library, who had a strong record of mentoring woman administrators.

Another type of positive interaction is the peer relationship, which differs from mentoring in that the interacting individuals are colleagues of relatively equal rank.[95] In this case the self-help is mutual, with both benefiting from the relationship. Peer relationship is especially beneficial in research projects or professional service. Again, the benefit goes not only to the individuals involved but also to the library profession. Academic librarians need to develop this peer relationship into the scientific model of an "invisible college," a concept that refers to a group of researchers organized around a research theme that could elevate research in librarianship. Members could come together, much like scientists, on the basis of their research interests rather than perceived status in the library world.[96]

Networking, another way to promote research among academic librarians, is used successfully in other disciplines, especially the sciences, and is a good way for a hesitant researcher to be launched into publishing.[97] Other disciplines use collaborative authorship much more than academic librarians. For instance, multiauthor research ranges from 67 to 83 percent in the physical and life sciences.[98] Library research resembles many networking patterns of the social sciences, with a multiple authorship of slightly over 20 percent.[99] Women have found collaborative research helpful in both the research and publishing phases. Finally, research based on collaborative efforts has a better chance of acceptance in refereed journals.[100]

Another criticism of research has been its effect on job performance—the belief that research takes away from job performance. Despite evidence to the contrary, this view is still widely held in certain library circles. One problem with countering this argument is that successful job-performance evaluation has been slow to develop. The difficulty in evaluating librarians has led to some interest in performance appraisal, which has both administrative and behavioral goals.[101] Administrative goals are information on which to base decisions on promotion, transfer, salary, and demotion or dismissal. Behavioral goals are directed toward improving performance. A study of these goals concluded that performance appraisal has been used almost exclusively for administrative (rather than behavioral) goals.[102] A 1971 survey of university libraries in the United States and Canada indicates that almost 95 percent of academic libraries conducts some sort of job appraisal.[103] More recent evidence reinforces the contention that all librarians are measured by some type of performance standard.[104] Usually it is a formal process that includes using written records for evaluation; other processes use appraisals in the form of annual reports or visiting committees of colleagues. Regardless of the method of appraisal, librarians are constantly scrutinized for job performance. Librarians with research responsibilities have been successful in meeting any type of job performance criteria, and they have tended to be more readily considered eligible for promotion and career advancement.

One of the major fears of faculty status is the loss of competent librarians in the pursuit of tenure. A mid-1980s study indicates that in the thirty-eight academic libraries that require research and publication for tenure, 81.5 percent of academic librarians received tenure.[105] This compares favorably to the national average of 58 percent for faculty of all disciplines. Nearly as many librarians were denied tenure for job performance and inadequate service records as for weaknesses in research and publication, but inadequate research/publication was still the major cause.[106] It was also found that considerable flexibility was accorded to the number of the subject fields of the publications accepted for the tenure process.[107] Nevertheless, some library administrators are still reluctant to believe that librarians should be subject to tenure requirements because, as one administrator put it, "We [librarians in academic institutions] are not the explorers or the teachers."[108] Yet some of these critics are not antiresearch, as long as the research is directed toward improvement of job performance.[109]

Another aspect of the faculty status issue is teaching. Most faculties in other disciplines have a teaching component as part of their job responsibilities, whereas a survey of librarians in the late 1960s indicated that only 2.75 percent of the professional staff was involved in formal classroom teaching.[110] While more academic librarians were involved in teaching in the 1980s, the percentage is still low. Still, many librarians have teaching responsibilities or quasi-teaching assignments, and most academic libraries have some type of bibliographic instruction or lecture program. In the mid-1970s, 83 percent of academic libraries offered a lecture program for graduate and undergraduate students.[111] While a majority of these programs are oriented toward undergraduate instruction, graduate students found this instruction helpful in starting their research topics.

Such instruction supports an institution's curriculum by aiding its students to find information and by examining different points of view.[112] One political leader attaches so much importance to bibliographic instruction that he recommends all undergraduates be given library-sponsored bibliographic instruction as an institutional requirement.[113] The only limit on bibliographic instruction in the past has been that the demand often exceeded the capacity of the library to supply librarians as instructors. Yet evidence exists that the teaching faculty seems less than enchanted about bibliographic instruction, even when faculty members admit that their bibliographic expertise is lacking.[114] Bibliographic instruction and other information programs, however, correspond to the teaching requirement of the more traditional disciplines. One university president has gone so far as to claim that librarians are "equal partners in the teaching-learning process." [115] Finally, one library educator maintains that "as librarians, we do better on teaching [broadly defined] and service than we do on research." [116]

Service is the third part of the responsibilities of faculty status for librarians. Participation in national, state, regional, and local organizations is rewarded by a "high profile" for both the university and the library. Professional service on campus is recognized, but it involves less prestige than similar activity at the state or national levels. Service remains important, but the rewards for librarians are dispensed at a lower rate than for research or job performance.[117] Academic librarians can make a name for themselves at conferences and meetings, but traveling and lodging are major expenses.

Another important aspect of librarianship is the impact of faculty status on the librarian-patron relationship. Patron service is recognized in the profession as one of the most important components of the job of the librarian. *Service* is an elastic term that includes working with and for faculty, students, staff, and other patrons in finding material to help them fulfill teaching and research needs. Consequently, reference service has to be provided at a variety of levels, from the expert to the novice. A 1970 survey of users indicated that the faculty, graduate students, and undergraduates were not homogeneous in their reasons for coming to the library or in their use of library materials.[118] The faculty used library facilities to do research for a publishable book or paper and to read for self-improvement.[119] In contrast, graduate students were more concerned about finding and reading required instructional material, and undergraduates about a place to do homework with their personal books.[120] Librarians have claimed bibliographical expertise as their specialty, and the weakness of the teaching faculty in this field has led librarians to claim superiority on bibliographical matters.[121] This type of feeling should be downplayed by librarians as much as possible.

Librarians work successfully with the overwhelming majority of their patrons, but they experience the most difficulty with their relationship with the scholarly expert. Discomfort between faculty members and librarians can come from an incompatibility of outlook. Librarians tend to be service oriented, and in their view all users deserve equal treatment, but this total-system orientation of the librarian can come into conflict with the faculty members' "sense of elite entitlement" to the library's books.[122] Hoarding of books by some of the faculty when students and other faculty members desire access to these books has long been a source of conflict between librarians and certain faculty members.[123] Disillusionment on both sides over this incompatibility of outlook can lead to difficulties between individual librarians and certain professors. The solution is for both sides to recognize the problem and for the librarian to educate the faculty on the nature of the difficulty. Another problem is that teaching departments often make curriculum decisions without considering the availability, cost, and lead time necessary to acquire materials.[124]

Librarians have to develop a close working relationship with the faculty that they serve. Too often librarians are passive, waiting for the faculty to seek out the librarian when looking for service. Instead, librarians should take the initiative and seek out the faculty.[125] Academic librarians are proud of their commitment to service, but they have to realize that every academic department is also a service unit.[126] Too much commitment to service by librarians, however, can lead to a passive attitude in the campus political arena.[127] It is in this delicate area of librarian-faculty relationships that the library and the librarian are at risk, unless there is some type of faculty or academic status system. Separate but equal systems have never worked well in the professional world, nor do they seem to function any better in the academic environment. The teaching faculty has had difficulty according equality to academic librarians, and it will not—unless a clear distinction is made between professional and nonprofessional activities.[128] Otherwise, the relationship is the one described by a president of a university: "The teaching faculty view professional librarians as they do residence hall directors, counselors in the career center, or athletic coaches." [129] Librarians have to be able to work with the teaching faculty as colleagues or the relationship is unequal. But this means that academic librarians must meet the professional standards of the teaching faculty. A survey of faculty attitudes toward librarians at the University of Manitoba shows that faculty perceptions of librarians were colored by their lack of knowledge of what librarians do.[130] The authors noted that implicit in these perceptions was the need for a higher profile and increased academic involvement in university affairs by the librarians.[131] Librarians also must be more active in helping faculty with their research projects.[132] This supportive stance will help improve relations between librarians and their scholar-clientele.

Sometimes a teaching faculty member's carelessness can cause difficulty in the library, most often between the librarian and the students over use of reserves. Students are sent by the instructor to use reserve materials that the instructor has either been late requesting or has not checked to see if the library possesses. The result is that the library appears inefficient or uncaring, and the students report this impression of slackness back to the instructor.[133] After this, the scenario worsens as blame is passed back and forth between the instructor and the library. Reserves are always a serious problem for libraries, and librarians have to be aware of the potential for danger in this area.

Selection of materials as a librarian's responsibility is a recent development. During most of the nineteenth century, books were purchased from departmental operating funds by the teaching faculty.[134] A survey conducted by the American Library Association in 1926 confirmed that more than 80 percent of academic libraries had collection-development policies determined by faculty committees.[135] Gradually, over the course of the twentieth century, book funds have been transferred from academic departments or library committees to the academic library. The growth of subject specialists has accelerated this transfer, but close contact between the subject specialist and the teaching faculty is mandatory. Exceptions are still numerous, but this transfer has been retarded more by a lack of librarians to assume this responsibility than by a conscious decision to retain teaching-faculty selection.

The librarian, in short, has an immense responsibility in book selection, and in more and more institutions librarians have assumed the selection of all materials, mainly because the teaching faculty is too busy with teaching and research. This attitude is reflected in the following statement of a prominent English professor at the University of Iowa:

> I would rather have that decision [on acquiring a book] made by an intelligent, humane, book-loving librarian, who is sensitive to the future and the past as well as the present, who respects his predecessors who have tried in their way to build a collection with integrity . . . than to trust a faculty committee or—God save the mark!—a computer analyzing utilization statistics.[136]

This statement places a conscious, deliberate responsibility for the selection of materials in the hands of librarians—but a type of librarian who loves books rather than a mere manager of collections. Such assumptions have been a positive sign of increased status for librarians.

Librarians have been less enthusiastic about weeding than selecting collections. One reason for their disinterest in weeding collections is that most of them subscribe to the doctrine that bigger is better.[137] Only when space problems are at their worst do academic librarians seriously consider weeding. Resentment by scholars toward any policy that deprives them of resources also makes librarians less than receptive to weeding. Weeding in the humanities and the social sciences is particularly difficult because of the inability of librarians or scholars to forecast research trends. Efforts to convince researchers that new technology will replace discarded materials often falls on deaf ears.

Resource sharing is always a popular topic during economic downturns that threaten library funding. Most of the large academic libraries have been reluctant to commit themselves to large-scale resource sharing, for a variety of political reasons, but many of the small academic libraries have had little choice and have cancelled serials.[138] Even the large research libraries have had large-scale serial cancellations in response to the increases in serial costs.

Librarians have to serve a varied and often difficult clientele, and often with limited resources. No library, not even the largest research library, has all the resources it needs to match patron demand. Rising expectations and limited resources are difficult to manage unless librarians have confidence in their ability to cope. Images of librarians as "warehouse custodians" make the jobs of academic librarians close to impossible. Librarians therefore have to work toward establishing their own expertise and "turf" in the university, or else they will be relegated to a lower status.[139] Some type of professional status, either faculty status or faculty rank, is required if academic librarians are to deal with the daily demands of the job. But this means that academic librarians have to start "selling" themselves as equals to the teaching faculty in the academic community. My experience has been that "separate but equal" only lowers the status of librarians. Although the teaching faculty has the three responsibilities of teaching, research, and service, significant portions of the faculty don't teach, don't conduct research, and don't perform any service for their profession or the university. Rather than accept low performance standards, academic librarians need to intensify their efforts, expanding research and service, and, if the opportunities present themselves, teach. Bibliographic instruction should count as teaching, because the librarian imparts knowledge to students. Also, professional librarians must not limit themselves to the forty-hour workweek, because they should be task driven rather than clock driven. At the same time, libraries have to give their librarians the flexibility to function as professionals. Higher expectations have to allow for more autonomy in the workplace. Autonomy will allow academic librarians to take their rightful place in the academic chain; now the emphasis is more on the institution and not on the academic librarians as the providers of the library's services.[140]

As for the future of libraries and librarians, new technologies will force libraries to change and librarians will adjust to these changes. One forecaster predicted in 1977 that librarians of the future would be identified in these terms:

> Melancholy as it may sound to some of you, librarians of the future must be budgeteers and systems managers, and conflict resolvers, and priority selectors, and superb academic politicians. They must be negotiators and compromisers and "Dear Abbies" and policemen. I know this, because what I have just said characterizes what the most successful of you are or do at present.[141]

The forecaster's scenario describes only part of what the future holds for academic librarians. The information age is upon us, and academic librarians will have to adjust to technological change at an accelerating rate. Predictions of the demise of the academic library are certainly premature, but librarians will have to make adjustments to the new world.[142] Some type of electronic library will develop in the future, yet the academic library will no doubt remain much the same, with a large book and journal collection available for both scholars and students. Most of the change will be in the form of increased access to nontraditional types of materials—CD-ROM, electronic journals, and the like. As the academic library comes closer to the electronic information age, a good working relationship will have to be established with the chief information officer and the computer center staff. This relationship will be at least as important as the interaction of librarians with the teaching faculty and the university administration. A continuing problem will remain of dealing with the university administration, teaching faculty, students, and general patrons on a daily basis with a declining percentage of the university's resources. Unless academic librarians learn to communicate and work hand-in-hand with the teaching faculty, the future of the academic library will be bleak. Always remember that administrations, faculties, and students come and go, but the university and the library will remain.

𝒩OTES

1. Edward G. Holley, "Defining the Academic Librarian," *College and Research Libraries* 46 (November 1985) 6:462.
2. Ed Neroda and Lana Bodewin, "Institutional Analysis for Professional Development," *Journal of Academic Librarianship* 9 (July 1983) 3:157.
3. Alfred North Whitehead, *Adventures in Ideas* (New York: Macmillan, 1933), p. 72.
4. J. Victor Baldridge, "Alternative Models of Governance in Higher Education," in *Governing Academic Organizations: New Problems, New Perspectives*, edited by Gary L. Riley and J. Victor Baldridge (Berkeley, Calif.: McCutchan, 1977), pp. 5–6.
5. Kenneth G. Peter, "Ethics in Academic Librarianship: The Need for Values," *Journal of Academic Librarianship* 9 (July 1983) 3:133.
6. Orvin Lee Shiflett, *Origins of American Academic Librarianship* (Norwood, N.J.: Ablex, 1981), p. 223.
7. Richard Hofstadter and C. DeWitt Hardy, *The Development and Scope of Higher Education in the United States* (New York: Columbia University Press, 1952), p. 170.
8. Ibid.
9. Andrew Abbott, *The System of Professions: An Essay on the Division of Expert Labor* (Chicago: University of Chicago Press, 1988), pp. 216–17.
10. Ibid., pp. 217–18.
11. Ibid., pp. 53–54.
12. Ibid., pp. 56–57.
13. Ibid., pp. 60–64.
14. Ibid., pp. 222–24.
15. Judy C. McDermott, "The Professional Status of Librarians: A Realistic and Unpopular Analysis," *Journal of Library Administration* 5 (Fall 1984) 3:17.
16. Eugene Brunelle, "New Learning, New Libraries, New Librarians," *Journal of Academic Librarianship* 1 (November 1975) 5:23.
17. Frank A. Lundy, "Faculty Rank of Professional Librarians—Part I," *College and Research Libraries* 12 (January 1951) 1:13.
18. Brunelle, "New Learning," p. 23.
19. Nancy A. Brown, "Managing the Coexistence of Hierarchical and Collegial Governance Structures," *College and Research Libraries* 45 (November 1985) 6:478.
20. Marion T. Reid, Anna H. Perrault, and Jane P. Kleiner, "The Role of the Academic Library Governance," in *New Horizons for Academic Libraries*, edited by Robert D. Stueart and Richard D. Johnson (New York: K. G. Saur, 1979), pp. 123–31.
21. Arthur M. McAnally, "Status of the University Librarian in the Academic Community," in *Research Librarianship: Essays in Honor of Robert B. Downs*, edited by Jerrold Orne (New York: Bowker, 1971), p. 22.
22. Patricia B. Knapp, "The College Librarian: Sociology of a Professional

Specialization," *College and Research Libraries* 16 (January 1955) 1:66–67.

23. George B. Weathersby, "Purpose, Persuasion, Backbone, and Spunk," in *Efficient College Management*, edited by William W. Jellema (San Francisco: Jossey-Bass, 1972), p. 4.

24. Janice C. Fennell, "The Woman Academic-Library Administrator: A Career Profile," in *The Status of Women in Librarianship: Historical, Sociological, and Economic Issues*, edited by Kathleen M. Heim (New York: Neal-Schuman, 1983), pp. 207–8.

25. W. C. Blankenship, "Head Librarians: How Many Men? How Many Women?" *College and Research Libraries* 28 (January 1967) 1:47.

26. Ibid.

27. Ronald Dale Karr, "The Changing Profile of University Library Directors, 1966–1981," *College and Research Libraries* 45 (July 1984) 4:282.

28. Arthur M. McAnally and Robert B. Downs, "The Changing Role of Directors of University Libraries," *College and Research Libraries* 34 (March 1973) 2:103.

29. William S. Wong and David S. Zubatsky, "The Tenure Rate of University Library Directors: A 1983 Survey," *College and Research Libraries* 46 (January 1985) 1:76.

30. John N. DePew and Anne Marie Allison, "Factors Affecting Academic Library Administration, 1976–1981," *Journal of Library Administration* 5 (Summer 1984) 5:13–57.

31. Ruth J. Person and George Charles Newman, "Selection of the University Librarian," *College and Research Libraries* 51 (July 1990) 4:347.

32. Paul L. Dressel, "Mission, Organization, and Leadership," *Journal of Higher Education* 58 (January–February 1987) 1:104.

33. Ibid., p. 109.

34. Robert S. Runyon, "Power and Conflict in Academic Libraries," *Journal of Academic Librarianship* 3 (September 1977) 4:200.

35. McAnally, "Status of the University Librarian," p. 20.

36. Shiflett, *Origins of American Academic Librarianship*, p. 225.

37. Mildred H. McAfee, "The College Library as Seen by a College President," *College and Research Libraries* 2 (September 1941) 4:302.

38. Robert B. Downs and Robert F. Delzell, "Professional Duties in University Libraries," *College and Research Libraries* 26 (January 1965) 1:30.

39. Robert E. Moody, "Our Academic Library Leadership: From the Faculty?" *College and Research Libraries* 21 (September 1960) 5:363.

40. Robert B. Downs, "Are College and University Librarians Academic?" *College and Research Libraries* 15 (January 1954) 1:10.

41. C. James Schmidt, "Faculty Status in Academic Libraries: Retrospective and Prospect," in *New Horizons for Academic Libraries*, edited by Robert D. Stueart and Richard D. Johnson (New York: K. G. Saur, 1979), pp. 411–12.

42. James A. McMillan, "Academic Status of Library Staff Members of Large Universities," *College and Research Libraries* 1 (March 1940) 2:138–40.

43. Arthur M. McAnally, "The Dynamics of Securing Academic Status," *College and Research Libraries* 18 (September 1957) 5:386.
44. Ibid.
45. Robert B. Downs, "Academic Status for University Librarians—A New Approach," *College and Research Libraries* 7 (January 1946) 1:7.
46. Lundy, "Faculty Rank of Professional Librarians," p. 13.
47. Virgil F. Massman, *Faculty Status for Librarians* (Metuchen, N.J.: Scarecrow Press, 1972), p. 5.
48. Robert D. Downs, "The Current Status of University Library Staffs," *College and Research Libraries* 18 (September 1957) 5:376.
49. Ibid.
50. Ibid.
51. Ibid. pp. 379–85.
52. Thomas G. English, "Librarian Status in the Eighty-nine Academic Institutions of the Association of Research Libraries: 1982," *College and Research Libraries* 44 (May 1983) 3:201.
53. Ibid., p. 200.
54. Ibid., pp. 204–7.
55. American Library Association, "Standards for Faculty Status for College and University Librarians," quoted by William Miller, "Faculty Status in the College Library," in *College Librarianship*, edited by William Miller and D. Stephen Rockwood (Metuchen, N.J.: Scarecrow Press, 1981), pp. 122–23.
56. Emily Werrel and Laura Sullivan, "Faculty Status for Academic Librarians: A Review of the Literature," *College and Research Libraries* 48 (March 1987) 2:96.
57. Knapp, "College Librarian," p. 68.
58. Harold V. Hosel, "Academic Librarians and Faculty Status: A Role Stress-Job Satisfaction Perspective," *Journal of Library Administration* 5 (Fall 1984) 3:57–66.
59. H. William Axford, "The Three Faces of Eve; or the Identity of Academic Librarianship: A Symposium," *Journal of Academic Librarianship* 2 (January 1977) 6:277.
60. Robert C. O'Reilly and Marjorie I. O'Reilly, *Librarians and Labor Relations: Employment under Union Contracts* (Westport, Conn.: Greenwood Press, 1981), p. 70.
61. This system is best described by Joan M. Bechtel, "Academic Profession Status: An Alternative for Librarians," *Journal of Academic Librarianship* 11 (November 1985) 5:289–92.
62. Fred Batt, "Faculty Status for Academic Librarians: Justified or Just a Farce?" in *Issues in Academic Librarianship: Views and Case Studies for the 1980s and 1990s*, edited by Peter Spyers-Duran and Thomas W. Mann (Westport, Conn.: Greenwood Press, 1985), pp. 115-16.
63. Nancy Davey and Theodora Andrews, "Implications of Faculty Status for University Librarians, with Special Attention to Tenure," *Journal of Academic Librarianship* 4 (May 1978): 71–74.

64. Irene Hoadley, director of the Evans Library of Texas A&M University, outlines the reasons against such a dual-track system. See Irene B. Hoadley, "The Role of Professionals in Technical Services," *Technical Services Quarterly* 6 (1988) 2:11–16.

65. Fred E. Hill and Robert Hauptman, "A New Perspective on Faculty Status," *College and Research Libraries* 47 (March 1986) 2:157–58.

66. Robert G. Sewell, "Faculty Status and Librarians: The Rationale and the Case of Illinois," *College and Research Libraries* 44 (May 1983) 3:212–22.

67. Dale S. Montanelli and Patricia F. Stenstrom, "The Benefits of Research for Academic Librarians and the Institutions which They Serve," in *Energies for Transition*, edited by Danuta A. Nitecki (Chicago: Association of College and Research Libraries, 1986), p. 18.

68. Thomas G. English, "Administrators' Views of Library Personnel Status," *College and Research Libraries* 45 (May 1984) 3:191–93.

69. Brunelle, "New Learning," p. 22.

70. Frederic Isaac, "Librarian, Scholar, or Author? The Librarian's New Dilemma," *Journal of Academic Librarianship* 9 (September 1983) 4:218.

71. Dorothy J. Anderson, "Comparative Career Profiles of Academic Librarians: Are Leaders Different?" *Journal of Academic Librarianship* 10 (January 1985) 6:329–30.

72. Chase Dane, "The Need for a Research Program in Library Problems," *College and Research Libraries* 16 (January 1955) 1:20–23.

73. For instance, a study of the research productivity of psychologists reveals that only 10 percent of such authors can be considered productive. William D. Garvey and Belver C. Griffith, "Scientific Communication: Its Role in the Conduct of Research and Creation of Knowledge," in *Key Papers in Information Science*, edited by Belver C. Griffith (New York: Knowledge Industry Publications, 1980), p. 41.

74. McAnally, "Status of the University Librarian," p. 44.

75. Richard Startup, "The Rewards of Research," *New Universities Quarterly* 30 (Spring 1976): 227–38.

76. Ibid., p. 229.

77. Barbara G. Petrof, "Theory: The X Factor in Librarianship," *College and Research Libraries* 16 (January 1955) 1:20–23.

78. Danny P. Wallace, "The Use of Statistical Methods in Library and Information Science," *Journal of the American Society for Information Science* 36 (November 1985) 6:408.

79. Holley, "Defining the Academic Librarian," pp. 465–66.

80. *Scholarly Communication: The Report of the National Enquiry* (Baltimore: Johns Hopkins Press, 1979), p. 48.

81. Daniel O'Connor and Phyllis Van Orden, "Getting into Print," *College and Research Libraries* 39 (September 1978) 5:391.

82. John Budd, "Publication in Library and Information Science: The State of the Literature," *Library Journal* (1 September 1988), p. 126.

83. Jack F. Pontius, "Faculty Status, Research Requirements, and Release

Time" (Arlington, Va.: ERIC Document Reproduction Service, ED 183147, 1978), p. 9.

84. Ibid.

85. W. Bede Mitchell and L. Stanislava Swieszkowski, "Publication Requirements and Tenure Approval Rates: An Issue for Academic Librarians," *College and Research Libraries* 46 (May 1985) 3:252.

86. Robert Boice, Jordan M. Scepanski, and Wayne Wilson, "Librarians and Faculty Members: Coping with Pressures to Publish," *College and Research Libraries* 48 (November 1987) 6:502.

87. Deborah E. Hunter and George D. Kuh, "The 'Write Wing': Characteristics of Prolific Contributors to the Higher Education Literature," *Journal of Higher Education* 58 (July–August 1987) 4:451.

88. Startup, "Rewards of Research," p. 232.

89. Hunter and Kuh, " 'Write Wing,' " p. 451.

90. Ibid., p. 452.

91. Ibid., p. 454.

92. Ibid., p. 453.

93. David Marshall Hunt and Carol Michael, "Mentorship: A Career Training and Development Tool," *Journal of Library Administration* 5 (Spring 1984) 1:78.

94. Ibid., p. 83.

95. Leslie M. Kong and R. A. H. Goodfellow, "Charting a Career in Research: The Motivations and Costs of Collaboration," *Journal of Higher Education* 55 (May–June 1984) 3:349.

96. Diana Crane, "Social Structure in a Group of Scientists: A Test of the 'Invisible College' Hypothesis," in *Key Papers in Information Science*, edited by Belver C. Griffith (White Plains, N.Y.: Knowledge Industry Publications, 1980), p. 23.

97. Mary Frank Fox and Catherine A. Faver, "Independence and Cooperation in Research: The Motivations and Costs of Collaboration," *Journal of Higher Education* 55 (May–June 1984) 3:349.

98. R. T. Bottle and E. N. Efthimiadis, "Library and Information Science Literature: Authorship and Growth Patterns," *Journal of Information Science: Principles and Practice* 9 (1984) 3:107.

99. Ibid.

100. Fox and Faver, "Independence and Cooperation in Research," pp. 350–51.

101. G. Edward Evans and Benedict Rugaas, "Another Look at Performance Appraisal in Libraries," *Journal of Library Administration* 3 (Summer 1982) 3:63.

102. Ibid., p. 64.

103. Marjorie Johnson, "Performance Appraisal of Librarians: A Survey," *College and Research Libraries* 33 (September 1972) 5:359.

104. Some of the evaluation measures are analyzed in J. Rebecca Kroll, "Beyond Evaluating: Performance as a Planning and Motivational Tool in Libraries," *Journal of Academic Librarianship* 9 (March 1983) 1:28–30.

105. Mitchell and Swieszkowski, "Publication Requirements and Tenure Ap-

proval Rates," p. 252.
106. Ibid., pp. 252–53.
107. Ibid.
108. Jerry D. Campbell, "An Administrator's View of the Negative Impact of Tenure on Librarians," *Technical Services Quarterly* 6 (1988) 2:4–5.
109. Ibid., p. 6.
110. Mary B. Cassata, "Teach-in: The Academic Librarian's Key to Status?" *College and Research Libraries* 31 (January 1970) 1:26.
111. Peter Hernon, "Library Lectures and Their Evaluation: A Survey," *Journal of Academic Librarianship* 1 (July 1975) 3:15.
112. Sonia Bodi, "Critical Thinking and Bibliographic Instruction: The Relationship," *Journal of Academic Librarianship* 14 (July 1988) 3:150.
113. Major R. Owens, "The Academic Library and Education for Leadership," in *Libraries and the Search for Academic Excellence*, edited by Patricia Senn Breivik and Robert Wedgeworth (Metuchen, N.J.: Scarecrow Press, 1988), pp. 14–16.
114. Constance McCarthy, "The Faculty Problem," *Journal of Academic Librarianship* 11 (July 1985) 3:142–43.
115. Gresham Riley, "Myths and Realities: The Academic Viewpoint II," *College and Research Libraries* 45 (September 1984) 5:369.
116. Holley, "Defining the Academic Librarian," p. 467.
117. Lynne E. Gamble, "University Service: New Implications for Academic Librarians," *Journal of Academic Librarianship* 14 (January 1989) 6:346.
118. Philip V. Rzasa and John H. Moriarty, "The Types and Needs of Academic Library Users: A Case Study of 6,568 Responses," *College and Research Libraries* 31 (November 1970) 6:407.
119. Ibid.
120. Ibid.
121. Shiflett, *Origins of American Academic Librarianship*, pp. 274–75.
122. Runyon, "Power and Conflict in Academic Libraries," p. 202.
123. Shiflett, *Origins of American Academic Librarianship*, pp. 235–36.
124. Donald A. Redmond, Michael P. Sinclair, and Elinore Brown, "University Libraries and University Research," *College and Research Libraries* 33 (November 1972) 6:451.
125. B. Anne Commerton, "Building Faculty/Library Relationships: Forging the Bond," *Bookmark* 45 (Fall 1986) 1:18.
126. Clyde Hendrick, "The University Library in the Twenty-first Century," *College and Research Libraries* 47 (March 1986) 2:129.
127. Ibid.
128. John M. Dawson, "Not Too Academic," *College and Research Libraries* 27 (January 1966) 1:37–38.
129. Riley, "Myths and Realities," p. 367.
130. Gaby Divay, Ada M. Ducas, and Nicole Michaud-Oystryk, "Faculty Perceptions of Librarians at the University of Manitoba," *College and Research Libraries* 48 (January 1987) 1:34.
131. Ibid.

132. Robert Grover and Martha L. Hale, "The Role of the Librarian in Faculty Research," *College and Research Libraries* 49 (January 1988) 1:113–14.
133. Knapp, "College Librarian," p. 70.
134. Jasper G. Schad, "Allocating Materials Budgets in Institutions of Higher Education," *Journal of Academic Librarianship* 3 (January 1978) 6:328.
135. American Library Association, *ALA Survey* (Chicago: American Library Association, 1926), p. 160.
136. Ray L. Heffner, "Zero Growth: When Is Not-Enough Enough? A Symposium," *Journal of Academic Librarianship* 1 (November 1975) 5:6.
137. Runyon, "Power and Conflict in Academic Libraries," p. 200.
138. Bernard H. Holicy, "Collection Development vs. Resource Sharing: The View from the Small Academic Library," *Journal of Academic Librarianship* 10 (July 1984) 3:146–47.
139. Stephen K. Bailey, "The Future of College and Research Libraries," *College and Research Libraries* 39 (January 1978) 1:5.
140. Allen B. Veaner, "1985 to 1995: The Next Decade in Academic Librarianship, Part I," *College and Research Libraries* 46 (May 1985) 3:211.
141. Herbert S. White, "Reactions to 'Defining the Academic Librarian,'" *College and Research Libraries* 46 (November 1985) 6:476–77.
142. Richard D. Hacken, "Tomorrow's Research Library: Vigor or Rigor Mortis?" *College and Research Libraries* 49 (November 1988) 6:489–91.

Conclusion

S*TUDIES OF THE ROLE* of the academic library in the university environment have been almost nonexistent because of the complexities of understanding the relationships between two related but in many ways different organizations. Neither the library nor the academic communities have taken the time or the effort to study the other, but both have to live in a symbiotic relationship. Decision making still remains at the university level, but decisions made in the library can affect university policies. A reduction in library hours by the library administration will cause the campus administration to react to numerous faculty complaints and to read hostile student newspaper articles.

Certain key points have emerged from this analysis of the relationship between the library and the university environment, and ten propositions can be said to contain the essence of this study.

1. *Academic libraries have always responded to trends in higher education.* A symbiotic relationship between the academic library and its host institutions has existed since the beginning of American higher education, at Harvard College in 1636. For the first 150 years libraries were considered by presidents, professors, and students to be tangential to the educational mission of the college, but with changes in philosophy toward research and teaching in the late nineteenth century the academic

library became more central to the goals of the institution. The need for more research materials started the drive at universities for massive collections of books and journals. Some of the prestige colleges and universities soon began to amass large collections of materials, with Harvard University leading the way. A large library became an indicator of the quality of the institution. By the beginning of the 1930s, about fifty institutions had formed large research libraries. These libraries, and a number of others in the postwar era, have become the trendsetters for the rest of the nation's academic libraries.

The nature of large research collections has changed during the course of the century. Early collections favored the humanities and the social sciences over the sciences because of the scholarly interests of the faculty and the lack of publications on scientific topics. World War II and the Cold War changed all this, with the federal government intervening with large grants for research and development in the sciences and technology. Academic libraries supplied the new demand for these types of materials simply by acquiring them, along with the others that they had been collecting. Large research libraries soon had collections in the millions of volumes. Yet the demand on libraries by faculty and students has expanded beyond the capacity of even the largest collections.

Now the issue has become whether to continue the building of always larger collections or to improve access to existing collections. Most of the large academic libraries are attempting to combine both approaches, but library administrators are encountering political problems from the teaching faculty on both sides of this issue. Smaller research libraries must choose between the two approaches because they are unable to acquire the funding for both.

2. *Despite academic libraries' matching or exceeding the universities in responding to the needs of the "information revolution," the role of academic librarians in the new world of information science remains uncertain.* The computer has had a dramatic impact on both the university and the academic library since its beginnings in the 1960s. While the academic world approached computers with interest for both academic and administrative reasons, it was not until the advent of the microcomputer that higher education has become totally committed to the computer. Large mainframe computers have always been considered important to the functioning of the research mission of the university, but now the microcomputer has reached down to the lowest faculty ranks, so that every faculty member may have access to a microcomputer before the turn of the century.

The academic library was an early candidate for computer applications because libraries were labor intensive and had many repetitive tasks. Library administrators were able to convince campus leaders that library automation could be justified as a "cost cutter," especially on personnel expenses. This initial expectation proved incorrect because rather than cutting costs significantly, computers improved library productivity. However, only a few libraries experimented with developing their own computer systems. Most libraries waited for others to develop systems before "buying into them." More and more academic libraries have adopted automated systems, but the future of computer development is hindered by its costs. University administrators are still reluctant to accept an unending demand for information services as a fact of life in the library. Progress on new systems will depend more on campus politics than on developments in the computer field.

The rivalry between the computer center and the academic library over the provision of information science is yet to be resolved. Librarians want to participate in the world of information science, but full participation depends on acceptance of their role by the academic community. This acceptance, moreover, has yet to be earned by academic librarians as they continue to perform in traditional patterns. Efforts to combine computer centers and academic libraries have therefore met with mixed success. Library leaders envisage the combined information science model as either a partnership or under library auspices, but it is not certain that the library will not come under a computer/information-science czar instead.

The easy part of library automation is over and now comes the hard part of active involvement in decision making on information-science issues.

3. *The academic library is receiving proportionally less and less of the resources of the university at a time when more and more demands are being made on it.*   The inability of universities to keep up with inflation in general and, specifically, in book and journal publishing over the last decade or so has had a detrimental impact on their libraries. Fiscal policies of the federal government, together with publishing trends, have produced a higher inflation rate for books and journals than for the economy as a whole. Although study after study has documented this fact, no one has initiated steps to correct the problem. (The only "solution" has been an impractical proposal to spend more money— at a time when university funds are in short supply.) Sharp debates between publishers and librarians have accomplished nothing, except to show the two sides of the issue. Efforts to hold serial collections steady have resulted in a drastic drop in the acquisition of monographs, and this has caused discontent in humanities and social sciences faculties, which depend on such materials for their research and teaching.

Caught between cancelling serials or reducing the number of mono-graphs, academic librarians have experienced considerable criticism for either action. Librarians believe that academic libraries have been given insufficient financial resources by their institutions to accomplish the job that the library has been given.

On the eve of the next big push into the information age, academic libraries find themselves lacking the financial resources to acquire the hardware and to access the new databases produced by technology. Busi-ness may count seven years as the life span of a computer system, but libraries have found it to be closer to five years for a new generation of systems. Therefore, using five years as their standard, academic libraries range from one to two generations behind the cutting edge of computer systems development. Computer centers average about one generation behind, as they too must come up with the huge capital investment to purchase equipment and software. Although the library was one of the first units in the university to use computer technology, the computer center now has the priority for expensive new systems. The extent to which budgets can absorb outlays for new systems for the library is a real conundrum, as universities either cannot or will not provide the necessary funding. Unless some new type of funding can be obtained for the new technology, this problem will only worsen.

4. *University administrators have little understanding of the func-tions of the library, and little time or energy to learn.* The benefits of the library and its role in the research and teaching mission of the uni-versity are often acknowledged by upper-level university administrators, but they have displayed little inclination, in the past or in the present, to support the library in its competition with other units for scarce funding. Part of the reason is that the academic library has always had a separate existence, and these administrators have little understanding of how it operates. Library directors and librarians have done a poor job in ed-ucating their academic counterparts in the university about the library. The library seems to rate attention from administrators only in times of financial or personnel crisis.

Librarians have cherished the library's autonomy, but it has been purchased at the exorbitant price of benign neglect. Two much atten-tion has been paid by library leaders to managing the library efficiently and not enough energy has been given to educating university leaders about the library. These leaders, however, need help from the rank-and-file librarians, who have the reasonable obligation to advance the cause of the library at every opportunity. This means that academic librari-ans have to create a high profile on campus by participating in faculty activities—senates and committees, as well as working with top schol-ars on research projects. Recruitment of high-quality individuals into academic librarianship is implied in this approach.

Library literature is full of ideas about the role of the academic library in the new information age, but these ideas have been addressed mostly to the already convinced librarian audience. Failure to commu-nicate these ideas to campus political leaders has real dangers in that university leaders may pick representatives from the higher-profile com-puter center to manage the information flow in the electronic journal age. If this happens, librarians will retain nothing but an archival function, and be even more isolated than before.

5. *The teaching faculty is divided between two types of library supporters: advocates of large collections and advocates of access to information.* Academic libraries are caught in the middle of the ongo-ing debate on the importance of applied versus liberal arts education. Fifty years ago this problem was not so apparent, because the consensus was on the primacy of a liberal arts education. Nowadays the emphasis has shifted toward the applied professions but not without protestations from adherents of the old order. This controversy takes the form in the academic library of a debate between access to current information or to large collections of books and journals. Engineering, medicine, business, law, and similar professions have opted for access to current information. Conversely, the traditional disciplines of history, English literature, political science, and the other humanities and social sciences still lobby for large collections of research materials. Thus academic librarians, caught in the middle of these conflicting demands, tend to be more sympathetic to the access side, because this side is closer to where librarians feel their future will be. The problem is that much of the political power in the university still resides on the side of the liberal arts. Moreover, the humanities faculty is vociferous in its demand for comprehensive collections for research. For them, resource sharing is not a substitute for large collections of books and journals.

Academic libraries will nevertheless have to take a middle-ground approach, or suffer the consequences. Many library leaders want the profession to take the "high road" to the information age by seizing on access as the key. Collection-development librarians, however, know that financial resources for such a strategy are lacking, and political pressures from unhappy faculty members will be directed against the library. Universities have always been conservative organizations, slow to opt for change, and the library proceeds at about the same pace. The library must make every effort to prepare for the information age, but campus political realities will have to be observed. These realities will be most apparent in efforts to obtain funding for further library technology.

   6. *The teaching faculty is lukewarm toward faculty status for librarians, but also has reservations about all applied disciplines.* Faculty status for academic librarians is one of the key components if the library is to operate successfully in the academic environment. The teaching faculty, however, has a proprietary attitude toward its rights and responsibilities. Faculty status, after all, was gained only after a long battle of individual professors and the American Association of University Professors (AAUP) against colleges and universities in the early twentieth century, and the teaching faculty is reluctant to extend these hard-won rights and responsibilities. Internal divisions between the traditional disciplines and the newer applied disciplines, which are openly displayed on most campuses, only reinforce faculty fears about their prerogatives. These disputes appear whenever the issues of curriculum, tenure, and status arise.

   Academic librarians have been one of the latecomers into the ranks of the applied professions, so they fall into the middle of the traditional-versus-applied controversy. Moreover, academic librarians have the misfortune to have no clearly defined teaching responsibilities. Librarians may teach in bibliographic instruction sessions, or even in the classroom, but teaching is not considered an essential part of their job responsibilities. These two factors have made faculty status for academic librarians a debatable issue.

   My personal experience is that only about 20 percent of the teaching faculty actively opposes faculty status for librarians, but it can be a very vocal minority. Danger looms when one of this 20 percent gets into a position of administrative responsibility at the university level. This individual can have a devastating impact on the library, regardless of what status librarians have in the institution. The other 80 percent of the teaching faculty is divided into approximately 60 percent who are neutral on the issue and 20 percent who support faculty status. These faculty members fluctuate from backing library initiatives to complete neutrality. Thus it is understandable why, with such lukewarm support, academic librarians are uneasy in their relationship with the teaching faculty.

   7. *Academic librarians have little understanding of the academic and administrative sides of the university.* Academic librarians have tended to overestimate the monolithic nature of the teaching faculty. They have extrapolated the behavior of *all* faculty from those whom they have come into contact with in the library. Professors who use the library

are some of the most dynamic and productive scholars on the campus; they are engaged both in teaching and research. Librarians only rarely have contact with the other, less productive members of the teaching faculty. Although the latter tend to restrict their activities to their offices and the classroom, they still play an active role in campus politics. Other disciplines also have few of their faculty using library facilities as these professors confine their research activities to laboratories or field experiments. Research on academic behavior has documented the fact that, on every teaching faculty, there are individuals who don't teach, don't do research, and don't provide service. Academic librarians, unfortunately, not aware of this, have compared themselves to an ideal standard and found themselves wanting. A more realistic attitude is for academic librarians to aim for the high end of the middle of academic standards, but to encourage the development of academic "stars" on the library faculty.

This misunderstanding of the academic side of the university extends to librarians' misconceptions about the administrative side. Even though many librarians perceive the difference between the rhetoric about the importance of the library and the reality of insufficient financial resources, this conflict between rhetoric and reality confuses some librarians because they are convinced that the library is making a positive contribution to the educational mission of the university. In short, librarians are going to have to learn to advance their own interests before they can prosper in the academic environment.

Twenty years ago, library leaders were passive during negotiations over the control of computer centers, and they lost the opportunity to have a say in their development. Similar passivity may be fatal in the future in a similar scenario. It is imperative for librarians to have a high profile on campus; otherwise, administrators will continue to pursue out-of-sight, out-of-mind policies.

8. *Academic librarians depend too much on the university librarian to protect them in the political arena of the university.* The university has an active political life, as does any other organization. Although participation in campus politics is recognized by all units as necessary for academic survival, academic librarians have been fearful to enter this arena. Somehow, they think, politics is demeaning, and the unfounded feeling among librarians is that the library will be rewarded, as it so richly deserves. Library directors, after all, are hired to represent the library, and it is their responsibility to see that the library gets its fair share. This attitude, and the general ineptness of library leadership, has resulted in the academic library's gradually losing its predominant role

in the university. For the most part, library directors are no more able to influence campus policy than individual librarians because neither group has realized the importance of constant interaction with campus leaders. Those library administrators who have mastered this behavior are some of the most successful of their brethren, but the record shows that there are not enough of them around. At one time the academic library could command total recognition of its role as the sole provider of information on campus, but now it has a serious rival, the computer center, as well as off-campus, private information networks. Efforts are now being made to regain the lost ground by allying with these rivals, but it may be too late.

Academic librarians can no longer leave the responsibility for the well-being of the library in the hands of one person. Too often, this individual is neutralized by coming in as an outsider or depending too much on personal relations with university administrators and faculty. Low-profile, rank-and-file librarians have likewise hurt the library when it comes to persuading policy leaders to allocate funds for materials and equipment.

9. *Some type of faculty status is imperative for academic librarians in the information age.*   Considerable debate has taken place over the last few decades on the desirability of faculty status for academic librarians. Various proposals have been advanced, such as unionization, separate status, and civil service, but none of them resolves the dilemma of librarians' working with the teaching faculty. The teaching faculty is jealous of its prerogatives, and will always be reluctant to accept any unit that approaches it as separate but equal. When a delegation of librarians approached representatives from the faculty senate at the University of Iowa in the late 1970s about faculty status for themselves, they received a chilly reception and were told that it was possible only if librarians were willing to meet research and publication standards for tenure. Unwillingness to accept this challenge has meant that librarians at Iowa have a separate rank, but they have been relegated to the campus status of scientific researchers.

Academic librarians have to be either similar to or profoundly different from the teaching faculty in form and function. Over the next decade or so, academic librarians will have both options available to them because of the advent of the information age. As more librarians become information specialists (rather than reference or cataloging librarians), the opportunity to elevate the status of librarians will appear. It is at this time that the decision on what direction academic librarians will go will have already been decided by others in the academic community. In the meantime academic librarians will have had to advance themselves, or they will be listed with the also-rans.

Research and publications are the lifeblood of any discipline. However, librarianship is one of the few disciplines in which nearly a third of its literature is provided by "experts" outside the profession. Besides the benefits of faculty status, research and publication are also the means for the library profession to form its own agenda for the future. Some critics have complained about weaknesses in the content and methodology of library research, and such criticism is not without merit, but criticism is easy whereas improving the quality and quantity of library scholarship is not. All academic librarians have the responsibility to elevate research and publication standards because each of us benefits in both the short and the long term. Freedom from the restraints of narrow scholarship is a strength, but inability to establish a research methodology is a weakness. Thus faculty status gives the librarian an "excuse" to do the things most beneficial both for career advancement and his or her profession.

My experience has been that librarians can only work effectively with the teaching faculty as equal partners in scholarship. Equality means that academic librarians have to function as closely as possible to the standards of the teaching faculty.

10. *Elevation of the library profession is a responsibility of all academic librarians.* Too often, responsibility for the image of the library profession has been left to library leaders and library educators; individual responsibility has been relegated to job performance or personal professional development. The library profession therefore suffers an image problem that it needs to address. Librarianship has been perceived as a second-class profession because of its low pay, low status, and gender imbalance. Women hold 65 percent of academic library positions, and this will probably never change more than a few percentage points, yet this can be a source of strength rather than a perceived weakness. Librarianship can serve as a model for other professions by *utilizing* this source of talent. Low salary and low status will become less important factors once the problem of equal access for women to upper-level management has been solved.

The means by which librarians can elevate their profession resides in a combination of mentoring and networking. Academic librarians have a vested interest in developing talent whenever and wherever it occurs. Senior librarians, moreover, have the responsibility of developing younger librarians into leaders of the profession, much as businesses develop leaders in the private sector of the economy. This means advising librarians at early stages of their careers and collaborating with them on research projects at later stages. The sciences developed the "invisible college" concept, forming teams around certain scientific problems, and librarians need to adopt and adapt this concept for librarianship. Professional associations, such as the American Library Association (ALA) or the Association of College and Research Libraries (ACRL), are good places to further mentoring and networking. Many library leaders learned this years ago, but many other librarians need to learn more about the benefits of professional activities.

Mentoring and networking will allow peer relationships to develop, and career opportunities will expand. Similar networks have existed in the past (and some of them were called old-boy networks). The need is to broaden this concept to include all elements of the library profession. In this scenario senior librarians, both men and women, would mentor young librarians, preparing them for future leadership positions. This mentoring would gradually change into a chain of peer relationships that would form "invisible colleges" for the study of library problems. The end result would be a stronger profession for the information age.

These propositions give an indication of the close relationship between the academic library and the university, a relationship that has withstood changes in the past and will do so in the future. The difference is that technology and people change at different rates. Technological change occurs at a faster rate than university leaders and academic librarians can assimilate. The latter, moreover, have to understand their academic environment before they can plan for change that might transform it. Library leaders have the responsibility to expand the debate over the future of the academic library to include others in the academic community. They also must become more attuned to campus politics, or the academic library will be excluded from future campus planning. These leaders therefore need all the help they can get from the lower ranks. Again, it is the responsibility of all academic librarians to advance their profession as well as their personal careers.

APPENDIX

Definitions

T HE 1987 CARNEGIE CLASSIFICATION includes all colleges and universities in the United States listed in the 1985–86 *Higher Education General Information Survey of Institutional Characteristics*. It groups institutions into categories on the basis of the level of degree offered—ranging from prebaccalaureate to the doctorate—and the comprehensiveness of their missions. The categories are as follows:

Research Universities I: These institutions offer a full range of baccalaureate programs, are committed to graduate education through the doctorate degree, and give high priority to research. They receive annually at least $33.5 million in federal support and award at least 50 Ph.D. degrees each year.

Research Universities II: These institutions offer a full range of baccalaureate programs, are committed to graduate education through the

Source: Carnegie Foundation for the Advancement of Teaching, *A Classification of Institution of Higher Education*, rev. ed., (Princeton, N.J.: Carnegie Foundation for the Advancement of Teaching, 1987), p. 7.

doctorate degree, and give high priority to research. They receive annually between $12.5 million and $33.5 million in federal support for research and development and award at least 50 Ph.D. degrees each year.

Doctorate-Granting Universities I: In addition to offering a full range of baccalaureate programs, the mission of these institutions includes a commitment to graduate education through the doctorate degree. They award at least 40 Ph.D. degrees annually in five or more academic disciplines.

Doctorate-Granting Universities II: In addition to offering a full range of baccalaureate programs, the mission of these institutions includes a commitment to graduate education through the doctorate degree. They award annually 20 or more Ph.D. degrees in at least one discipline or 10 or more Ph.D. degrees in three or more disciplines.

Comprehensive Universities and Colleges I: These institutions offer baccalaureate programs and, with few exceptions, graduate education through the master's degree. More than half of their baccalaureate degrees are awarded in two or more occupational or professional disciplines such as engineering or business administration. All of the institutions in this group enroll at least 2,500 students.

Comprehensive Universities and Colleges II: These institutions award more than half of their baccalaureate degrees in two or more occupational or professional disciplines, such as engineering or business administration, and many also offer graduate education through the masters degree. All of the colleges and universities in this group enroll between 1,500 and 2,500 students.

Liberal Arts Colleges I: These highly selective institutions are primarily undergraduate colleges that award more than half of their baccalaureate degrees in arts and science fields.

Liberal Arts Colleges II: These institutions are primarily undergraduate colleges that are less selective and award more than half of their degrees in liberal arts fields. This category also includes a group of colleges (identified with an asterisk) that award *less* than half of their degrees in liberal arts fields but, with fewer than 1,500 students, are too small to be considered comprehensive.

Two-Year Community, Junior and Technical Colleges: These institutions offer certificate or degree programs through the Associate of Arts level and, with few exceptions, offer no baccalaureate degrees.

BIBLIOGRAPHY

Books

Abbot, Andrew. *The System of Professions: An Essay on the Division of Expert Labor*. Chicago: University of Chicago Press, 1988.

Academic Librarianship: Yesterday, Today, and Tomorrow. Edited by Robert Stueart. New York: Neal-Schuman, 1982.

Academic Libraries by the Year 2000: Essays Honoring Jerrold Orne. Edited by Herbert Poole. New York: Bowker, 1977.

The Academic Library: Essays in Honor of Guy R. Lyle. Edited by Evan Ira Farber and Ruth Walling. Metuchen, N.J.: Scarecrow Press, 1974.

Access to Scholarly Information: Issues and Strategies. Edited by Sul H. Lee. Ann Arbor, Mich.: Pierian Press, 1985.

American Council on Education. *Graduate Education Today*. Washington, D.C.: American Council on Education, 1965.

———. *Higher Education in the United States*. Washington, D.C.: American Council on Education, 1965.

American Library Association. *ALA Survey*. Chicago: American Library Association, 1926.

The American University: A Public Administration Perspective. Edited by Clyde J. Wingfield. Dallas: Southern Methodist University Press, 1970.

Arnett, Trevor. *College and University Finance.* New York: General Education Board, 1922.

ASHE Reader on Finance in Higher Education. Edited by Larry L. Leslie and Richard E. Anderson. Lexington, Mass.: Ginn Press, 1986.

Association of Governing Boards of Universities and Colleges. *Composition of Governing Boards, 1985.* Washington, D.C.: Association of Governing Boards, 1986.

Atelsek, Frank J., and Irene L. Gomberg. *Tenure Practices at Four-Year Colleges and Universities.* Washington, D.C.: American Council on Education, 1980.

Axt, Richard G. *The Federal Government and Financing Higher Education.* New York: Columbia University Press, 1952.

Balderston, Frederick E. *Managing Today's University.* San Francisco: Jossey-Bass, 1974.

Bess, James L. *Collegiality and Bureaucracy in the Modern University.* New York: Teachers College Press, 1988.

Bloom, Allan. *The Closing of the American Mind: How Higher Education Has Failed Democracy and Impoverished the Souls of Today's Students.* New York: Simon and Schuster, 1987.

Bornheimer, Deane G., Gerald P. Burns, and Glenn S. Dumke. *The Faculty in Higher Education.* Danville, Ill.: Interstate, 1973.

Bowden, Henry L. *Boards of Trustees: Their Organization and Operation at Private Colleges and Universities.* Macon, Ga.: Mercer University Press, 1982.

Bowen, Howard R., and Jack H. Schuster. *American Professors: A National Resource Imperiled.* New York: Oxford University Press, 1986.

Brough, Kenneth J. *Scholar's Workshop: Evolving Conceptions of Library Service.* Urbana: University of Illinois Press, 1953.

Brown, William R. *Academic Politics.* University, Ala.: University of Alabama Press, 1982.

Brubacher, John S., and Willis Rudy. *Higher Education in Transition: A History of American Colleges and Universities, 1636–1976.* 3d ed. New York: Harper and Row, 1976.

Burke, Colin B. *American Collegiate Populations: A Test of the Traditional View.* New York: New York University Press, 1982.

Cahn, Steven M. *Saints and Scamps: Ethics in Academia.* Totowa, N.J.: Rowman and Littlefield, 1986.

Campus Computing Strategies. Edited by John M. McCredie. Dedford, Mass.: Digital Press, 1983.

Carnegie Foundation for the Advancement of Teaching. *A Classification of Institutions of Higher Education.* Berkeley, Calif.: Carnegie Commission on Higher Education, 1973.

―――. *A Classification of Institutions of Higher Education.* Rev. ed. Berkeley, Calif.: Carnegie Council on Policy Studies in Higher Education, 1976.

―――. *A Classification of Institutions of Higher Education.* Rev. ed. Princeton, N.J.: Carnegie Foundation for the Advancement of Teaching, 1987.

―――. *1984 Faculty Survey.* Princeton, N.J.: Carnegie Foundation for the Advancement of Teaching, 1984.

Caruthers, J. Kent, and Melvin Orwig. *Budgeting in Higher Education.* Washington, D.C.: American Association for Higher Education, 1979.

Clark, Burton R. *The Academic Life: Small Worlds, Different Worlds.* Princeton, N.J.: Carnegie Foundation for the Advancement of Teaching, 1987.

Cline, Hugh F., and Loraine T. Sinnott. *The Electronic Library: The Impact of Automation on Academic Libraries.* Lexington, Mass.: Lexington Books, 1983.

Cohn, Michael D., and James G. Marsh. *Leadership and Ambiguity: The American College President.* 2d ed. Boston: Harvard Business School Press, 1986.

Cummings, Martin M. *The Economics of Research Libraries.* Washington, D.C.: Council on Library Resources, 1986.

The Dilemma of the Deanship. Edited by Daniel E. Griffiths and Donald J. McCarty. Danville, Ill.: Interstate, 1980.

Dressel, Paul L. *Administrative Leadership: Effective and Responsible Decision Making in Higher Education.* San Francisco: Jossey-Bass, 1981.

Dressel, Paul L., F. Craig Johanson, and Philip M. Marcus. *The Confidence Crisis.* San Francisco: Jossey-Bass, 1970.

Efficient College Management. Edited by William W. Jellema. San Francisco: Jossey-Bass, 1972.

Energies for Transition. Edited by Danuta A. Nitecki. Chicago: Association of College and Research Libraries, 1986.

Evaluation of Management and Planning Systems. Edited by Nick L. Poulton. San Francisco: Jossey-Bass, 1981.

Ferrari, Michael R. *Profiles of American College Presidents*. East Lansing, Mich.: Michigan State University Graduate School of Business Administration, 1970.

Garvin, David A. *The Economics of University Behavior*. New York: Academic Press, 1980.

Geiger, Roger L. *To Advance Knowledge: The Growth of American Research Universities, 1900–1940*. New York: Oxford University Press, 1986.

Gerould, J. T. *Statistics of University Libraries*. Princeton, N.J.: Princeton University Press, 1913.

Governing Academic Organizations: New Problems, New Perspectives. Edited by Gary L. Riley and J. Victor Baldridge. Berkeley, Calif.: McCutchan, 1977.

Grant, W. Vance, and Thomas D. Snyder. *Digest of Education Statistics, 1985–86*. Washington, D.C.: U.S. Government Printing Office, 1986.

Hackett, E. Byrne. *Trade Bibliography in the United States in the Nineteenth Century*. New York: Brick Row Book Shop, 1939.

Hamlin, Arthur T. *The University Library in the United States: Its Origins and Development*. Philadelphia: University of Pennsylvania Press, 1981.

Harding, Thomas S. *The College Literary Societies: Their Contribution to Higher Education in the United States, 1815–1876*. New York: Pageant Press, 1971.

Harvey, L. James. *Managing Colleges and Universities by Objective: A Concise Guide to Understanding and Implementing MBO in Higher Education*. Littleton, Colo.: Ireland Educational Corporation, 1976.

———. *Zerobase Budgeting in Colleges and Universities*. Littleton, Colo.: Ireland Educational Corporation, 1977.

Helsabeck, Robert E. *The Compound System: A Conceptual Framework for Effective Decisionmaking in Colleges*. Berkeley, Calif.: Center for Research and Development in Higher Education, 1973.

Hofstadter, Richard, and C. DeWitt Hardy. *The Development and Scope of Higher Education in the United States*. New York: Columbia University Press, 1952.

Hyatt, James A., and Aurora A. Santiago. *University Libraries in Transition*. Washington, D.C.: NACUBO, 1987.

Irvine, Betty Jo. *Sex Segregation in Librarianship: Demographic and Career Patterns of Academic Library Administrators*. Westport, Conn.: Greenwood Press, 1985.

Issues in Academic Librarianship: Views and Case Studies for the 1980s and 1990s. Edited by Peter Spyers-Duran and Thomas W. Mann. Westport, Conn.: Greenwood Press, 1985.

Johnson, Elmer. *A History of Libraries in the Western World*. New York: Scarecrow Press, 1965.

Key Papers in Information Science. Edited by Belver C. Griffith. New York: Knowledge Industry Publications, 1980.

Lancaster, F. Wilfrid. *Toward Paperless Information Systems*. New York: Academic Press, 1978.

Leadership Roles of Chief Academic Officers. Edited by David G. Brown. San Francisco: Jossey-Bass, 1984.

Lehmann-Haupt, Helmut. *The Book in America: A History of the Making and Selling of Books in the United States*. New York: Bowker, 1951.

Libraries and the Search for Academic Excellence. Edited by Patricia Senn Breivik and Robert Wedgeworth. Metuchen, N.J.: Scarecrow Press, 1988.

The Library in the University. Edited by John David Marshall. Hamden, Conn.: Shoe String Press, 1979.

Lyle, Guy R. *The President, the Professor, and the College Library*. New York: Wilson, 1963.

Massman, Virgil F. *Faculty Status for Librarians*. Metuchen, N.J.: Scarecrow Press, 1972.

McGrath, Earl James. *The Evolution of Administrative Offices in Institutions of Higher Education in the United States from 1860 to 1933*. Chicago: University of Chicago Libraries, 1938.

McVey, Frank L., and Raymond M. Hughes. *Problems of College and University Administration*. Ames: Iowa State College Press, 1952.

Metzger, Walter P. *Academic Freedom in the Age of the University*. New York: Columbia University Press, 1955.

Millett, John D. *The Academic Community: An Organizational Essay*. New York: McGraw-Hill, 1962.

———. *Politics and Higher Education*. University, Ala.: University of Alabama Press, 1974.

Molyneux, Robert E. *The Gerould Statistics, 1907/08–1961/62*. Washington, D.C.: Association of Research Libraries, 1986.

Moran, Barbara B. *Academic Libraries: The Changing Knowledge Centers of Colleges and Universities*. Washington, D.C.: Association for the Study of Higher Education, 1984.

Morton, Herbert C., Anne J. Price, and Robert Cameron Mitchell. *The ACLS Survey of Scholars: Final Report of Views on Publications, Computers and Libraries*. Washington, D.C.: Office of Scholarly Communication and Technology, American Council of Learned Societies, 1989.

Mott, Frank Luther. *A History of American Magazines, (1885–1905)*. Cambridge, Mass.: Belknap Press, 1957.

Nauratil, Marcia J. *The Alienated Librarian*. New York: Greenwood Press, 1989.

New Horizons for Academic Libraries. Edited by Robert D. Stueart and Richard D. Johnson. New York: K. G. Saur, 1979.

O'Harra, Downing Palmer. "Book Publishing in the United States, 1860 to 1901." M.A. thesis, University of Illinois, 1928.

O'Reilly, Robert C., and Marjorie I. O'Reilly. *Librarians and Labor Relations: Employment under Union Contracts*. Westport, Conn.: Greenwood Press, 1981.

Orlans, Harold. *The Effects of Federal Programs on Higher Education: A Study of 36 Universities and Colleges*. Washington, D.C.: Brookings Institution, 1962.

Osburn, Charles B. *Academic Research and Library Resources: Changing Patterns in America*. Westport, Conn.: Greenwood Press, 1979.

Research Librarianship: Essays in Honor of Robert B. Downs. Edited by Jerrold Orne. New York: Bowker, 1971.

Rider, Fremont. *The Scholar and the Future of the Research Library: A Problem and Its Solution*. New York: Hadham Press, 1944.

Rudolph, Frederick. *The American College and University: A History*. New York: Knopf, 1965.

Schmidt, George P. *The Old Time College President*. New York: Columbia University Press, 1930.

Scholarly Communication: The Report of the National Enquiry. Baltimore: Johns Hopkins University Press, 1979.

Shiflett, Orvin Lee. *Origins of American Academic Librarianship*. Norwood, N.J.: Ablex, 1981.

Shils, Edward. *The Academic Ethic*. Chicago: University of Chicago Press, 1983.

Shipton, Clifford K. *American Bibliography of Charles Evans: A Chronological Dictionary of All Books, Pamphlets, and Periodical Publications Printed in the United States of America from the*

Genesis of Printing in 1639 Down to and Including the Year 1800 with Bibliographical and Biographical Notes. Worcester, Mass.: American Antiquarian Society, 1955.

Shores, Louis. *Origins of the American College Library.* Nashville, Tenn.: George Peabody College Press, 1934.

Smith, Eldred. *The Librarian, the Scholar, and the Future of the Research Library.* New York: Greenwood Press, 1990.

Snyder, Thomas D. *Digest of Education Statistics, 1987.* Washington, D.C.: Center for Education Statistics, 1987.

———. *Digest of Education Statistics, 1989.* Washington, D.C.: Center for Education Statistics, 1989.

Sortie, Catharine Penniman. "What Contributions Did the American College Society Make to the College Library: A Supplementary Chapter in the History of the American College Library." M.A. thesis, Columbia University, 1938.

The Status of Women in Librarianship: Historical, Sociological, and Economic Issues. Edited by Kathleen M. Heim. New York: Neal-Schuman, 1983.

Taylor, Bettey W., Elizabeth B. Mann, and Robert J. Munro. *The Twenty-first Century: Technology's Impact on Academic Research and Law Libraries.* Boston: Hall, 1988.

Technology for the '90s: Microcomputers in Libraries. Edited by Nancy Melin Nelson. Westport, Conn.: Meckler, 1990.

Tebbel, John. *A History of Book Publishing in the United States.* 4 vols. New York: Bowker, 1972–81.

Tewksbury, Donald G. *The Founding of American Colleges and Universities before the Civil War.* Hamden, Conn.: Archon Books, 1965.

Thomison, Dennis. *A History of the American Library Association.* Chicago: American Library Association, 1978.

Thwing, Charles F. *The American University and the German University.* New York: Appleton, 1928.

———. *A History of Higher Education in America.* New York: Appleton, 1906.

Tucker, Allan, and Robert A. Bryan. *The Academic Dean: Dove, Dragon and Diplomat.* New York: Macmillan, 1988.

U.S. Bureau of Statistics. *Historical Statistics of the United States, Colonial Times to 1970.* Washington, D.C.: Bureau of the Census, 1975.

Universities, Information Technology, and Academic Libraries: The Next Twenty Years. Edited by Robert M. Hayes. Norwood, N.J.: Ablex, 1986.

The University an an Organization. Edited by James A. Perkins. New York: McGraw-Hill, 1983.

University Library History: An International Review. Edited by James Thompson. New York: Saur, 1980.

Veyser, Laurence R. *The Emergence of the American University.* Chicago: University of Chicago Press, 1965.

Weber, Max. *The Theory of Social and Economic Organization.* New York: Free Press, 1964.

Whitehead, Alfred North. *Adventures in Ideas.* New York: Macmillan, 1933.

Wiegand, Wayne A. *The Politics of an Emerging Profession: The American Library Association, 1876–1917.* New York: Greenwood Press, 1986.

Wilson, Logan. *American Academics: Then and Now.* New York: Oxford University Press, 1979.

Women and Library Management: Theories, Skills and Values. Edited by Darlene E. Weingard. Ann Arbor, Mich.: Pierian Press, 1982.

Zuboff, Shoshana. *In the Age of the Smart Machine.* New York: Basic Books, 1988.

Articles

Altick, Richard D. "The Scholar's Paradise." *College and Research Libraries* 15 (October 1954) 4:375–82.

Anderson, Dorothy J. "Comparative Career Profiles of Academic Librarians: Are Leaders Different?" *Journal of Academic Librarianship* 10 (January 1985) 6:326–32.

Atkinson, Hugh C. "A Brief for the Other Side." *Journal of Academic Librarianship* 9 (September 1983) 4:200–201.

Axford, H. William. "The Three Faces of Eve; or the Identity of Academic Librarianship: A Symposium." *Journal of Academic Librarianship* 2 (January 1977) 6:276–85.

Bailey Stephen K. "The Future of College and Research Libraries." *College and Research Libraries* 39 (January 1978) 1:4–9.

Bartlett, Richard A. "The College Library and the Recruiting Process." *Journal of Library History* 4 (July 1969) 3:253–55.

Barzun, Jacques. "The Scholar Looks at the Library." *College and Research Libraries* 7 (April 1946) 2:113–17.

Battin, Patricia. "The Library: Center of the Restructured University." *College and Research Libraries* 45 (May 1984) 3:170–76.

Bechtel, Joan M. "Academic Professional Status: An Alternative for Librarians." *Journal of Academic Librarianship* 11 (November 1985) 5:289–92.

Bergen, Daniel Patrick. "Librarians and the Bipolarization of the Academic Enterprise." *College and Research Libraries* 24 (November 1963) 6:467–80.

Birnbaum, Robert. "Consistency and Diversity in the Goals of Campus Leaders." *Review of Higher Education* 12 (Fall 1988) 1:17–30.

Blanchard, J. R. "Departmental Libraries in Divisional Plan University Libraries." *College and Research Libraries* 14 (July 1953) 3:243–48.

Blankenship, W. C. "Head Librarians: How Many Men? How Many Women?" *College and Research Libraries* 28 (January 1967) 1:41–48.

Bodi, Sonia. "Critical Thinking and Bibliographic Instruction: The Relationship." *Journal of Academic Librarianship* 14 (July 1988) 3:150–53.

Boice, Robert, Jordan M. Scepanski, and Wayne Wilson. "Librarians and Faculty Members: Coping with Pressures to Publish." *College and Research Libraries* (November 1987) 6:494–503.

Bonner, Thomas N. "The Unintended Revolution in America's Colleges since 1940." *Change* 18 (September–October 1986) 5:44–51.

Bottle, R. T., and E. N. Efthimiadis. "Library and Information Science Literature: Authorship and Growth Patterns." *Journal of Information Science: Principles and Practice* 9 (1984) 3:107–16.

Briscoe, Peter, et al. "Ashurbanipal's Enduring Archetype: Thought on the Library's Role in the Future." *College and Research Libraries* 47 (March 1986) 2:121–26.

Broadbent, Elaine. "A Study of Humanities Faculty Library Information Seeking Behavior." *Cataloging and Classification Quarterly* 6 (Spring 1986) 3:23–37.

Brock, Clifton. "The Rising Tide: Some Implications for College and University Libraries." *College and Research Libraries* 19 (January 1958) 1:12–16.

Brown, Nancy A. "Managing the Coexistence of Hierarchical and Collegial Governance Structure." *College and Research Libraries* 46 (November 1985) 6:478–82.

Bruder, Isabelle. "The Library of the Future—Now." *Electronic Learning* 7 (March 1988) 6:22.

Brundin, Robert E. "Justin Winsor of Harvard and the Liberalizing of the College Library." *Journal of Library History* 10 (January 1975): 57–70.

Brunelle, Eugene. "New Learning, New Libraries, New Librarians." *Journal of Academic Librarianship* 1 (November 1975) 5:327–40.

Bryant, Douglas W. "Centralization and Decentralization in Academic Libraries: A Symposium." *College and Research Libraries* 22 (September 1961) 5:328–34.

Buckland, Michael K. "Foundations of Academic Librarianship." *College and Research Libraries* 50 (July 1989) 4:389–95.

Budd, John. "Publication in Library and Information Science: The State of the Literature." *Library Journal* (1 September 1985): 125–31.

Bundy, Mary Lee. "Conflict in Libraries." *College and Research Libraries* 27 (July 1966) 4:253–60.

Burke, Dolores, L. "The Academic Marketplace in the 1980s: Appointment and Termination of Assistant Professors." *Review of Higher Education* 10 (Spring 1987) 3:199–214.

Cahners Publishing Company. "Upgrading Systems, Software, and Microcomputers." *Library Journal* 114 (15 September 1989): 56–59.

Campbell, Jerry D. "An Administrator's View of the Negative Impact of Tenure on Librarians." *Technical Services Quarterly* 6 (1988) 2:3–9.

Carnegie Foundation for the Advancement of Teaching. "The Faculty: Deeply Troubled." *Change* (September–October 1985): 31–34.

———. "The Satisfied Faculty." *Change* (March–April 1986): 31–34.

———. "The Ups and Downs of Federal Funding for R&D." *Change* (November–December 1987) 6:35–39.

Carrigan, Dennis P. "The Political Economy of the Academic Library," *College and Research Libraries* 49 (July 1988) 4:325–31.

Cassata, Mary B. "Teach-in: The Academic Librarian's Key to Status?" *College and Research Libraries* 31 (January 1970) 1:22–27.

Cimbala, Diane J. "The Scholarly Information Center: An Organizational Model." *College and Research Libraries* 48 (September 1987) 5:393–97.

Clark, Thomas D. "Building Libraries in the Early Ohio Valley." *Journal of Library History* 6 (April 1971) 2:101–19.

Clayton, Howard. "The American College Library, 1800–1860." *Journal of Library History* 3 (April 1968) 2:120–37.

Cohen, Arthur M., and John Lombardi. "Can the Community College Survive Success?" *Change* 11 (November–December 1979) 8:24–27.

Collier, Douglas J. "Making Financial Assessment More Meaningful." *New Directions in Higher Education* 38 (June 1982) 2:85–94.

Commerton, B. Anne. "Building Faculty/Library Relationships: Forging the Bond." *Bookmark* 45 (Fall 1986) 1:17–20.

Crossland, Fred E. "Preparing for the 1980s: Learning to Cope with a Downward Slope." *Change* 12 (July–August 1980) 5:18–25.

Culley, James D., Denis F. Healy, and Kermit G. Cudd. "Business Students and the University Library: An Overlooked Element in the Business Curriculum." *Journal of Academic Librarianship* 2 (January 1977) 6:293–96.

Dane, Chase. "The Need for a Research Program in Library Problems." *College and Research Libraries* 16 (January 1955) 1:20–23.

Dawson, John M. "Not Too Academic." *College and Research Libraries* 27 (January 1966) 1:37–39.

Divay, Gaby, Ada M. Ducas, and Nicole Michaud-Oystryk. "Faculty Perceptions of Librarians at the University of Manitoba." *College and Research Libraries* 48 (January 1987) 1:27–35.

Dix, William. "The Financing of the Research Library." *College and Research Libraries* 35 (July 1974) 4:252–58.

Dougherty, Richard M. "Libraries and Computing Centers: A Blueprint for Collaboration." *College and Research Libraries* 48 (July 1987) 4:289–96.

Douglas, Joel M. "Faculty Collective Bargaining in the Aftermath of Yeshiva." *Change* 13 (March 1981) 2:36–43.

Downs, Robert B. "Academic Status for University Librarians—A New Approach." *College and Research Libraries* 7 (January 1946) 1:6–9.

———. "Are College and University Librarians Academic?" *College and Research Libraries* 15 (January 1954) 1:9–14.

———. "The Current Status of University Library Staff." *College and Research Libraries* 18 (September 1957) 5:375–85.

Downs, Robert B., and Robert F. Delzell. "Professional Duties in University Libraries." *College and Research Libraries* 26 (January 1965) 1:30–39.

Dressel, Paul L. "Mission, Organization, and Leadership." *Journal of Higher Education* 58 (January–February 1987) 1:101–9.

Eisenberg, Daniel. "Problems of the Paperless Book." *Scholarly Publishing* 21 (October 1989) 1:11–26.

Ellsworth, Ralph E. "Trends in University Expenditures for Library Resources and for Total Educational Purposes, 1921–41." *Library Quarterly* 14 (January 1944) 1:1–8.

English, Thomas G. "Administrators' Views of Library Personnel Status." *College and Research Libraries* 45 (May 1984) 3:189–95.

———. "Librarian Status in the Eighty-nine U.S. Academic Institutions of the Association of Research Libraries: 1982." *College and Research Libraries* 44 (May 1983) 3:199–211.

Evan, Luther H. "The Librarians' Agenda of Unfinished Business." *College and Research Libraries* 12 (October 1951) 4:309–13.

Evans, G. Edward, and Benedict Rugaas. "Another Look at Performance Appraisal in Libraries." *Journal of Library Administration* 3 (Summer 1982) 2:61–69.

Fields, Dennis C. "Library Management by Objectives: The Humane Way." *College and Research Libraries* 35 (September 1974) 5:344–49.

Finn, Chester E. "The Future of Education's Liberal Consensus." *Change* 12 (September 1980) 6:25–27.

Fisher, Francis Dummer. "Higher Education circa 2005: More Higher Learning, but Less College." *Change* 19 (January–February 1987) 1:40–46.

Fisher, James L. "Presidents Will Lead—If We Let Them." *NACUBO Business Officer* 18 (March 1985) 9:37–38.

Fleit, Linda H. "Computerizing America's Campuses: How Technology Is Changing Higher Education." *Electronic Learning* 6 (March 1987) 6:18–23.

Fox, Mary Frank, and Catherine A. Faver. "Independence and Cooperation in Research: The Motivations and Costs of Collaboration." *Journal of Higher Education* 55 (May–June 1984) 3:347–59.

Freedman, Mervin, and Nevitt Sanford. "The Faculty Member Yesterday and Today." *New Directions for Higher Education* 1 (Spring 1973): 1–9.

Gamble, Lynne E. "University Service: New Implications for Academic Librarians." *Journal of Academic Librarianship* 14 (January 1989) 6:344–47.

Gapen, D. Kaye. "Myths and Realities: University Libraries." *College and Research Libraries* 45 (September 1984) 5:350–61.

Getz, Malcolm. "More Benefits of Automation." *College and Research Libraries* 49 (November 1988) 6:534–44.

Gilman, Henry. "What the Scientist Expects of the Librarian." *College and Research Libraries* 8 (July 1947) 3:329–32.

Ginsburg, Sigmund G. "Understanding Administrators." *NACUBO Business Officer* 17 (June 1984) 12:26–27.

Gore, Daniel. "Zero Growth: When Is Not-Enough Enough? A Symposium." *Journal of Academic Librarianship* 1 (November 1975) 5:4–5.

Graham, Peter S. "Research Patterns and Research Libraries: What Should Change?" *College and Research Libraries* 50 (July 1989) 4:433–40.

Graziano, Eugene E. " 'Machine-Men' and Librarians: An Essay." *College and Research Libraries* 28 (November 1967) 6:403–6.

Grieder, Elmer M. "The Reorganization of the Stanford University Libraries." *College and Research Libraries* 13 (July 1952) 3:246–52.

Gross, Francis M. "Formula Budgeting and the Financing of Public Higher Education: Panacea or Nemesis for the 1980's?" *Association for Institutional Research Professional File* 3 (Fall 1979): 1–7.

Grossman, Robert J. "The Great Debate over Institutional Accountability." *College Board Review* 147 (Spring 1988): 4–11.

Grover, Robert, and Martha L. Hale. "The Role of the Librarian in Faculty Research." *College and Research Libraries* 49 (January 1988) 1:9–15.

Guskin, Alan E., Carla J. Stoffle, and Barbara E. Baruth. "Library Future Shock: The Microcomputer Revolution and the New Role of the Library." *College and Research Libraries* 45 (May 1984) 3:177–83.

Hacken, Richard D. "Tomorrow's Research Library: Vigor or Rigor Mortis?" *College and Research Libraries* 49 (November 1988) 6:485–93.

Hart, James D. "Search and Research: The Librarian and the Scholar." *College and Research Libraries* 19 (September 1958) 5:365–74.

Heffner, Ray L. "Zero Growth: When Is Not-Enough Enough? A Symposium." *Journal of Academic Librarianship* 1 (November 1975) 5:5–6.

Heinritz, Fred J. "Quantitative Management in Libraries." *College and Research Libraries* 31 (July 1970) 4:232–38.

Hendrick, Clyde. "The University Library in the Twenty-first Century." *College and Research Libraries* 47 (March 1986) 2:127–31.

Hernon, Peter. "Library Lectures and Their Evaluation: A Survey." *Journal of Academic Librarianship* 1 (July 1975) 3:14–18.

Herricks, Mary D., and N. Arvin Rush. "Early Literary Societies and Their Libraries in Colby College, 1824–78." *College and Research Libraries* 6 (December 1944) 1:58–63.

Hill, Fred E., and Robert Hauptman. "A New Perspective on Faculty Status." *College and Research Libraries* 47 (March 1986) 2:156–59.

Hoadley, Irene B. "The Role of Professionals in Technical Services." *Technical Services Quarterly* 6 (1988) 2:11–26.

Holicky, Bernard H. "Collection Development vs. Resource Sharing: The View from the Small Academic Library." *Journal of Academic Librarianship* 10 (July 1984) 3:146–47.

Holley, Edward G. "Academic Libraries in 1876." *College and Research Libraries* 37 (January 1976) 1:15–47.

_____. "Reaction to 'A Brief for Centralized Library Collections.'" *Journal of Academic Librarianship* 9 (September 1983) 4:201–2.

_____. "Defining the Academic Librarian." *College and Research Libraries* 46 (November 1985) 6:462–68.

Hosel, Harold V. "Academic Librarians and Faculty Status: A Role Stress-Job Satisfaction Perspective." *Journal of Library Administration* 5 (Fall 1984) 3:57–66.

Hunt, David Marshall, and Carol Michael. "Mentorship: A Career Training and Development Tool." *Journal of Library Administration* 5 (Spring 1984) 1:77–95.

Hunter, Deborah E., and George D. Kuh. "The 'Write Wing': Characteristics of Prolific Contributors to Higher Education Literature." *Journal of Higher Education* 58 (July–August 1987) 4:443–62.

Hyatt, James A. "Incentives and Disincentives for Effective Management." *NACUBO Business Officer* 18 (October 1984) 4:19–22.

Isaac, Frederick. "Librarian, Scholar, or Author? The Librarian's New Dilemma." *Journal of Academic Librarianship* 9 (September 1983) 4:216–20.

Jahoda, Gerald. "Planning Improved Library Service for Scientists in Universities." *College and Research Libraries* 28 (September 1967) 5:343–46.

Jenkins, William A. "The Role of the Chief Financial Officer in Large Public Universities." *NACUBO Business Officer* 18 (January 1983) 7:27–30.

Johnson, Edward R. "Financial Planning Needs of Publicly Supported Academic Libraries in the 1980s: Politics as Usual." *Journal of Library Administration* 3 (Fall–Winter 1982) 3,4:23–36.

Johnson, Marjorie. "Performance Appraisal of Librarians: A Survey." *College and Research Libraries* 33 (September 1972) 5:359–67.

Karr, Ronald Dale. "The Changing Profile of University Library Directors 1966–1981." *College and Research Libraries* 45 (July 1984) 4:282–86.

Kasten, Katherine Lewellan. "Tenure and Merit Pay as Rewards for Research, Teaching, and Service at a Research University." *Journal of Higher Education* 55 (July–August 1984) 4:500–514.

Kellar, Herbert A. "American Reference Libraries in the Postwar Era." *College and Research Libraries* 3 (September 1942) 4:293–302.

Kilpela, Raymond. "The University Library Committee." *College and Research Libraries* 29 (March 1968) 2:141–43.

Knapp, Patricia B. "The College Librarian: Sociology of a Professional Specialization." *College and Research Libraries* 16 (January 1955) 1:66–72.

Koenig, Michael E. D., and Victor Alperin. "ZBB and PPBS: What's Left Now That the Trendiness Has Gone?" *Drexel Library Quarterly* 21 (Summer 1985) 3:19–38.

Kong, Leslie M., and R. A. Goodfellow. "Charting a Career Path in the Information Professions." *College and Research Libraries* 49 (May 1988) 3:211–12.

Kopmeyer, Norman J. "Yeshiva Revisited: Alternative Remedies." *Footnotes* (Spring 1989): 1.

Kraus, Joe. "The Book Collections of Early American College Libraries." *Library Quarterly* 43 (1973): 142–59.

————. "The Qualifications of University Librarians, 1948 and 1933." *College and Research Libraries* 11 (January 1950) 1:17–21.

Kroll, J. Rebecca. "Beyond Evaluating: Performance as a Planning and Motivational Toll in Libraries." *Journal of Academic Librarianship* 9 (March 1983) 1:27–32.

Krukowski, Jan. "What Do Students Want? Status." *Change* 17 (May–June 1985) 3:21–28.

Lancaster, J. Wilfrid. "Whither Libraries? or, Wither Libraries?" *College and Research Libraries* 39 (September 1978) 3:345–57.

Lee, Barbara A. "Contractually Protected Governance Systems at Unionized Colleges." *Review of Higher Education* 5 (Winter 1982) 2:69–85.

Lewis, David W. "Inventing the Electronic University." *College and Research Libraries* 49 (July 1988) 4:291–304.

Lewis, Ralph W. "User's Reaction to Microfiche: A Preliminary Study." *College and Research Libraries* 31 (July 1970) 4:260–68.

Little, Evelyn Steel. "War Activities of College and Research Libraries." *College and Research Libraries* 4 (July 1943) 3:179–211.

Lohela, Shari, and F. William Summers. "The Impact of Planning on Budgeting." *Journal of Library Administration* 2 (Summer–Fall–Winter 1981) 2,3,4:173–85.

Lundy, Frank A. "Faculty Rank of Professional Librarians—Part I." *College and Research Libraries* 12 (January 1951) 1:11–19.

MacVicar, Robert. "The President Views the Campus Library." *Journal of Academic Librarianship* 3 (September 1977) 4:196–97.

Mapp, Edward. "The Library in a Community College." *College and Research Libraries* 19 (May 1958) 3:194–96.

Marshall, Joan L. "The Effects of Collective Bargaining on Faculty Salaries." *Journal of Higher Education* 50 (May–June 1979) 3:310–22.

Martin, Susan K. "Information Technology and Libraries: Toward the Year 2000." *College and Research Libraries* 50 (July 1989) 4:397–405.

Martin, Warren Bryan. "The Limits to Diversity." *Change* 10 (December–January) 11:41–45.

McAfee, Mildred H. "The College Library as Seen by a College President." *College and Research Libraries* 2 (September 1941) 4:301–5.

McAnally, Arthur M., and Robert B. Downs. "The Changing Role of Directors of University Libraries." *College and Research Libraries* 34 (March 1973) 2:103–25.

McCarthy, Constance. "The Faculty Problem." *Journal of Academic Librarianship* 11 (July 1985) 3:142–45.

McDermott, Judy C. "The Professional Status of Librarians: A Realistic and Unpopular Analysis." *Journal of Library Administration* 5 (Fall 1984) 3:17–21.

McGee, Gail W., and Robert C. Ford. "Faculty Research Productivity and Intention to Change Positions." *Review of Higher Education* 11 (Autumn 1987) 1:1–16.

McMillan, James A. "Academic Status of Library Staff Members of Large Universities." *College and Research Libraries* 1 (March 1940) 2:138–40.

McNeal, Archie L. "Ratio of Professional to Clerical Staff." *College and Research Libraries* 17 (May 1956) 3:219–23.

Michalak, Thomas J. "Library Services to the Graduate Community: The Role of the Subject Specialist Librarian." *College and Research Libraries* 37 (May 1976) 3:257–65.

Miller, Donald E. "Genteel Poverty: Reflections of an Assistant Professor." *Change* 11 (May–June 1979) 4:10–11.

Mitchell, Mary B. "The Process of Department Leadership." *Review of Higher Education* 11 (Winter 1987) 2:161–76.

Mitchell, W. Bede, and L. Stanislava Swieszkowski. "Publication Requirements and Tenure Approval Rates: An Issue for Academic Librarians." *College and Research Libraries* 46 (May 1985) 3:249–55.

Moody, Robert E. "Our Academic Leadership: From the Faculty?" *College and Research Libraries* 21 (September 1960) 5:362–68.

Moore, Kathryn M. "The Structure of Administrative Careers: A Prose Poem in Four Parts." *Review of Higher Education* 8 (Fall 1984) 1:1–13.

Moran, Barbara B. "The Unintended Revolution in Academic Libraries: 1939 to 1989 and Beyond." *College and Research Libraries* 50 (January 1989) 1:25–41.

Moran, Barbara B., James T. Suprenant, and Merrily E. Taylor. "The Electronic Campus: The Impact of the Scholar's Workstation Project on the Libraries at Brown." *College and Research Libraries* 48 (January 1987) 1:5–16.

Morris, Dilys E. "Electronic Information and Technology: Impact and Potential for Academic Libraries." *College and Research Libraries* 50 (January 1989) 1:56–64.

Neal, James G., and Barbara J. Smith. "Library Support of Faculty Research at the Branch Campuses of a Multi-Campus University." *Journal of Academic Librarianship* 9 (November 1983) 5:276–80.

Neroda, Ed, and Lana Bodewin. "Institutional Analysis for Professional Development." *Journal of Academic Librarianship* 9 (July 1983) 3:156–60.

Oakeshot, Priscilla. "The 'BLEND' Experiment in Electronic Publishing." *Scholarly Publishing* 17 (October 1985): 25–36.

O'Connor, Daniel, and Phyllis Van Orden. "Getting into Print." *College and Research Libraries* (September 1978) 5:389–96.

Oh, Tai Keun. "New Dimensions of Management Theory." *College and Research Libraries* 27 (November 1966) 6:431–38.

Olum, Paul. "Myths and Realities: The Academic Viewpoint." *College and Research Libraries* 45 (September 1984) 5:362–66.

O'Neil, Robert M. "Academic Libraries and the Future: A President's View." *College and Research Libraries* 45 (May 1984) 3:184–88.

———. "The President Views the Campus Library." *Journal of Academic Librarianship* 3 (September 1977) 4:195.

———. "The University Administrator's View of the University Library." *New Directions for Higher Education* 39 (1982) 5–12.

O'Toole, James B. "Tenure: A Conscientious Objection." *Change* 10 (June–July 1978) 6:24–31.

Parker, Ralph H. "Libraries in an Inflationary Cycle." *College and Research Libraries* 12 (October 1951) 4:338–42, 348.

Person, Ruth J., and George Charles Newman. "Selection of the University Librarian." *College and Research Libraries* 51 (July 1990) 4:346–59.

Peter, Kenneth G. "Ethics in Academic Librarianship: The Need for Values." *Journal of Academic Librarianship* 9 (July 1983) 3:132–37.

Peterson, Marvin W., and Robert Blackburn. "Faculty Effectiveness: Meeting Institutional Needs and Expectations." *Review of Higher Education* 9 (Autumn 1985) 1:21–34.

Petrof, Barbara G. "Theory: The X Factor in Librarianship." *College and Research Libraries* 26 (July 1965) 4:316–17.

Phillips, E. D. "The Elective System in American Education." *Pedagogical Seminary* 8 (June 1901): 206–30.

Pontius, Jack E. "Faculty Status, Research Requirements, and Release Time." Arlington, Va.: ERIC Document Reproduction Service, ED183147 (1978), 9–12.

Posvar, Wesley, W. "The President Views the Campus Library." *Journal of Academic Librarianship* 3 (September 1977) 4:193.

Rayward, W. Boyd. "Melvil Dewey and Education for Librarianship." *Journal of Library History* 3 (October 1968) 4:297–312.

Redmond, Donald A., Michael P. Sinclair, and Elinore Brown. "University Libraries and University Research." *College and Research Libraries* 33 (November 1972) 6:447–53.

Reeves, Floyd W., and John Dale Russell. "The Relation of the College Library to Recent Movements in Higher Education." *Library Quarterly* 1 (January 1931) 1:57–66.

Reichmann, Felix. "Hercules and Antaeus." *College and Research Libraries* 14 (January 1953) 1:22–25, 34.

Riley, Gresham. "Myths and Realities: The Academic Viewpoint II." *College and Research Libraries* 45 (September 1984) 5:367–69.

Rogers, Sharon, and Charlene S. Hurt. "How Scholarly Communication Should Work in the 21st Century." *College and Research Libraries* 51 (January 1990) 1:5–8.

Rumsey, Eric. "The Power of the New Microcomputers: Challenge and Opportunity." *College and Research Libraries* 51 (March 1990) 2:95–99.

Rundell, Walter. "Relations between Historical Researchers and Custo-
    dians of Source Materials." *College and Research Libraries* 29
    (November 1968) 6:466–76.
Runyon, Robert S. "Power and Conflict in Academic Libraries." *Journal
    of Academic Librarianship* 3 (September 1977) 4:200–205.
Rzasa, Philip V., and John H. Moriarty. "The Types and Needs of Aca-
    demic Library Users: A Case Study of 6,568 Responses." *College
    and Research Libraries* 31 (November 1970) 6:403–9.
Schad, Jasper G. "Allocating Materials Budgets in Institutions of Higher
    Education." *Journal of Academic Librarianship* 3 (January 1978)
    6:328–31.
Sellen, Mary, and Dana Anderson. "Faculty Library Committees: Eval-
    uations from the Librarians' Perspective." *Journal of Library Ad-
    ministration* 5 (Summer 1984) 2:79–86.
Sewell, Robert G. "Faculty Status and Librarians: The Rationale and the
    Case of Illinois." *College and Research Libraries* 44 (May 1983)
    3:212–22.
Seymour, Daniel T. "Higher Education as a Corporate Enterprise." *Col-
    lege Board Review* 147 (Spring 1988): 2–4.
Shalvoy, Mary Lee. "College Workstations: Vendors Line Up for a
    Multi-Billion Dollar Market." *Electronic Learning* 7 (November–
    December 1987) 3:26–34.
Startup, Richard. "The Rewards of Research." *New Universities Quar-
    terly* 30 (Spring 1976): 227–38.
Stewart, M. A. "The Duality of Demand on University Libraries." *Col-
    lege and Research Libraries* 8 (October 1947) 4:396–98.
Tinker, C. B. "The University Library." *Yale Alumni Weekly* 33 (February
    1924): 649–51.
Trow, Martin. "American Higher Education: Past, Present, and Future."
    Educational Researcher 17 (April 1988) 3:13–23.
Trueswell, Richard W. "Zero Growth: When Is Not-Enough Enough?
    A Symposium." *Journal of Academic Librarianship* 1 (November
    1975) 5:6–7.
Van Erde, John. "The Library and the Researcher." *College and Research
    Libraries* 19 (March 1958) 2:1104–6, 1164.
Veaner, Allen B. "Librarians: The Next Generation." *Library Journal*
    109 (April 1984): 623–25.
———. "1985 to 1995: The Next Decade in Academic Librarianship,
    Part I." *College and Research Libraries* 46 (May 1985) 3:209–29.
Volkwein, J. Fredericks. "State Financial Control of Public Universities
    and Its Relationship to Campus Administrative Elaborateness and

Cost: Results of a National Study." *Review of Higher Education* 9 (1986) 3:267–86.

Waldron, Rodney K. "Implications of Technological Progress for Librarians." *College and Research Libraries* 19 (March 1958) 2:118–25, 146.

Wallace, Danny P. "The Use of Statistical Methods in Library and Information Science." *Journal of the American Society for Information Science* 36 (November 1985) 6:402–10.

Watts, Thomas D. "A Brief for Centralized Library Collections." *Journal of Academic Librarianship* 9 (September 1983) 4:196–97.

Weber, David C. "A Quagmire of Scientific Literature." *College and Research Libraries* 18 (March 1957) 2:103–6.

––––––. "University Libraries and Campus Information Technology Organizations: Who Is in Charge Here?" *Journal of Library Administration* 9 (1988) 4:5–19.

White, Herbert S. "Reactions to 'Defining the Academic Librarian.'" *College and Research Libraries* 46 (November 1985) 6:474–77.

Williams, Joyce E., and Elinor Johansen. "Career Disruption in Higher Education." *Journal of Higher Education* 56 (March–April 1985) 2:144–60.

Wilson, Francis G. "The Library Catalog and the Scholar." *College and Research Libraries* 3 (June 1942) 3:201–6.

Wong, William S., and David S. Zubatsky. "The Tenure Rate of University Library Directors: A 1983 Survey." *College and Research Libraries* 46 (January 1985) 1:69–77.

Woodsworth, Anne. "Computing Centers and Libraries as Cohorts: Exploiting Mutual Strengths." *Journal of Library Administration* 9 (1988) 4:21–34.

Yenawine, Wayne S. "Education for Academic Librarianship." *College and Research Libraries* 19 (November 1958) 6:479–86.

INDEX

MARC (Machine-Readable Cataloging) 54
Marsh, James G. 97
Massachusetts Institute of Technology 73
mentoring 125, 174, 197, 198
microfiche 141
microform 141
Morrill Act of 1862 12
Morrill Act of 1890 12

National Center for Higher Edu-
cation Management Systems
(NCHEMS) 72
National Labor Relations Act 113
networking 175, 197, 198
North Central Association of Col-
lege and Secondary Schools
23
Northwest Ordinance of 1787 6
Northwestern University 26, 55
NOTIS (Northwestern Online Total
Integrated System) 55

Ohio College Library Center
(OCLC) 54
Ohio State University 147
Online Public Access Catalogs
(OPACs) 55
organized anarchy 95, 97, 98
Oxford University 2

paperless society 56
peer evaluations 122, 126, 160
peer relationship 124, 125, 174,
175, 198
peer reviews 127
Pennsylvania State University 144
percentage of instruction 74
performance appraisal 175
Phoenix model 86
Phyrr, Peter 71
Planning, Programming, and Budgeting Systems (PPBS) 70, 74
political model 95, 98
postaudit of funds 66

Princeton University 26, 102
private schools 22, 26, 27, 45, 66,
68, 77
private universities 66, 68, 111, 135
production 56, 96, 99, 127, 131,
137
professional status 161, 162, 170,
172, 180
professionalism 160, 161, 162
public school movement 15
public universities 21, 26, 111, 135,
163

qualitative information 160, 161

racial unrest 47
rare-book room 141
rate per student 74
Reagan administration 50
recitation 3, 8, 13, 16
reference assistance 148
reform of higher education 12
reforms 5
release time 173, 174
religious denominations 2, 6
remote storage 147
reorganization 150, 166
Report of the Committee on Academic Freedom and Tenure,
1915 19
research allocation 99
Research Libraries Information Network (RLIN) 54
research reputation flow 67, 68
research universities 41, 42, 43, 50,
67, 72, 126, 127, 129, 133,
140
resource acquisition 99
resource allocation 99
Resource Requirement Prediction
Model (RRPM) 72
resource sharing 37, 87, 149, 180,
193

St. Cloud University 171
Scholarly Communication System
52, 57, 145

scholarly journals 14, 16, 57, 127
scientific model 95, 96
scientists 56, 105, 141, 142, 143,
    161, 168, 175
search committees 164
senate library committee 111, 148
serials 52, 87, 127, 180, 192
service 23
social scientists 143, 144
special collections 86, 141
Standards for Faculty Status for
    College and University Librar-
    ians 170
Stanford University 14, 21, 26, 150
state legislatures 7, 55, 102
state regulatory agencies 74
state universities 7, 13, 15, 68
student enrollment 3, 22, 27, 36,
    38, 41, 45, 48, 49, 95
student flow model 72
subject specialists 147, 179
System Dimensions Ltd. (SDL) 72

Tappan, Henry P. 14
Taylor, Frederick 96
teachers' colleges 42
teaching faculties 8, 27, 36, 37, 40,
    59, 85, 87, 111, 121, 122, 146,
    147, 148, 150, 151, 159, 163,
    170, 171, 174, 176, 178, 179,
    180, 181, 190, 194, 196, 197
teaching loads 133, 134
technical literature 28
technical services 53, 54, 55, 75
technological revolution 52, 53
tenure 19, 69, 77, 96, 105, 107,
    124, 134, 135, 136, 137, 165,
    171, 173, 174, 176, 194, 196
Texas Instruments Company 71
Tinker, Chauncy Brewster 23
tuition 7, 48, 66, 68, 69
turnkey systems 55
two-year colleges 43

U.S. Supreme Court 7, 113
uniform percentage adjustment 69

unionization 113, 114, 125, 171,
    196
university administrators 38, 54, 73,
    75, 94, 99, 115, 172, 191, 192,
    196
university committees 148
University of California–Berkeley
    26, 83
University of Chicago 14, 21, 23,
    26, 52
University of Florida 57
University of Illinois 26, 106, 107,
    147, 166, 167, 169, 172, 174
University of Iowa 26, 179, 196
University of Kansas 26
University of Manitoba 178
University of Michigan 14, 26
University of Minnesota 26
University of Missouri 26
University of Montana 169
University of Nebraska 169
University of Pennsylvania 26
University of Utah 141
University of Virginia 12
University of Washington–Seattle
    26, 50
University of Wisconsin 26
university presidents 14, 20, 36, 77,
    103, 104, 105, 106, 107, 122,
    165, 167, 177, 178

Veaner Theorem 85
veterans 35, 38
vice-president for academic affairs
    107, 108, 167
vice-president for administrative
    affairs 107
Vietnam War 125

Washington Library Network
    (WLN) 54
Weber, Max 96
weeding 165, 179
Wellesley College 168
Western Interstate Commission for
    Higher Education (WICHE) 72

Stephen E. Atkins is the head of the Resource Development Division at the Evans Library, Texas A&M University. He has worked as an academic librarian at the University of Illinois, Urbana-Champaign and Texas A&M University, and as a library assistant at the University of Iowa. His research has focused around two subjects: arms control and disarmament issues and the relationship between academic librarians and the university. Atkins is an active member of ALA and ACRL.